# Praise for *Digital Marketing for Law Firms*

"*Digital Marketing for Law Firms* is a comprehensive guide on how to create and build an engaging online campaign to attract new clients. A must-read for any lawyer who is serious about growth in this highly competitive environment."

—Andy Citrin, Andy Citrin Injury Attorneys

"*Digital Marketing for Law Firms: The Secrets to Getting More Clients and Better Cases* offers exactly what its subtitle claims: it takes the mystery out of online marketing. This helpful guide explains, in simple terms, not only why but also how to adopt internet marketing strategies that will result in a return on investment for your law firm. *Digital Marketing for Law Firms* is broken down into seventeen easily digestible chapters. My (nonlegal!) advice? It's worth the purchase just for the opportunity to read and implement the steps described in the first chapter, on building a brand, and the sixth chapter, on writing online content that will turn potential clients into your clients.

—Amanda Narvaes, partner at Drew Cooper & Anding, director-at-large at the Women Lawyers Association of Michigan, 2018-2020

"Informative and insightful. Chip has taken what he has learned from his years of experience and put that information in an easy to understand format that provides answers to what works in digital marketing."

—Matthew R. Myers, Myers Law Firm, PLLC

"The foundation of all marketing is defining your brand, being true to your brand, and being open to the evolution of your brand as your firm grows. 'Build it and they will come,' stay true to your brand and the results will come!"

—Jason A. Plotkin, Esq., CEO of the Pinder Plotkin Legal Team, a Maryland Personal Injury and Workers' Compensation law firm

"LaFleur breaks down what it takes to take [your] law firm to the next level. This book offers practical guidance to law firms of all sizes, but I especially like that the solo practitioner can implement these strategies and tips.

—Kari Santana, law offices of Kari Santana

# DIGITAL MARKETING FOR LAW FIRMS

## The Secrets to Getting More Clients and Better Cases

**Chip LaFleur**

with

Steven Kent and Leigh Ebrom

TRIAL GUIDES™

Trial Guides, LLC, Portland, Oregon 97210



ISBN: 978-1-951962-07-4



Trial Guides, LLC
Attn: Permissions
2350 NW York Street
Portland, OR 97210
(800) 309-6845
www.trialguides.com

Managing Editor: Tina Ricks

Production Editor: Travis Kremer

Copyeditor: Patricia Esposito

Cover Designer: Lee Gullet

Original Interior Template Design by Laura Lind Design

Interior Layout by Travis Kremer

Printed and bound in the United States of America.

Printed on acid-free paper.

*To my wife, Sarah, whose support and trust helped me complete this project, and to my sons, Lucien and Leif, who did everything they could to foil her efforts.*

—Chip LaFleur

# TABLE OF CONTENTS

# PUBLISHER'S NOTE

This book is intended for practicing attorneys. This book does not offer legal advice and does not take the place of consultation with an attorney or other professional with appropriate expertise and experience.

Attorneys are strongly cautioned to evaluate the information, ideas, and opinions set forth in this book in light of their own research, experience, and judgment; to consult applicable rules, regulations, procedures, cases, and statutes (including those issued after the publication date of this book); and to make independent decisions about whether and how to apply such information, ideas, and opinions to their own marketing activities.

Although the authors mention various legal restrictions that apply to attorney advertising and marketing, this book is not a compliance manual. Attorneys are cautioned to satisfy themselves that their advertising and marketing activities are consistent with applicable laws, rules, and regulations.

All references to the trademarks of third parties are strictly informational and for purposes of commentary. No sponsorship or endorsement by, or affiliation with, the trademark owners is claimed or implied by the author or publisher of this book.

Recommendations of third-party providers of goods and services that may be useful in attorney advertising and marketing are based on the experience of the authors in using these resources. No endorsement of these providers, and no endorsement of this book by these provided, is stated or implied by the authors or the publisher. Readers should satisfy themselves that the third-party providers are appropriate for their needs.

This book contains illustrative examples of advertising and marketing issues that focus on a law firm called "Webster, Webster & Cohen" (sometimes referred to as "WWC") and its various personnel, vendors and clients, all of which are wholly imaginary. The firm name is a light-hearted and parodic homage to the fictional brokerage firm that appears in the film *Cool Runnings*, an iconic artifact of American pop culture. No connection between the film and this book is claimed or implied. Any similarity between the fictional names of individuals and business entities and those of real persons is strictly coincidental.

The author and publisher disclaim any liability or responsibility for loss or damage resulting from the use of this book or the information, ideas, or opinions contained in this book.

# FOREWORD

All good trial lawyers have one thing in common: the ability to take complicated, nuanced topics and make them seem simple—even crystal clear. Most of an effective courtroom advocate's knowledge is not acquired in law school; they learn it later on. Successful lawyers know that they must understand their cases' subject-matter well enough to converse with experts and cross-examine any opposing doctor or product engineer.

However, the ability to translate sophisticated legal, medical, or technical issues into plain English takes time and practice. We work diligently to become armchair experts.

Imagine that your next trial is on the subject of digital marketing. How would you prepare? You would probably read books and articles on the subject. You would ask questions, lots of questions. You would consult with your own experts. You might question the other side's experts. You would attempt to become conversant in the field of digital marketing because the better you understand it, the more likely you will be successful in your case.

I believe that developing a good understanding of digital marketing is just as important to your practice as winning your next trial. It is the present and the future. Lawyers who hope to market their firms on the web must learn enough to converse intelligently with digital marketers. That's where this book comes in.

Like the practice of law, marketing has its own language and alphabet soup. Marketers love to talk about PPC, SEO, CTRs, and KPIs as if everyone understands these terms. Unless you've built up your expertise, it's easy to spend too much money on misguided marketing efforts. For example, I know lawyers who believe that paid advertising is a scam because of their negative experiences with unscrupulous or inexperienced paid advertising managers.

Admittedly, my early experiences with large legal marketing companies tarnished my opinion of the industry, too. Before I founded Crosley Law, I worked for a firm that spent massive amounts of money on advertising. To me, the legal advertisers I encountered seemed more concerned with separating law firms from their money than with delivering measurable results. I recall meeting with website reps who wanted to upsell me additional services and tried to pressure me into matching what my competitors were doing. Every law firm's website started to look and sound the same, and we were all paying outrageous amounts of money for cookie-cutter content and designs. I figured there had to be a better way.

In 2005, as I began to build Crosley Law, I wanted to chart my own marketing path. I needed to stand out, and I didn't want to waste my money on ineffective tactics.

Based on my research, I concluded that phonebook advertising was a dying industry and that TV ads were too pricey. I decided that the web was my best option. I built a basic website and started to look for people who could help me stand out and connect with the right clients. That's when I met Chip LaFleur.

At the time, Chip worked for an SEO (search engine optimization) firm in San Antonio, Texas. Unlike the typical digital marketing professional, Chip valued transparency and education. There wasn't much geek speak. Instead, he took the time to answer my questions, explain his strategies, and empower good decision-making. He gave me the time and information that I needed, just like I would with one of my clients.

Quickly, I realized that Chip wasn't just a marketing provider; he was my partner. He didn't want to hide behind technical jargon and the typical smoke and mirrors used to overcharge attorneys. Instead, he believed that candor, client education, and meaningful data are mutually beneficial for lawyers and their marketing teams.

When Chip opened LaFleur Marketing, Crosley Law was one of its first clients. His team continues to teach my firm about the latest advances in digital marketing. We're continually improving my online presence, and his team is always ready to answer my tough questions.

This book is a continuation of Chip's mission to educate lawyers about the power of digital marketing. In it, you'll find detailed information about how to build your law firm's brand, create a website, and connect with people through compelling blogs, ad campaigns, and social media platforms. The text is filled with practical information, examples, and anecdotes. Even after many years of working with Chip and his team, I learned some new things while reading it.

Even if you decide to hire an agency to build and implement your digital marketing plan, *Digital Marketing for Law Firms* is a valuable tool. As you read, you'll gain the expertise and confidence you need to make smart decisions, identify the best partner, review proposals, and assess their performance. Pretty soon, you'll be able to poke holes in an unscrupulous salesperson's assertions, just like you would an independent medical examiner's report. And if more complicated questions arise, you can always follow my lead and call Chip. He'll happily answer your questions.

—Tom Crosley, founder of Crosley Law

# ACKNOWLEDGMENTS

Like everything we do at LaFleur, this book was a team effort. I am humbled by everyone's dedication, attention to detail, and sacrifice. I especially want to thank my cowriters, Steven Kent and Leigh Ebrom, who helped put my thoughts and approach to digital marketing into words, and Catherine Smyka, who kept the project on track and encouraged us at every step.

However, we were never alone in our effort. Jason Brower and Sowmya Padigi pitched in, offering their expertise and insight into the world of paid advertising; Jason gets cowriting credits for the chapter on paid social media advertising. Falon Peters and Jane Newton had the unenviable task of reviewing and reading our first draft; their feedback was invaluable. Nick Wright created the majority of the graphics in the book. Amy Hinman helped craft the title. Our project and account managers, Eric Rosbury, Rosemarie Falsetta, Becky Zobl, and Pat Kose, provided support and managed our workloads and client relationships to give us time to breathe and focus on the book's content. Our friend Kyle McCarthy helped get this project off the ground in the early days and contributed to our discussion of paid advertising.

I also want to thank Tom Crosley for writing the foreword and putting his trust in our skills. I'm proud to work with an attorney with as much integrity and intelligence as Tom.

Personally, our families deserve a lot of credit. Sarah LaFleur, Matt Ebrom, and Regina Berlin gave us an incredible amount of support and encouragement throughout the writing and editing process. Similarly, Leif, Lucien, and Drew get thanks for (occasionally) being patient while Dad or Mom wrote a book.

# INTRODUCTION

## Beyond Winning: Leverage Your Success and Get More Clients

Most lawyers are good at winning. They win in courtrooms, in negotiations, and in casual discussions over a few drinks. Winning propels them forward in their careers and, in some cases, to start their own firms. But a lot of lawyers struggle when success at their vocation doesn't translate to success as a stakeholder or owner at a firm.

Part of this struggle stems from gaps in training. Most lawyers we've spoken with have taken a handful of business or marketing classes over the course of their career, and even the best of those classes at law schools and CLE events have been described to us as "cursory" or "required." High praise.

The other primary struggle that attorneys have is one of capacity. If you're like the lawyers we partner with, you're a quick learner and you are good at a variety of things. But even if you could meticulously plan out the ten thousand hours you need to invest in new skills to truly master them, no one person can keep a firm running, deftly manage their caseload, respond to clients (let alone everyone else), carve out enough time for themselves to maintain their sanity, and, of course, effectively market their practice to get new clients and (hopefully) hire some more staff who can free up some of their time to focus on more important things.

Digital marketing isn't a panacea for the perennial struggles that attorneys face as they set out on their own, grow their practice, or try to maintain their established position in the market. Digital marketing can, however, give law firms of any size a scalable, sustainable model for revenue growth. It can also provide frameworks, methodologies, and tools that will improve the way your law firm operates as a business.

Most importantly, a well-developed holistic marketing strategy can take one of the most difficult and time-consuming aspects of running a law firm (attracting new business) off your plate so you can focus on what you do best: winning.

## The Inspiration for This Book Is ROI

The inspiration for this book stems from a professional relationship and friendship with an incredibly talented trial lawyer whom I have been working with for nearly ten years. As it turns out, great trial lawyers also tend to be some of the most demanding—and rewarding—digital marketing clients.

Long before I opened my own digital marketing agency, that attorney, Tom Crosley of San Antonio, Texas, challenged me to show him the return on his digital marketing investment. In response, I showed him a graph, lists of keywords, some charts, and other data points that I (at the time) thought looked polished and compelling.

Like the great negotiator and lawyer that Tom is, he saw that what I presented was superficial. He kept coming back to the original question, and it's one that we return to every day and in every marketing tactic that we consider and execute:

> How can we clearly determine and report return on investment (**ROI**) for lawyers?

# The Only Metrics That Matter: Clients and Cases

Finding an answer to that question is challenging, and the solution is rarely neat and tidy. But with diligence and inquisitiveness, we have mapped potential client journeys, tracked their interactions, and built a model for legal marketing success. That's a model we'll be sharing with you for the rest of this book.

Throughout, we will help you do the following:

- Understand your potential clients and how they pursue legal services.
- Determine whether your marketing efforts are effective at attracting actual clients.
- Analyze how your marketing budget correlates with new client acquisition.
- Improve your marketing efforts to more effectively target your ideal audience and increase ROI.

We're not interested in creating a cloud of mystery around digital marketing. Yes, it can be very technical and demanding. But you should never get distracted by software, the alphabet soup of acronyms, or any of the other trappings of digital marketing.

Whether you're hoping to launch your first **website** or you've been at this for forty-five years, all of your marketing should help you bring in more—and better—clients and cases.

# What This Book Is Really About: Helping You

This simple fact leads us to the purpose of this book. We know you don't like spending your marketing budget on tactics that don't produce ROI. Many of our clients come to us after they've sunk money into strategies that didn't pan out. We don't beat ourselves up over every experiment that doesn't succeed. Instead, we learn from every tactic and initiative, whether it delivers results or fails, and we've been learning with law firms from across the United States.

# Who Is LaFleur?

When I founded LaFleur, my mission was to create an agency that created brilliant digital marketing for law firms. In my opinion, too many marketing agencies use smoke and mirrors to upsell law firms on services and tactics that they don't need. We do things differently, creating legal brands, websites, ad campaigns, and content that is unique, compelling, and effective. Headquartered in Grand Rapids, Michigan, our Midwestern work ethic and practicality is reflected in everything we do.

While we've broadened our clientele over the years, legal marketing is still our main focus and passion. We've worked with attorneys who are just starting out and firms that have been succeeding for decades. Our clients have come from across the nation and from a vast range of practice areas. We've partnered with attorneys in personal injury, tax law, family law, estate planning, business law, mediation, and a wide variety of other areas.

My team includes talented writers, editors, designers, web developers, paid advertising experts, video producers, and project managers, many of whom contributed their time, words, and insight to this book. Of special note is our content team; my first hire after I created the company was a writer; my second was an editor—because the importance of outstanding content within a marketing strategy cannot be overstated. We take a conscientious, strategy-first approach to every initiative we employ on behalf of our clients. We familiarize ourselves with their businesses, their unique needs, and their specific goals to develop a customized suite of marketing services that delivers maximum value.

This careful analysis helps us understand exactly how you can tell your story online in a way that resonates with your audience. Then we apply proven marketing strategies that attract the right people and convince them to hire your firm.

The knowledge and data we've been able to acquire through years of learning and refining is highly valuable, and we don't believe you need to hire an agency like ours to benefit from it. We know that we're good at what we do and that we can execute the tactics and strategies we lay out in this book.

Because of our confidence, we're open to sharing—in detail and in a way that you can use—the approach we've taken to help our clients achieve success in digital marketing. We wholeheartedly invite you to review the chapters that follow and apply the experience we've gained for your own benefit.

In each of the chapters that follow, we'll outline the approach from a crawl-walk-run perspective. We'll address what you can do right now and what you could do if you applied some budget or people to the strategy. We'll also discuss what you could do if you hired a marketing coordinator or director and what you could do if you worked with an agency or freelancer to help you.

Each chapter closes with a checklist to help you start implementing these strategies and tactics. The checklist will also serve as a quick reference you can share with your team to track progress and increase accountability as you work on implementation.

Finally, we realize that, like law, marketing has its own vernacular. To help you build your marketing literacy, we've included a detailed glossary of terms. When you see a word or phrase in bold, you can find its definition in the glossary.

We trust that you'll enjoy this book, but more than that, we hope the proven strategies and tactics you learn will grow your practice and allow you to serve more clients who need your knowledge and expertise.

One final note: we are not compensated for referring software, providers, tools, and so on. Our recommendations throughout this book simply come from experience in marketing and with law firms in particular.

# 1

# Foundations: Your Brand

Most lawyers worry they won't succeed at online marketing efforts for one or more of the following reasons:

- They're not creative enough.
- They're not technical enough.
- They don't have enough time.

Thinking you're not creative enough to create great marketing messages is nonsense. In fact, the most famous and acclaimed marketing genius of all time, David Ogilvy, said:

> When I write an advertisement, I don't want you to tell me that you find it "creative." I want you to find it so interesting that you buy the product.[1]

Notice the focus on "you": the audience for the ad. Marketing is about capturing the attention of your audience and speaking to them with messages that address their needs. And you're in the right field to focus on straightforward messaging without a lot of fluff. People who need a lawyer have real problems, and they don't have time for whimsical ads that tickle their imaginations.

If you're afraid you're not technical enough, well, I'm not a technical person—I mostly work with words, like you. However, I am a detail-oriented person, also probably like you. And here I am, working as a professional online marketer and writing a book about digital marketing. I'm not great with math or numbers, but if you can look at two numbers and tell which is bigger, you've got enough math skills to handle your online marketing efforts.

Not having enough time to devote to marketing is the only legitimate concern, and it's the main reason why lawyers hire our marketing agency (or any other agency). But many of those attorneys we work with either wouldn't or couldn't devote time to pick up this book, so you're already ahead of the game. By reading these chapters and developing your understanding, you can avoid blind alleys and false starts, which will make the time you do spend on marketing much more efficient.

1. David Ogilvy, *Ogilvy on Advertising* (New York: Crown, 1983).

# Why Do Marketing Efforts Fail?

Most law firms don't get great results from their digital marketing efforts for three reasons:

1. They don't have a strong sense of how they want to present themselves (branding).

2. They don't have a clear understanding of who they're marketing to (audience).

3. They're not using the right methods for their budget and their audience (tools).

For the next three chapters, we'll talk about how to build your brand, how to understand your audience, and how to select the right tools. We'll devote this chapter to developing your brand.

# What's in a Brand?

When you think of **brands**, you probably think of big, multinational corporations: Walmart, Apple, Amazon. They have flashy logos, and they can afford television ads: that's what makes a brand!

That's not how we think of brands in marketing. To us, every business has a brand, including your law firm. The definition we use for a brand is this: your brand is whatever your clients think of when they think about your company.

People often associate brands with logos, like Apple's apple or Nike's swoosh. However, that's only because people are very visual by nature, so they're more likely to make a connection between a company name and a picture than between a company name and words.

Sometimes, words are powerful enough to define a brand too, like the slogan "Just Do It" for Nike. But most companies change slogans every few years while they rarely or never change their logo.

To understand branding better, let's think about Beyoncé. She's one of the most fiery and fearless performers of her generation, but did you know she's a quiet and reserved person outside of the stage?

"I'm better at one-on-one conversations," she told *Dazed & Confused* magazine. "I become shy and a bit intimidated when it's a large group of people. At a big dinner, I just hope no one expects anything from me. I wish I'd disappear."

Watching Beyoncé onstage, no one would ever guess she's shy. Beyoncé also does lots of other things we never see or think about. She attends business meetings, hires and fires people, and has bad days. Once in a while, she probably lounges on the couch in sweatpants and eats junk food. Those things are part of Beyoncé's life, but we don't see them, so we don't think about them when we hear the name Beyoncé. They aren't part of her brand.

Just because Beyoncé's brand is different from the real Beyoncé doesn't mean it's phony or disingenuous. After all, no one could be Beyoncé onstage except Beyoncé. Her onstage performance is an expression of parts of who she is and parts of who she wants to be, all carefully selected and honed through planning and practice.

So, your law firm is the "full Beyoncé": it includes meetings, personnel changes, payroll, casual Fridays, and all the other stuff your clients don't care about. Your brand is Beyoncé onstage: every move and note thought through, practiced, and designed to communicate meaningful messages to your potential clients.

# Defining Your Brand

Creating a successful brand doesn't have to be incredibly complicated. In fact, the most successful brands keep things very simple. Again, think about ads you see from brands like Nike, Apple, and Target. Their ads don't use a lot of words, and their logos are basically just a few lines and one or two colors. Simple means easy to remember, which is critical in branding.

To define your brand, your law firm needs to answer one two-part question: Who are we, and what separates us from the competition?

This sounds like a simple question, but it can be difficult to answer, especially for lawyers who've been practicing for a long time. When you spend every day in the trenches, operating your law firm and handling cases, it's easy to lose sight of the larger picture of your potential clients' options and why they might choose you over any of them.

The single best way to nail down the core elements of your brand is to talk with current and past clients. Find out what made them choose you over all the other lawyers in the area and what they liked about the experience of working with you. Learn what your attorneys and support staff did that made them feel confident and gave them peace of mind. And take the opportunity to find out whether there were parts of the experience your clients didn't like and figure out how you can improve in those areas.

After speaking with your clients, see if you can provide concise (one or two sentences) answers to the following questions. To help, we'll create a fictional law firm—the firm of Webster, Webster & Cohen (WWC for short, internally) in Hazardville, Florida—and we'll imagine how they might answer the following questions:

1. **What does my law firm excel at?**

    » At Webster, Webster & Cohen, we're able to handle complex cases other injury attorneys can't by using cutting-edge investigative techniques and the best expert witnesses. We also have some of the most efficient and streamlined client communications practices in the industry thanks to technology that we use to schedule consultations, bring clients onboard, and stay in touch throughout cases.

2. **Who is my ideal client?**

    » We want to focus on the people who need our help the most, so we want to reach severely injured victims of negligence in and around Hazardville, especially people with brain injuries and those who have suffered serious injuries in car accidents and truck wrecks.

3. **How do I want my clients to feel when they interact with or think about my law firm?**

    » We want our clients to feel confident that someone capable is looking out for them, and we want them to feel that their case really matters to everyone at our firm who touches it.

4. **What do I want someone's first impression of my law firm to be?**

    » We want a potential client to say, "Wow, these are smart lawyers who don't make me feel dumb. They listen to me, care about my story, and talk to me in language I can understand."

5. **What makes my law firm different?**

» We have a track record of taking and winning cases that other attorneys viewed as unwinnable, and we also use the best technology and investigative methods without losing sight of the human element of our work. To that end, we stay in touch with our clients throughout their cases and pick up the phone whenever they call, or make sure someone returns their call within an hour if we can't.

6. **How are my competitors branding themselves, and what needs are they failing to address among potential clients?**

» Our biggest competitors focus their messaging on themselves—their credentials, their accomplishments, how much money they've won. We want our potential clients to feel like they come first at WWC, and our messaging should reflect that by addressing their needs, concerns, hopes, and fears. All our messaging should tie back to the fundamental question for our clients: "How will my life get better if I work with WWC?"

Based on your answers to these questions, you should be able to come up with a clear, overarching brand concept that you can articulate in just one or two sentences. For example:

- **Webster, Webster & Cohen:** We're a personal injury law firm that handles complex injury cases other attorneys can't win and treats our clients like friends and equals.

- **Another example:** We're a small-town general practice firm that not only gets to know our clients and gives them the best service but also gives back to the community.

Remember, features that don't differentiate you from the competition don't matter for branding. So, if you run a personal injury law firm, potential clients need to know you offer free consultations. However, so does every other personal injury lawyer in town. That's a feature of your industry, not your brand. Likewise, your practice areas are not defining features of your brand—at least not unless you have no competitors in those practice areas.

There's a joke in an episode of *The Simpsons* where Homer tries to hire Surly Joe's Foundation Repair, and when he doesn't like the quote he gets, he tells Surly Joe to get lost: "You're not the only foundation guy in town!" Then Homer opens up the phone book (it's an old episode) to the foundation repair section and sees one entry: "Surly Joe's: The ONLY Foundation Repair Company in Town!"

With no competition, heck, that's all the branding you need. However, if you don't have Surly Joe's situation, then you can't rely on just being this or that type of lawyer to convince someone to hire you.

A lot of attorneys we work with mention to us during branding conversations that they have great client communications practices. That's laudable but not really something to build a brand around. People expect good customer service from every business they interact with. Far too many law firms fail to meet this expectation, but that still doesn't mean you can stake your brand on "our industry is below average for customer service, but we're doing what we're supposed to be doing!"

Now, if you're the type of lawyer who will take a client's call at 9:30 p.m. just before you get into bed for the night, that's unusual dedication to customer service for any industry, and maybe that's something to highlight in your brand concept.

Remember also that your brand needs to make sense based on the type of people you want to market to (your target audience, which we'll talk more about in chapter 2, "Foundations: Your Audience"). If you and your fellow attorneys have exceptional credentials and you're smarter than the average bear, you may lean toward a high-end, sophisticated feel for your brand. This might work if your firm primarily focuses on, say, intellectual property law.

However, let's go back to Webster, Webster & Cohen, who mostly handle car accident cases. A car wreck caused by another driver is equally likely to happen to anyone, so their target audience is essentially the average person. Average people don't gravitate toward high-end, sophisticated brands like Rolex or Calvin Klein. They like brands that are approachable, empathetic, and simple, like Betty Crocker and Home Depot. Unless WWC practices in and only wants clients from a wealthy, highly educated community (which isn't the case), developing a luxury-type brand for a firm that focuses on injury law probably doesn't make sense.

## Your Brand Needs a Visual Identity

It's important to translate your brand into not just words but also images. Pictures evoke stronger feelings in most people than words, and people are much more likely to remember a striking image than a phrase. This is where the need for artistically creative people comes in, so if you're anything like me—can't draw a straight line and partially color-blind—then you need to hire a professional who can help you define the visual elements of your brand.

However, hiring a graphic designer can feel like plunging a net into the ocean and coming up with thirty types of fish you've never seen before. Once you start your search—for example, by looking up "graphic designers near me," or checking a site like Upwork for freelance professionals, or asking friends and colleagues for recommendations—you'll quickly realize there are all sorts of options. You could partner with a graphic design agency, for example, or a freelancer designer who works solo. Not only that, but you'll find that *graphic designer* is a blanket term and that many design professionals have different specializations within the field. You may encounter the following:

- logo designers
- brand identity designers and branding specialists
- web designers
- user experience (designers)
- packaging designers
- 3D graphics designers
- motion designers
- art directors

The type of designer you want for your initial branding project is someone who has extensive experience with branding and logo design. Ask to see their portfolio and look for evidence of professional-quality logos and brand designs that appeal to you on a visual level. Also, ask the designer to talk about some recent experiences they've had creating brands and logos for other businesses and describe how those processes played out.

A good designer will be able to listen to what you've developed so far about your brand—your one-sentence brand concept, how you want your clients to feel, the impression you want to make, what makes your firm unique—and work with you to translate these words into a logo, a color palette, and an overall visual feel. You'll draw from these elements again and again when executing the digital marketing strategies we describe in later chapters.

As an example, let's say Sarah Webster of Webster, Webster & Cohen asks some of her peers in other states about graphic design firms. She receives a referral for the design agency Blitzer Studios and sets an initial meeting with them. After viewing work and agreeing to terms, WWC goes through the logo and brand design process during a series of meetings with Blitzer: an initial information-gathering call, a follow-up in which WWC reviews initial ideas and various logo options, and then a final presentation in which Blitzer unveils the finalized logo, color palette, and visual strategy for the brand. WWC wants a relatively classic logo that still has a modern feel, and Blitzer comes up with a stylized "WWC" design that everyone at Webster loves. The agency also draws from WWC's feedback and general principles of color theory to choose a brand palette for WWC: navy blue, black, and white as the core colors, with gold and a lighter shade of blue as secondary accent colors.

Creating a logo and color palette is the bare minimum, but if your firm has the resources, you can also invest in a full brand design. In this case, the designer or design agency will go further and create a detailed set of visual branding guidelines that will instruct you and anyone else who reads them (other people at your firm, other designers) how to use the design elements they created. Those elements should include the following:

- *Logo:* You should receive a package of graphic files that depict your logo. To put the logo on a website, you'll need the logo as a digital image file, like a .JPG or a .PNG. However, these digital image files aren't easy for designers to edit, so make sure the designer gives you the original design file. It's probably an Adobe Illustrator file (.AI). If you ever work with other designers and they need to make tweaks to your logo, like making it a different color, they'll need the design file. Finally, make sure the designer gives you a **.PDF** file of the logo as well. This file is useful for printing, among other things.

  Also, you'll probably want at least one alternative version of your logo. For example, let's say your primary logo is blue. If you find yourself in a situation where you have to print your logo on a blue background, it will be very hard for your blue logo to stand out. So, an alternative version of the logo will cover situations like this. Make sure the designer gives you the same files we described for any alternative versions of your logo as well.

- *Color palette:* The designer will probably choose one or two colors that will serve as your core colors. This doesn't mean your website and ads can never use other colors, but you'll use your core colors almost everywhere. Make sure the designer gives you the *hex codes*, the *CMYK profiles*, and the *Pantone values* for your color palette. These codes will let designers and printers you hire in the future match the colors exactly without having to guess. The hex codes are for digital purposes, like your website, and they will look like this: #1C4792. The CMYK profiles and Pantone values are for printing, and they will look like this: CMYK 100, 85, 10, 0, Pantone 2738.

- *Font:* If your logo includes your firm's name or other text (which most law firm logos do), make sure you know which font the designer used. If the designer decided on other fonts for your firm's print materials and website copy, make sure you have a record of those fonts as well. If they aren't fonts that come standard with the computers you have, then you'll need the font files (.OTF) as well.

Also, the visual branding guidelines should include instructions about photography and icons. These instructions should describe in detail which types of images are and aren't appropriate for your marketing **assets**. (An *asset* is a marketing term for any type of marketing material—so an email message, a flyer, a website, and a **YouTube** video are all different types of assets.) The designer should help you work through these choices, so don't worry about them for now.

If you have a small firm with a team of just a few people and you're handling your own marketing, you probably don't need to invest in a full-on set of visual brand guidelines—just the logo and color palette will do, and your hands-on management of your own assets will keep everything consistent. However, as your firm grows, you'll probably delegate more of the marketing internally or hire an outside partner. The more people who are involved in marketing your firm, the more valuable it is to have a detailed set of brand guidelines that keep everyone on the same page.

It probably won't be cheap to hire a talented designer who has real-world branding experience, but developing the visual identity for your brand is one area where you don't want to skimp. Someone with little or no formal training can accomplish almost everything else we'll describe in this book, including building a respectable website and copywriting, which is what I do. However, trying to cheap out and hire your niece or nephew who's in the first year of art school to craft your firm's visual identity will just set all your later marketing and branding efforts on a weak foundation.

And finally, remember that your brand needs to express real aspects of you and your firm's key team members if you want it to be distinctive. If you just go along with other people's ideas of what your brand should be, you'll wind up with a generic brand that only reflects people who have no actual stake in your law firm, which is bad.

So, working with a designer is a good opportunity to learn how to collaborate with someone on your brand without losing your way. Listen to the designer and respect their expertise, but don't go with a logo and color palette that everyone in your firm hates just because the designer recommends it. Voice your feelings when the designer shows you their work, don't be afraid to ask for revisions, and keep pushing until you receive something you love.

At our agency, we went through a rebranding process a few years ago where we just couldn't seem to find a logo we were excited about. Everyone started to get fatigued of looking at endless rounds of options, and eventually, we began to feel like we were waiting for some divinely created logo that wasn't coming. We almost went with a logo that everyone was just okay with. One key person held out and said: "We've come this far, and we need a logo that's more than okay, or we're just going to do this all again in a few years."

The next designer we brought in created something our whole team loved, and the excitement after the unveiling meeting energized everyone in our agency for months. We still love the logo and visual identity we ended up with by holding out until something truly felt right.

# Finding Your Voice

Even though the visual elements of your brand carry enormous weight, the words you choose matter too. So, you'll want to establish some guidelines for copy as well. *Copy* is marketing-speak for any text (like what you're reading right now).

For marketing purposes, most lawyers are terrible writers. Copywriting is about communication, and the way most lawyers write prevents them from communicating effectively with anyone except another lawyer. If you're hopelessly addicted to long, winding sentences full of commas and sprinkled with occasional Latin, then you may need to hire professional writers as well as a professional designer.

However, all is not lost. If you can hold a conversation with anyone who's a nonlawyer, you can write effective marketing copy for your website, your **blog**, and any other purposes you need. Just think about the way you talk with a new client—how you ease their fears, address their anxieties, help them understand their situation and how you can help. There's no right answer here, just an approach that's unique to you: maybe you have a relaxing, calming style, or maybe you win clients over by getting them fired up and making them feel like they can take on the world.

Also, think about how your clients talk to you. Understand how language makes sense to them, the words they use, and the words they respond to. Use that type of language in your marketing copy and get away from how you think your potential clients expect a lawyer to write. This authentic, distinctive, client-focused language we're now focusing on should serve as your brand voice.

Here's an example of the kind of overly erudite, unapproachable, non-client-focused language you find on far too many law firm websites when they explain their services:

## Typical Law Firm Web Text

According to the Florida Department of Motor Vehicles (DMV), a vehicle crash happens roughly every four minutes on the Commonwealth's roads. Collisions most often involve cars, pickups, commercial trucks, and busses. Statistics show that more than 120,000 crashes occurred on our streets and highways, resulting in 764 deaths and over 63,000 injuries, many of which were serious. Insurance companies are generally responsible for paying claims when wrecks occur, and they are motivated to protect their interests. That means that aggressive action needs to be taken to protect victims' rights. If you were injured by a negligent, careless, or reckless driver, you may be entitled to recover damages. Our accident lawyers work with forensic experts to determine causes of accidents and prove a defendant's fault and breach of care. Contact our law office today for a free consultation to discuss your options for a claim.

Now, let's see how Webster, Webster & Cohen talks about their services after considering their audience and thinking about their ideal clients' needs and concerns.

## Webster, Webster & Cohen Web Text

After a car wreck, it's easy to feel overwhelmed. You and your loved ones are probably facing a long and difficult recovery. You may be concerned about how you'll pay all those bills that are piling up. And to top it off, you're probably getting a lot of different advice about what to do next.

The team at Webster, Webster & Cohen is here to help you cut through the noise and get the answers and compensation you deserve. We know how important your case is to you, which is why we keep in touch at every step of the process and keep you informed. We hire the nation's leading expert witnesses and use cutting-edge investigative techniques, all so we can build the strongest case possible and get you the best results. And our track record speaks for itself: we've recovered millions of dollars for injured victims like you.

You can get an assessment of your case from one of our experienced attorneys at no cost and with no financial commitment. Just contact us to schedule your free initial consultation, and let us take care of the rest.

Notice how WWC begins by focusing on the potential client's concerns and only frames the firm's own services and selling points in terms of how they will translate to better results for the client. It's not about *selling*—it's about explaining, in clear and empathetic terms, why the potential client will be better off if they choose you.

Establishing your brand voice is up to you, but in our experience, most potential clients care a lot less about you seeming lawyerly than you care about it. They care much more about finding someone who can help them solve their issue and communicate with them in language they understand. Remember that people hire lawyers for the same reason they buy any product: they want to have more happiness afterward than before. If your brand voice makes them feel depressed, intimidated, confused, or talked down to, they probably won't feel like that's what they'll get if they hire you.

# Consistency Is Key for Branding

Branding is kind of like physical fitness: it's defined by consistency. No matter how in shape you are, if you stop working out, you'll lose everything you gained. Likewise, if you get lazy about your brand, you can undo any amount of hard work.

One example we see all the time among attorneys is an inability to adhere to a consistent brand name. We'll see them variously refer to themselves as, for example, Webster, Webster & Cohen PLLC, Webster Law Firm, Webster Legal Team, or WWC Legal.

Imagine you went to the store to buy a can of Coca-Cola, and some of the cans said "Coca-Cola," some of them said "The Coca-Cola Company," and some of them just said "Coca." Think how bizarre that would feel. Would a person trying Coca-Cola for the first time feel sure these are all the same flavor? How would they recommend the soda to someone? If they wanted to search online for more info about the soda, which name would they use?

To make sure branding stays consistent, marketers use **branding guidelines**. A branding guidelines document packages together all the most important information about your brand. With all this information bundled together, anyone can refer to it when creating a marketing asset like a television ad, a website page, or a print mailer. If the marketing asset doesn't align with the directives in the branding guidelines document, then someone needs to change that asset and bring it into alignment before it gets released to the public.

Let's go through a sample branding guidelines document for Webster, Webster & Cohen. This document should contain the following:

- **Your (one and only) brand name.**
    - » **Example:** Webster, Webster & Cohen. Technically, the firm's name as a legal entity is Webster, Webster & Cohen, PLLC, but their clients don't need to know and don't care that the firm is a professional

limited liability company. So, the firm will use "Webster, Webster & Cohen" as its brand name for all public-facing materials.

- **Vision statement.** This is the one-sentence, overarching brand concept we described earlier.
  - » **Example:** Webster, Webster & Cohen is a personal injury law firm that handles complex injury cases other attorneys can't win and treats our clients like friends and equals.
- **Mission statement:** This statement explains what you do for your clients that your competitors can't.
  - » **Example:** We pioneer new investigative techniques and stay on the cutting edge of brain science to win unwinnable cases.
- **Visual guidelines:** We described these earlier in the section about visual identity. Your visual guidelines should include your logo, fonts, and core colors as well as instructions about how to use them, and it should also contain instructions about how to pick photos and icons.
- **Copy guidelines:** Copy guidelines describe the voice of your brand and how to convey that voice through copywriting. These guidelines will apply to written text as well as any marketing materials that begin with written text (for example, a television ad, which starts from a written script). Effective copy guidelines don't focus on particular word choices so much as describing what the brand voice is trying to capture as well as the preferred tone and style for copy. These elements can be hard to articulate if you're not a trained writer, but just do your best. You can always revise these guidelines later as you continue to develop a sharper sense of your brand. You can also include any information you think would help a writer understand your brand or your potential clients. For example, you

should keep vocabulary at an eighth-grade reading level.[2] (This doesn't mean you need to "dumb" your content down, *Time* and *Newsweek*'s content is typically at an eighth-grade reading level. It does, however, mean that you need to use plain English and avoid flowery, multisyllabic words when simpler ones will suffice.)

## Webster, Webster & Cohen Copy Guidelines

Our voice at Webster, Webster & Cohen is approachable, compassionate, empathetic, and welcoming. We never make our clients feel alienated by complex legalese. Instead, we talk in everyday terms our clients understand and translate legal concepts for the general public using images, analogies, and plain language. Our content should always strive to connect with, educate, and empower our clients so they can make the best decisions. We don't boast about our accomplishments or frighten the client into thinking we're the only option. And we avoid writing styles that make it hard for our clients to follow. Instead, we communicate with simple, clear sentences in active voice, with no unnecessary Latin or legal jargon. Our clients should be able to skim through the headings, introductions, and calls to action of any page or asset to understand the overall message and the next steps they should take.

If you're a solo practitioner or you have a very small team, you might not need to make a full branding guidelines document right away. If you have a strong enough sense of your brand and you can

2. If you need help assessing your content's reading level, there are a variety of tools you can use. Microsoft Word can analyze a document's reading level. To do this, you'll need to go to "Options" or "Preferences" in MS Word's menu and click the box that says "show readability statistics." When you run the spell check, it will automatically report your content's reading level. You can also use a website like http://gunning-fog-index.com.

personally review everything, it's possible to stay consistent without having an authoritative document you can refer to. However, the larger your firm gets, the harder it will become to get your hands on every marketing asset that goes out the door.

# Evaluating What You Have

Once you have a clear idea of the brand you want to convey, it's time to start evaluating what marketing assets you already have and what you need. Your brand needs to stay consistent at every point the public could interact with it.

For Webster, Webster & Cohen, they're just beginning this process. After creating their logo, color palette, and guidelines document, they're going back and looking at their major marketing materials and **touchpoints**, including the following:

1. Printed materials, like letterhead

    » All the office letterhead has an old logo, so WWC should probably order new letterhead as soon as it's feasible.

2. Their website and everything on it (text, images, videos)

    » WWC hasn't put money into their website in a long time, so it looks like it was designed by a college student in 1997. They know they'll need to build a completely new site in the near future. (We'll talk more about the process of building a website in chapter 4, "Build Your Core Website," and 5, "Upgrade and Optimize Your Website.")

3. Billboards

» WWC hasn't invested in billboards since they're prohibitively expensive. So, nothing to worry about here.

4. Radio and TV ads

» WWC runs a few radio spots and local television ads that regularly bring in leads. For the radio spots, the content could be better, but it's good enough for now, and since it's audio-only, there are no worries about logo discrepancies. The television ads were shot on digital media with a local video marketing firm, so WWC should contact the firm and ask them to replace the firm's old logo in the ads, then resubmit the updated ads to the advertising reps at the relevant stations. WWC would like to create new ads that align better with the firm's updated branding, but they don't have the budget right now with a website redesign looming. So, updating the existing TV ads with the new logo will do until the website project gets completed.

5. Social media profiles (**Facebook, LinkedIn**)

» WWC should assign an intern or someone from the support staff to update the company's existing Facebook and LinkedIn profiles with the new logo and to make sure the company name and all contact info are consistent across platforms. Over time, WWC will roll out a strategy to publish social media content that's in line with the updated brand. See chapter 7, "Engage Your Followers on Social Media," for more information about social media marketing.

» Make sure that one key employee has the log-in and password data for each account. Otherwise, you may face problems if the intern or staff member leaves your firm and forgets to transfer the passwords over. At LaFleur, we use password management software to ensure that our passwords remain safe and accessible.

6. Listings on **directory** sites (Avvo, Justia, FindLaw)

   » The directory listings for WWC are all over the place because of the naming consistency problems we mentioned earlier. WWC should assign someone (maybe an intern or a member of the office support staff) to go through all the directories and make sure the firm's name and contact information are standardized, both in any listings for the firm and any profiles for individual attorneys. This is a medium-priority item, not as important as overhauling the website and updating social profiles.

7. Your office environment (interior and exterior)

   » The offices at WWC are a bit dingy and sterile. The firm would like to get out of its location in a strip mall, but they don't have the resources right now. However, they can still take some steps to update the location in the meantime: working with a local printing company to get updated signage and stickers for the door, for example, and putting on some fresh paint in the new brand colors. (Stores like Lowe's and Home Depot can actually mix paint that matches custom colors if you give them the Pantone values we mentioned earlier during the section on visual brand guidelines.)

8. Intake processes and employee training

   » WWC is a small team with three attorneys and a few paralegals and support staff, so they don't have any elaborate training or intake materials to update. Most employee training is hands-on. However, WWC should have everyone in the firm attend the final meeting where the design agency unveils the brand guidelines, so each employee understands what the updated brand is trying to accomplish and where the firm wants to go. Going forward, everyone in the firm should have access to a PDF version of the brand guidelines document in case they need to review it.

If you're starting up a brand-new firm and you don't have any of these major touchpoints in place yet, then you have a great foundation to start building them. On the other hand, if you already spent lots of money building all these touchpoints and now you realize none of them align with what you want your brand to represent, that can feel devastating. Overhauling all this stuff can be a massive undertaking, which is why large companies spend years to rework their brands.

When you find yourself with a lot of assets that don't align with your brand and not enough money to update them all, don't despair. If needed, meditate for a while or find one of those inflatable clown-shaped punching bags and give it a good whacking. Then move forward by doing what you can when you can. Start making a realistic plan to make changes over time based on whatever resources you can devote to it.

# Summary

Remember that well-built brands endure for decades or even longer, so it's okay for a branding or rebranding process to take time. Eventually, you may reevaluate parts of your brand and make tweaks and updates, but if you take a thoughtful, thorough path through the branding process, you should come up with a core concept for your law firm's brand that's essentially timeless.

# Branding Guidelines Checklist

Based on what you learned in this chapter, you can create these things, or work with an agency to create them with you:

- Vision statement
- Mission statement
- Logo
- Color palette
- Visual guidelines
- Copy guidelines

# 2

# Foundations: Your Audience

Have you ever had a fascinating story you told in a few different settings? If so, you'll probably realize when you look back that the telling turned out just a bit different each time, even if the essential facts stayed constant.

If you told your story to a good friend over a drink or two, then you might have stretched out and spun a full-on yarn, knowing your friend was completely focused. Later, at a party or social dinner with a couple loudmouths lurking around, you might have pared your long and winding tale down to a few highlights as you competed for attention.

If the story centered on a case or court proceeding, then maybe you filled in all the legal details when you told fellow attorneys, knowing they'd salivate over these morsels. But when you told the same story to family or friends from outside the legal world, you knew from experience that their eyes glaze over whenever you get into the weeds of litigation and legal work, so you avoided that path and focused on the indelible characters and the unforgettable outcome.

If you've ever tailored a story to your listeners like this, then you intuitively understand that different audiences have different needs, interests, and priorities. Not everyone responds to a story the same way, so it's important to know your listeners and adjust your language, pacing, and choice of details to keep them rapt at attention. This is true in social life, and it's true in marketing as well.

In the previous chapter, we learned about the process of defining your brand, which involved planning out the story you want to tell when marketing your law firm. Now, in this chapter, we'll learn how to zero in on your most valuable potential clients—your target audience—so you can adjust *how* you tell your story to create the greatest impact.

## Target Market versus Target Audience

If you've read books about business or are otherwise familiar with business language, you might have heard the term *target market* before. *Target market* generally means "the group of consumers most likely to buy a company's products or services." So, what's the difference between your **target market** and your **target audience**?

The answer: your target market is the group of people whom you want to buy your products or services, and your target audience is the group of people whom you want to receive and respond to your advertising messages.

Why even distinguish between the two? Would your law firm ever want to create marketing messages aimed at people who would never buy your products or services? Well, yes, you might. For example, you might at some point create a web page and some supporting blog content designed to generate referral cases from other attorneys. The attorneys won't be the ones who actually sign on as clients, but they can send folks your way who will. In this case, the attorneys are your target audience while the referred clients are your target market.

In most situations, though, target audience and target market mean roughly or even exactly the same thing. Advertisers tend to prefer the term *target audience* because it specifically refers to people who will receive advertising messages.

## Breaking an Audience into Segments

So, let's return to the example of your killer story from the introduction to this chapter. Technically, anyone who will listen to your story is part of your overall target audience. But we broke down that larger group into a few distinct groups, each of which requires a slightly different telling of the story to keep them interested:

1. **Lawyer friends:** You already have an existing relationship with them, and they love listening to interesting legal details as well. Assuming your story involves your work, they'll not only listen to your story at length but also eat up any information about the legal aspects of the case or the litigation process that you can throw at them.

2. **Friends and family:** They already know you and like you, so they're happy to listen to your story for quite a while. However, they don't understand the finer points of the law, so you'll lose them if you try to focus too much on the legal elements of your story. You can tell a lengthier version of your tale, but it's best to focus on the more universal human elements: the characters, the events, and the outcome.

3. **Strangers at a party or social event:** They don't know you, so you have no existing goodwill with them, and there's a lot going on around them. You could easily lose their interest, so you need to keep your story short and to the point.

In marketing, we call this process of breaking down a larger audience into identifiable groups **audience segmentation**, and we would call each of these groups we came up with audience segments.

Whenever you can identify distinct groups within your overall target audience who may respond best to different types of messages, you'll need to separate those groups into segments and create separate ad campaigns and content for each segment.

# Defining Your Target Audience through Research

Your target audience (and the various segments within that audience) shouldn't come from a gut feeling or your recall. It's important to gather as much data about your most valuable potential clients as you can to sharpen your picture of who you're marketing to. To learn more about your audience, follow these initial steps:

## 1. Get Information about Your Current and Past Clients

One of the simplest and most effective ways you can figure out which types of people are likely to become clients is to look at the clients you've already signed. Once you understand some of the essential characteristics that define them, you can try to create messages that target other people with similar characteristics.

Fortunately, compared to, say, a company that sells products over the web to customers they've never met, law firms tend to have a lot of information about their clients. If you're not already recording detailed information about your clients, preferably using some type of client intake and case management software, then it's time to start. Here are some data points you'll want to consider:

- age
- stage of life (single, parent, retired, and so on)
- gender
- location (where they live)
- language
- education
- income

Even for practice areas that can seem demographic-agnostic at first glance, like car accident law, it's important to gather this data and look for trends. Although car accidents and the resulting injuries can happen to anyone, that doesn't mean every car accident victim is equally likely to receive medical treatment for their injuries and hire an attorney.

## 2. View Analytics Data from Your Website

Analytics tools on your website can provide lots of useful demographic and behavioral information about the people who visit. However, since you're reading a chapter about the basics of digital marketing, there's a good chance you may not have a website at all, let alone a high-traffic website with analytics tools in place. That's okay. We'll talk more about website analytics and what you can learn from them in chapter 16, "Going Beyond the Basics: Analytics." For now, we'll stick to low-tech fundamentals.

## 3. Study Your Competitors

Every small law firm has those competitors—the bigger firms that seem to vacuum up clients effortlessly. Most likely, those firms have done lots of work over the years to understand their target audience. However, marketing isn't a perfect science, and markets and audiences change over time, so even the most successful firms can overlook lucrative sources of potential clients.

Ask yourself: How are your competitors positioning themselves in the market? Are they going after the same potential clients that you are? Are they targeting demographics or types of cases you've never tried to focus on? Is there a valuable type of client or case out there that they're overlooking?

Of course, you probably can't just call up your competitors and ask them for this information. But what you can do is browse their website, check out their social media profiles, and sign up for their emails and e-newsletters. By studying their marketing messages, you can probably make some educated inferences about the types of clients and cases they're working hardest to bring in. You might even notice some obvious mistakes in their strategy.

### Webster, Webster & Cohen's Competition

Webster, Webster & Cohen (WWC for short) checks out a top competing injury law firm. The competing firm maintains an active blog and publishes almost exclusively about car accidents and truck crashes,[1] so it seems like these are the cases they're trying hardest to bring in.

1. We know that many injury attorneys dislike the terms *car accident* and *truck accident*, because they minimize the negligent party's negligence. However, your clients aren't searching *truck wreck* and *car crash* as frequently as accident-related terms. For example, Ahrefs (a respected data analytics company) reports that *car accident lawyer* gets roughly fifteen thousand monthly searches on Google. *Car crash lawyer* gets only one hundred searches.

However, WWC notices that the blogs the competing law firm publishes are overly verbose and written at a reading level that's way above average. In WWC's experience, car crash victims tend to come from a fairly average educational background, so the competing law firm's approach doesn't seem to make sense. The competing law firm might not be doing a good job of communicating with their target audience, and WWC may be able to reach those potential clients more effectively with simpler **blog articles** that are written at a reading level appropriate for the general public.

Not only that, but even though the competing firm lists bicycle accidents and pedestrian accidents as practice areas, they don't blog about these topics at all. WWC has handled several cases involving bike crashes in the past, and those cases turned out to be lucrative ones. If top competitors aren't focusing on these types of cases, then injured cyclists might be a very valuable target audience segment that's currently flying under the radar.

## 4. Learn Why Clients Choose You

Marketers often distinguish between features and benefits of products, and this is still true when the products are legal services. Many attorneys focus on the features of their law firm: the number of cumulative years of experience, the certifications they've received, the dollar amounts for past settlements and verdicts.

However, what potential clients really care about are benefits: the results they get from working with your law firm. Your clients want to feel more confident, more at peace, more secure, and above all happier after working with you. Features—experience, credentials, case results—only matter to the extent you can convince potential clients they will translate to benefits—confidence, peace of mind, happiness.

One of the best ways to learn about the benefits of your services is to ask your current and past clients why they chose you and how they felt about their experience working with you. After candid conversations with a few of your past clients, you may find that the reasons you think your firm is a better option than the competition are completely different from the reasons potential clients make that determination. Maybe you think clients love your credentials and your success rate in trials, but they actually chose you because you were a good listener and your support staff was extremely responsive, which made the clients feel heard and cared for.

## 5. Create a Brand Positioning Statement

Using all the information you've gathered so far, it's time to create a single, succinct statement that defines your overall target audience and the benefits you offer them over the competition. Marketers call these declarations **brand positioning statements**, and they usually follow a fairly standard format:

For [target audience] who [target audience need], [brand name] provides [primary benefit]. [Brand name] stands out from the competition by [reasons target audience should choose brand].

If you find it hard to believe that a powerful brand positioning statement can follow a simple template, then consider these fictional examples we created for two global brands:

### Amazon

For consumers who want affordable products with lightning-quick delivery, Amazon offers an easy-to-use shopping platform. Amazon outpaces other online retail sites with its diverse catalog of offerings, innovative tech solutions, and obsession with the customer experience.

### Coca-Cola

For people who crave refreshing beverages, Coca-Cola provides a wide range of exciting, enjoyable options. Coca-Cola is associated worldwide with joy, friendship, and a unwavering commitment to its customers.

It's really that simple. You don't need to try to identify every different segment of your target audience in your brand positioning statement.

### Webster, Webster & Cohen's Brand Positioning Statement

For injured victims in the Hazardville area, Webster, Webster & Cohen listens to their stories, answers their questions, and uses the best available witnesses, investigation techniques, and legal strategies to win their cases. Webster, Webster & Cohen strives to make clients' lives better—not only by getting the best case results but also by treating clients with compassion and staying in touch with them at every step of their case.

Once you have a final brand positioning statement, you can add it to the brand guidelines document we described in the previous chapter. Make sure everyone who handles marketing for your brand has read the positioning statement and that you refer to the statement for guidance whenever you create new marketing materials and campaigns.

## 6. Revisit Your Audience Research Over Time

The target audience for most law firms probably won't change as rapidly as the audiences do for soft drinks and fall fashions. However, it's still important to stay in touch with your clients and keep track of any changes in their demographic information as well as in their values, attitudes, and responses to your firm.

There are at least two important reasons to do this. First of all, new generations of younger people constantly enter adulthood and begin to need legal services, and they change the market as they do so. And second, changes in buying experiences and customer service practices in other industries influence how people view their interactions with law firms too.

To stay ahead of shifts in attitudes and expectations among potential clients, you need to keep conducting the research we described in this section on a regular basis. Aim to survey a small sample of clients about their experiences and review demographic information on all your clients at least once every year.

# Personas: Imaginary Clients That Make You Real Money

A marketing **persona** (sometimes called a buyer persona) is a semi-fictional distillation of an audience segment based on research and experience. From the outside, personas appear to be one of the more fanciful elements of marketing, and they seem not very scientific at all: Can we really make up fictional clients and use them to improve our marketing efforts?

The answer is yes. However, personas can quickly devolve into a vanity exercise for creative types. (I know, because in the past I and other members of my team created personas that fell victim to this.) A persona should never turn into a Dickensian life story about the subject, replete with colorful but pointless details. Every detail contained in the persona should help inform marketing decisions.

Here are some essential elements that your personas should describe:

- age
- gender
- location
- primary language
- education
- job title
- average income
- buying behavior
- interests and activities
- life stage
- problems
- goals

Personas seem like a creative exercise at first, but they really shouldn't be. Any details that you make up are liable to be irrelevant or flat-out wrong. Instead, every detail in your personas should come from information you gathered through conversations with clients, analysis of existing client data, or study of competitors.

How many personas you need to create depends on how many practice areas you have (and regularly take cases for). Remember that your marketing personas don't need to encompass everyone who could possibly become a client. They only need to translate a few of your most valuable potential client archetypes into memorable characters you can easily reference and share. For some businesses with a very narrow focus, even a single persona might do, but for most law firms, three to five personas is probably a good range to start with.

## Persona: Ray Velo

After realizing that competitors aren't creating content that targets injured cyclists, Webster, Webster & Cohen decides to create a marketing persona that represents this valuable audience segment.

- Name: Ray Velo
- Age: 37
- Gender: Male
- Location: Victory, Vermont
- Primary language: English
- Education: Bachelor's degree
- Job title: Software developer
- Average income: $85,000 per year
- Buying behavior: Dedicated to online research; always reads reviews before buying
- Interests and activities:
    - » Cycling
    - » Health and fitness
    - » Healthy eating (organic, locally sourced)
    - » Technology
- Life stage:
    - » Married parent with two young children
- Problems:
    - » Experiencing back and neck pain after a car hit him while riding his bike, despite following all doctors' recommendations and treatment plans
    - » Can't work normal hours or keep up with normal fitness regimen, so feels depressed
    - » Struggling to pay medical bills
- Goals:
    - » Get help with medical bills
    - » Feel motivated again

Reviewing this persona, we can pick up a few details about Ray that might help inform some strategic marketing decisions. For example, Ray is struggling with mental health issues after his crash since he can't exercise or work at his normal capacity anymore. He may be searching for information about how to deal with depression after a car accident, which is the type of information WWC can provide through their blog.

Ray is also an avid reader of online reviews, so if WWC isn't already making a concerted effort to generate more positive reviews, they may need to make that a priority.

## Embrace the Journey: The Marketing Funnel

Every client goes through a **buyer's journey** to sign on with you and bring their case to your firm. You understand this intuitively to some degree: never has a potential client called your firm because an alien mothership beamed your phone number into their head. Somehow or other, the client learned about you, gathered information, and chose you from among their potential options.

Marketing professionals like to get a bit more formal about the actions that lead people to sign on as customers or clients, and we do that by visualizing the process as a **funnel**. We say *funnel* because the goal is to help the potential client narrow down their options until you're the only one that remains.

At first, the potential client is looking at a wide range of potential solutions to their problem, so the diameter of the funnel is wide; by the end of their journey, you've hopefully narrowed their focus to your firm exclusively, at which point you're likely to take them on as a client.

## Phases of the Marketing Funnel

The classic conception of the marketing funnel has four distinct phases, each one corresponding with the potential client's focus getting narrower:

1. *Awareness:* The potential client has never heard of your firm and may not even know they have a case. In this stage, the goal is to make them aware that your firm exists and can help solve the potential client's problem.

2. *Discovery:* In this phase, the potential client knows they have a legal issue and wants to learn more about how a lawyer can help them. They're likely to consume informational content like blog articles and e-books during this stage, so your goal is to give them the information they need and keep them engaged with your firm.

3. *Consideration:* Now, the potential client knows they want to hire a law firm, and they begin to look at available options. They're still doing research, but now they're looking for information that can differentiate one firm from another, like reviews and testimonials. Your goal during this stage is to make the case for your firm as the best solution and get the client to fill out a **contact form** so they become a **lead**. Once they become a lead, you can follow up through phone calls and automated emails until they schedule a consultation.

4. *Conversion:* The client schedules a consultation and chooses your firm to represent them.

The funnel is a useful concept since it will help you create a range of marketing materials that connect with potential clients no matter where they are in the process of choosing a law firm. But in real life, a client's journey rarely resembles a neat and orderly progression through a series of stages. We use digital tools to track the journey of every client we partner with at our marketing agency, and some of our current and past clients opened emails or read blogs from us for months or years before they contacted us. Leads go cold and stop responding for weeks or months before suddenly turning up again. In short, life happens.

Some types of law firms have the benefit of urgency and statutes of limitations to speed clients along, but you can still bet that most leads will require a multitude of engagements and follow-ups before they ever seriously consider hiring your firm to handle their case.

The important thing to understand about the digital marketing funnel is that potential clients have different needs at different stages of the funnel, even if they're part of the same audience.

## Ray Velo's Journey

Ray Velo, the ideal potential bicycle accident client for Webster, Webster & Cohen, starts his journey by searching for "back pain won't go away after a bike accident." WWC needs to have a well-written article on their blog about back pain after a bike accident if they hope to show up in the Google search results and connect with Ray.

Even if the firm has a phenomenal practice area page about bicycle accidents along with many testimonials from bike accident victims, Ray isn't looking for lawyers yet, and he's not browsing law firm websites to look at practice area pages and testimonials. If WWC doesn't have a blog article available that can pop up in Ray's Google search about back pain, then some other law firm most likely will—and then Ray is starting down their funnel, not WWC's. Ray will still probably compare options later, so all hope isn't lost, but the competing firm already has an advantage if Ray engages with them first.

# Summary

So far, we've laid a foundation that establishes two of the most important elements of marketing in any medium: your brand and your target audience. Now, we can move on and start talking about the information you're probably most interested in: the specific digital marketing tools and tactics that will deliver the most clients and cases for your money.

# Audience Research Checklist

Based on what you learned in this chapter, you can create these things or work with an agency to create them with you.

- Brand positioning statement
- Audience personas (three to five)

# 3

# Foundations: Tools and Tactics

If your digital marketing education is like a James Bond film, then congratulations—you've made it through the part where 007 gets an extended lecture on the fundamentals of spying. (Come to think of it, I'm sure that part was in all the scripts, but it never seemed to make the final cuts of the films.) Now, we get to the crowd-pleasing part where I play Q and walk you through all the mind-blowing gadgets you'll use in your exploits.

In other words: in this chapter, we're going to preview the various digital marketing tools and tactics that we'll discuss throughout later chapters and explain how they all fit together. And it all starts with...

## Your Website

As far as digital marketing assets go, your website is the granddaddy of them all. Your website should serve as the hub for your online presence and unify all your other digital marketing efforts. If you don't have a visually appealing, user-friendly website that's filled with content your target audience finds helpful, there's not much point in pursuing the other strategies we'll discuss.

Content marketing? Why bother publishing content on a website no one wants to spend time on? Social media? Good luck rustling up phone calls directly from YouTube and Facebook; users want to learn more about you before they'll call. Paid advertising through search engines? You won't get results without website landing pages designed to convert visitors into leads.

Since your website should serve as the sun in your digital marketing solar system, we've devoted two full chapters to the process of building, optimizing, and maintaining a website. Chapter 4, "Build Your Core Website," and chapter 5, "Upgrade and Optimize Your Website," will both focus on this topic.

## Content Marketing

Many digital marketing agencies love to advertise their **search engine optimization** (SEO) services front and center. Search engine optimization, if you're not familiar with it, is the process of tuning a website so that it ranks higher in **search engines** and therefore attracts more visitors from the **search engine results pages**.

Nothing sounds more appealing to most law firms than having an agency sprinkle some special sauce on their website and then suddenly getting lots of **website traffic** from **Google** searches. But in this guide, we haven't even devoted a chapter to SEO. Why? Because for the most part, content marketing *is* SEO.

If you don't believe me, then take it from Google. In their guide "Steps to a Google-Friendly Site," Google says:

> Provide high-quality content on your pages, especially your homepage. This is the single most important thing to do [to create a Google-friendly site].[1]

In the past, search engines were fairly primitive, and they relied on a fixed set of rules to decide whether a web page was relevant for a search. For example, they often looked for specific keywords without assessing the overall quality of the content. Marketing agencies and website management companies figured out some of these signals and abused them, creating web pages stuffed with unrelated strings of keywords.

The search engines, not knowing any better, ranked these **spam**-filled pages very high in search results. This type of loophole gave rise to SEO as a pursuit separate from content creation.

However, search engine companies never wanted SEO to work this way. They quickly caught on and knew they had to make their **algorithms** better so they could avoid these types of cheap exploits.

Today, Google and the other leading search engines (like **Bing** and **Yahoo!**, if you're into that) use a very complicated (and somewhat secretive) mix of criteria to decide which web pages should appear in searches and in what order. The goal is to craft algorithms that sort pages as a discerning human would, with an eye for quality and relevance—and those algorithms fare quite well compared to years past.

So, to recap: Google says that creating high-quality content is the most important thing you can do to get your website to rank well in Google searches, which is where most **organic** (nonpaid) website traffic comes from. And your website is the most important component of your digital marketing strategy. It stands to reason that as soon as you've got a functioning website, creating additional content like blog articles is the next avenue you should explore, and that's exactly what we recommend for most of our clients.

It's important to understand that content marketing doesn't just refer to creating written text. In fact, many web users prefer more visual

1. Google, "Steps to a Google Friendly Site" (2020), available at www.support.google.com/webmasters/answer/40349.

types of content over plain old paragraphs. A robust content marketing strategy can use any combination of these:

- blog articles
- videos
- frequently asked questions (FAQs)
- checklists
- case studies
- interactive content (like quizzes)
- in-depth content with visual elements (like e-books and infographics)

We'll discuss content marketing in greater detail in chapter 6, "Plan and Maintain a Content Strategy," and in chapter 10, "Use Visual Content to Hold Attention."

## Other SEO Activities

Even though content marketing should take up most of your attention when it comes to improving your site's performance in search **rankings**, there are a couple of other things you can do. First, you need to make sure your site is sewed up on a technical level. Specifically, your site needs to load fast, meet Google's security expectations, and have a logical structure that makes sense to the bots that crawl search engine results. You also need to make sure your content uses **header tags** and various other on-page technical elements that send the proper signals to search engines regarding the subject matter of your content. We'll go over these on-site optimizations in chapter 5, "Upgrade and Optimize Your Website."

Besides those technical concerns, you can also improve your site's search performance by reaching out to legitimate, established websites and getting them to link to yours. Usually, the best way to do this is to find a news article or blog that touches on or ties in with a topic you've written about. Then you can email the webmaster of that site directly with a link to your content and ask if they'll update their article with a link to yours. While this tactic can be time-consuming, it requires no budget or technical expertise, so it's something to consider. Of course, if you haven't invested in creating worthwhile content, then you'll have nothing to send along, so this approach only makes sense when you've got an ongoing blog content strategy in place.

## Social Media

Compared to other types of businesses, most law firms struggle to get engagement on social media. After all, many people only need a lawyer when something bad happens; on a typical day, lawyers and law firms are the furthest thing from people's minds.

However, social media marketing has several important points going for it that apply just as well to law firms as any other type of business. Number one, it's low risk and low cost: it takes very little effort to create LinkedIn and Facebook profiles so you can promote your content, share occasional snapshots of life at your office, and make yourself available to potential clients who prefer to interact via social channels. And compared to offline advertising and even your website, social media lets you build relationships faster and reach different audiences.

Finally, don't forget that for younger audiences, who get a bit older and more likely to need a lawyer every single day, using social media platforms is like breathing. For potential clients who were born after

1990 and have grown up with smartphones in hand, not using social media can make you seem aloof, unapproachable, and out of touch.

We'll sort out the finer points of social media marketing in chapter 7, "Engage Your Followers on Social Media," and chapter 12, "Paid Advertising: Start with Social."

# Email Marketing

**Email marketing** involves using email messages to move leads along the marketing funnel and to keep your existing and past clients engaged. Remember how we talked in chapter 2, "Foundations: Your Audience," about the ideal concept of the digital marketing funnel versus how it works in the real world? Well, in the ideal world, where your potential clients do exactly what you want and move through the stages of the funnel in an orderly fashion, you hardly need email marketing at all.

In the real world, where leads regularly go dormant and stop progressing for no reason you can discern, and where it sometimes take dozens of engagements with your firm before a potential client decides to call your firm and schedule a consultation, automated emails can help keep potential clients in your orbit until they come back around and become an active lead again.

But even for leads who stay constantly engaged with your firm, email marketing can play a valuable role. Sending email content lets you do the following:

- Deliver targeted content based on a client's specific area of interest.
- Personalize email content based on information you gathered from contact forms.

- Provide in-depth and exclusive information beyond what's available on your website.

- Maintain relationships with past clients so they can refer friends and family to your firm.

We'll talk about how to get the best results from email marketing in chapter 8, "Email Newsletters That Engage Your Followers," and chapter 9, "Nurture Leads with Email Automation."

# Networking

No, thankfully, I don't mean making small talk over watered-down cocktails at a local industrial-chic bar that no one actually likes. Digital networking is more about building mutually beneficial relationships with other law firms and content creators online to generate referrals and create promotional opportunities.

With a little effort and almost no expenditure, you can expand your reach to new audiences online by doing the following:

- Adding peers and media contacts to segmented marketing lists.

- Reaching out to **influencers** to share content and ideas (an influencer is someone who has an online following in a particular niche and can use their authority, knowledge, or relationship with their audience to influence others' purchasing decisions).

- Seeking opportunities to publish **guest blogs** on other websites.

We'll go over how to build a network and use it to maximum effect in chapter 11, "Networking and Creating Brand Ambassadors."

# Paid Advertising

The tools we've discussed so far generate **organic traffic**, which means traffic you don't pay for directly. It takes investment to generate the marketing assets, but once they exist, they deliver clicks and website visitors for free. However, as anyone who's clicked on a website's **banner ad** or closed a pop-up window can attest, conventional forms of advertising where you pay to place ads in front of potential clients are alive and well online.

Compared to traditional ad media like billboards, TV commercials, and radio spots, paid online advertising can be much more cost-effective. (Emphasis on *can* be.) Today's online paid advertising platforms let you observe your results and make immediate adjustments as needed, and they also give you the power to make your ads appear only for users who resemble your target audience (whom you distilled into the marketing personas you made after reading chapter 2, "Foundations: Your Audience," right?).

Probably the most important type of paid advertising is **pay-per-click (PPC) advertising**, in which you **bid** on paid ad slots in search engine results pages. Have you ever used Google to do a search and noticed the results marked "AD" at the top of the page? These spots are extremely desirable because they show up first in Google searches, which means they get lots of clicks. The only way you can get your law firm to appear in these slots is by bidding on them through PPC advertising tools.

Following are some other types of paid advertising:

- **Display advertising:** With this type of advertising, you create banner-style advertisements and then buy space for them on desirable websites through a display advertising network such as MMedia, Adknowledge, or Taboola.

- **Native advertising:** If you visit a major news website like CNN or MSNBC and browse around their homepage, you'll see a collection of links with a label that may say "From Around the Web" or "Paid Content." These links won't look much different from the site's regular articles, which is the point; many users end up clicking on these links because they don't obviously look like ads. These ads are called native advertising, and you can purchase space among collections of native ads by using a platform like Outbrain or Nativo.

- **Over-the-top (OTT) advertising:** OTT is a fast-growing form of advertising that involves delivering targeted video ads on streaming devices, gaming platforms, and internet-connected smart TVs. OTT ads are like traditional television ads in their content, but they work differently. While everyone who watches a television program on cable or network TV sees the same ads, two people who watch a show or movie on a streaming service like Hulu will see different sets of ads based on data gathered about their viewing and browsing preferences.

- **Retargeting:** This type of advertising uses the **cookies** (small pieces of data that get placed on users' devices, allowing your website to identify users and record information about them) from your website to "follow" site visitors to other websites and show them display ads to try to get them to return to your site.

We'll talk more about PPC and other types of paid advertising in chapter 12, "Paid Advertising: Start with Social," and chapter 13, "Paid Advertising: Pay per Click."

Of all the tools and tactics discussed in this book, paid advertising—and especially PPC—is the one you're most likely to fail at handling yourself. That's because running paid advertising campaigns takes technical know-how combined with constant attention. To succeed, you'll need to train yourself on how to use the (often not very user-friendly) paid advertising platforms effectively. Then, once you've launched ad campaigns, you'll have to monitor and adjust them almost every day. And the legal field is one of the most competitive and expensive industries for online paid advertising, so if you make mistakes during the learning process, they can cost you fistfuls of money.

I have a friend who's been teaching himself how to do home repairs and maintenance for several years. He once told me, "I'll take a shot at anything that doesn't involve plumbing. I leave that to the experts." Well, paid advertising is the plumbing of digital marketing. Even if you're ready to learn and have a can-do spirit, there's a strong case to be made for handling all the other tactics in this book yourself and hiring an agency to run your paid advertising campaigns.

None of this is meant to dissuade you from trying to learn about paid advertising. All I'm trying to provide is a reality check. Worst case: you read our chapter about paid advertising, and if you have to hire an agency to handle your paid campaigns, you'll be armed with an excellent BS detector. You can go into any paid advertising partnership understanding the terminology and the fundamentals of what your agency partner is doing.

We'll explain how to build and maintain paid advertising campaigns that don't burn through your budget in chapter 13, "Paid Advertising: Pay per Click," and chapter 14, "Paid Advertising: Monitoring."

## Lead Follow-Up

No matter how successful your digital marketing campaigns are, they can only get you leads. At some point, it's up to you and your team to get in touch with those leads and create the one-on-one interaction that's required to schedule their consultation, get them in the door, and sign them on as a client.

For too many law firms we've worked with at our agency, they tell us that their website and other digital marketing campaigns aren't generating clients or cases. When we examine their analytics data and lead history, we can see we're getting them many more leads per month than they've seen in the past. But when we ask about their lead follow-up practices, we hear something like: "We get back to them as soon as we can. At least within a day or two."

This type of response shows a lack of understanding of the urgency of lead follow-up in today's web-driven marketplace, and make no mistake: poor lead follow-up practices can destroy your ability to get strong returns from your investment in digital marketing, even when everything else falls into place.

Do you still think it's acceptable to contact a new potential client within a day or two? If so, consider the following statistics for website leads from a large-scale 2010 study conducted by InsideSales.com:

- Just one hour after a lead fills out a contact form, your chances of calling and reaching them are 10 percent of what they were in the first five minutes after they filled out the form.

- After twenty hours have passed from the time a lead fills out a contact form, every phone call you make actively hurts your chances of getting more information from them—you're technically better off doing nothing and waiting for them to reach out again.

We know what you're thinking: "Five minutes? My team can't just sit around waiting to pounce on every lead. How on earth can we achieve a five-minute average response time? And website leads come in at all hours—am I supposed to bolt out of bed at midnight and call if someone fills out a website form?"

Well, no. It's vitally important to examine your in-office lead-follow-up practices to look for ways you can become more efficient and responsive, but at the end of the day, you'll never be able to drop everything every single time someone fills out your website's contact form.

However, digital tools like automated email responses and automated live chat services can help do some of the lifting. These tools can keep leads engaged until someone from your team can reach out and get more information.

We'll discuss these tools in greater detail and explain how to sharpen your firm's lead follow-up practices in chapter 9, "Nurture Leads with Email Automation," and chapter 15, "Practical Client Acquisition Strategies."

## Analytics

The single greatest advantage of digital marketing tools compared to traditional advertising methods is that the digital tools generate data that you can use to improve your campaigns so you can keep getting better and better results.

When you buy an ad through traditional media—a billboard or a television spot, say—you're shooting in the dark. Sure, the company selling the ads can give you estimates of impressions based on highway traffic or TV viewership. However, once your TV ad airs, you can never know how many people stayed in front of their TVs and paid attention to your ad versus how many reached for their phones or got up for a pit stop.

With digital marketing tools, you won't have to accept guesses about how many people saw your ads, and you don't need to wonder whether that recent uptick in cases happened because of an ad campaign or a change in the weather. Even at the beginner level and using the simplest tools, digital marketing analytics tools can tell you vital information such as the following:

- How many people are visiting your website.
- Where those visitors are coming from (**organic search results**, paid ads, other websites, and so on) and where they go after visiting your website.
- How many pages people view on your website during an average visit.
- Which website pages are most popular.

- How many people are reading your blog articles and other content.
- How long people spend on your website in general and on each page.
- Which pages people often visit before filling out a contact form.
- What percentage of visitors fill out a contact form (also known as a **conversion rate**).
- The total number of leads you get via your website.
- The average cost you're paying per lead.
- Which pages cause people to leave your website.

Now, given that the above is just an incomplete list of some of the most essential website analytics (and we haven't even mentioned analytics from other tools like email and social media), there's a valid concern here: information overload. Sorting through analytics as a beginner can feel like hacking your way through dense underbrush with a rusty machete, especially since many of the platforms that provide analytics data won't seem easy to navigate at first.

Don't fret, because we'll devote an entire chapter to talking through analytics: which metrics to prioritize, which ones are mostly a vanity exercise, and how to generate reports that give you insights you can act on instead of drowning you in a sea of data points. We'll discuss this information in chapter 16, "Going Beyond the Basics: Analytics."

# How It All Fits Together

If you can think back to high school biology class, do you remember looking at an illustration of the water cycle? You know, one of those circular illustrations that shows how water moves through the environment: condensation, precipitation, collection, evaporation.

Done right, digital marketing campaigns work in the same sort of closed-loop cycle, which in an illustration should look like the water cycle:

And round and round we go. This type of relationship is why our agency likes to refer to our digital marketing services as *holistic*. This may sound slightly new age, but it captures the interrelated nature of digital marketing services, which should all tie in with each other to create an online ecosystem of sorts.

Here are the keys to seeing that ecosystem teeming with life:

1. Laying a strong foundation during your website build or rebuild.

2. Regularly publishing informative, helpful content (blog articles videos, e-books) that attracts potential clients to your website via search and gives you items to share on your social channels and in your email newsletters.

3. Keeping your brand consistent across all channels and strategies.

4. Staying focused on the target audience for each campaign.

5. Using analytics data to determine which campaigns or tactics aren't working and adjust them quickly.

# Establishing a Budget

At this point (or maybe long before), you're probably wondering: How do I translate all this into a monthly digital marketing budget? As an attorney, you're probably all too familiar with the line I'm about to give you, which is no less annoying than it is true: It depends. Your firm's business goals and unique circumstances will dictate how much you can spend and where you should put your resources first, and it would be irresponsible to give you hard-and-fast suggestions without a personalized assessment.

However, we can provide some general information about which tools you should treat with the highest priority, and we can even give you a sample monthly marketing budget for a small firm that's just getting its web presence off the ground.

If you're starting from a place where you have absolutely no online presence or everything needs work, then you should "triage" in the following order:

1. **Your website:** If your firm doesn't have a website or your existing website looks badly out of date or contains dated information, then getting your website up to speed should be your highest priority.

2. **Lead follow-up:** All digital marketing can do is get you leads, and if you can't follow up on them in a timely manner and turn them into clients, then generating leads is a pointless activity.

3. **Social media:** There's plenty of room to get sophisticated with social media, but at the minimum, creating profiles on the most popular platforms (definitely Facebook and LinkedIn, possibly **Twitter**) and posting once or twice per week requires such little investment that you can't afford not to do it.

4. **Content marketing:** Like planting a garden, getting a content marketing strategy up and running takes work, and the early results will probably fail to impress. Over time and as you get more comfortable and experienced, the work levels off while you reap continually greater benefits.

5. **Paid advertising:** Online paid advertising can deliver very impressive results very fast, but it's high-maintenance, and it can burn up cash quickly without accomplishing much—especially if you don't have other more fundamental tools and strategies in place.

6. **Networking and guest blogging:** Unless the opportunities find you, don't worry about this until you've got the other tools and strategies in place.

As for the sample monthly budget, keep in mind that it's just a starting point to get you thinking about realistic numbers, and the figures will vary widely depending on your market and the exact services you need. Rather than pay attention to the exact numbers, note the percentages, which indicate how much of the total budget each strategy takes up.

| Tactic | Budget | Percent |
|---|---|---|
| **Content marketing** | **$1,750.00** | **35 percent** |
| Blog content | $1,050.00 | 60 percent |
| Video content | $700.00 | 40 percent |
| **Paid digital advertising** | **$1,750.00** | **35 percent** |
| Google (PPC) | $787.50 | 45 percent |
| YouTube (PPC) | $350.00 | 20 percent |
| Display, native, and retargeting | $612.50 | 35 percent |
| **Website management** | **$750.00** | **15 percent** |
| Site management and hosting | $525.00 | 70 percent |
| Ongoing modifications | $225.00 | 30 percent |
| **Email marketing** | **$500.00** | **10 percent** |
| Email newsletter | $225.00 | 45 percent |
| Email campaigns | $175.00 | 35 percent |
| Hosting (for platform) | $100.00 | 20 percent |
| **Social media** | **$250.00** | **5 percent** |
| Facebook | $137.50 | 55 percent |
| Twitter | $25.00 | 10 percent |
| LinkedIn | $12.50 | 5 percent |
| YouTube | $75.00 | 30 percent |
| **TOTAL** | **$5,000.00** | **100 percent** |

# Summary

From here on, no more lectures about how the game works—it's time to play ball. Now that you've got your tools laid out in front of you and you understand how each one fits into the larger task of marketing your law firm online, we'll spend the remaining chapters teaching you how to maximize your results from each of the essential strategies we outlined in this chapter.

# 4

# Build Your Core Website

Your website is both a representation of and a tool for your law firm. All your other marketing strategies depend on having a user-focused, conversion-driven website. Your website should both stand on its own and support your other marketing initiatives—online and off.

To build a successful website, you need to focus on two key goals:

1. Provide a simple, reliable way for potential clients to contact you (and for you to add those contacts to a database).

2. Publish and promote relevant, compelling content that resonates with potential clients and gets noticed by search engines like Google.

In short, your website should be *functional* and *findable*.

# A Word about Building Your Website

Before we go any further, let's set expectations for this chapter: our goal here is to teach you the principles that go into building a good website. However, we can't actually provide detailed and illustrated step-by-step instructions about how to create your own site in this chapter. To do so would require much more than a single chapter, and we'd have to write it several times over since the process will look very different depending on which platform you choose (WordPress? Wix? Squarespace? Something else?).

Instead, we'll use this chapter to show you how a good website looks and how it works so you understand the endpoint you're trying to reach. You can use the information you learn here to inform and evaluate your website build, whether you choose to hire someone else to do it or embrace a DIY approach using one of the many available tools.

If you decide you want to build your website yourself using WordPress, then review the recommended resources at the end of this chapter, which can provide more of the step-by-step instructions that can actually help turn your website vision into reality. If you use this chapter as a companion piece with a true how-to resource that focuses on the platform you've chosen for your site, you should have all the tools you need to create a successful site that advances your firm's most important business goals.

If you choose a more beginner-friendly web builder like Wix, Weebly, or Squarespace, the platform will provide detailed instructions and tutorials to show you how to build your site. Later in this chapter, we'll talk about the pros and cons of these simplified website builders.

# Setting Goals, Avoiding Pitfalls

Whether you're building a brand-new website for your law firm or considering upgrades to your existing site, planning is the most important step to prevent headaches and skyrocketing costs. That planning needs to focus on your primary site objectives.

Unfortunately, law firms often sink disproportionate amounts of time, energy, and money into aspects of their site that won't yield a return on their investment. They mistakenly assume that their website is primarily for these uses:

- A tool for showcasing their accomplishments.
- A way to show up in Google searches.
- A first impression that needs to convey professionalism, excellence, experience, and more.

These considerations should factor into your website planning, but only as secondary concerns. First and foremost, your website is an extension of your business, so it needs to help you achieve your fundamental business goals. For most law firms, here's what your website needs to do:

- Attract site visitors who need your services.
- Encourage potential clients to provide their contact information.
- Help you and your staff follow up with **qualified leads**.

In other words, your website should help visitors move forward through the buyer's journey (defined next). This fundamental goal will inform practical decisions about site structure, design, content, and more as you plan your site.

# The Buyer's Journey on Your Home Page

Below is an example of a typical buyer's journey through the digital marketing funnel (which we introduced in chapter 2, "Foundations: Your Audience"), including details about how your understanding of that journey should inform decisions about your website's home page. For this example, we'll continue to use our fictional firm of Webster, Webster & Cohen (WWC for short). Imagine you work at WWC and are responsible for the firm's website.

Luke has been in a car crash. He is an informed consumer and knows that he needs a lawyer, so he searches online for "car accident lawyer." Your home page shows up in the search results:

websterwebsterandcohen.com ▾
Webster, Webster & Cohen: Experienced Hazardville Personal Injury Attorneys
We help victims get the justice and compensation they deserve. Call (800) 932-7837 to schedule a free consultation.

Luke clicks on it. What do you want him to accomplish once he gets to that page? Ideally, you want him to contact your firm, especially if he has an issue you can help resolve.

To encourage this outcome, you want to explain how you can help him with his issue, give him a clear **call to action** (CTA), and provide an obvious path for him to accomplish that action.

Here's a boilerplate example:

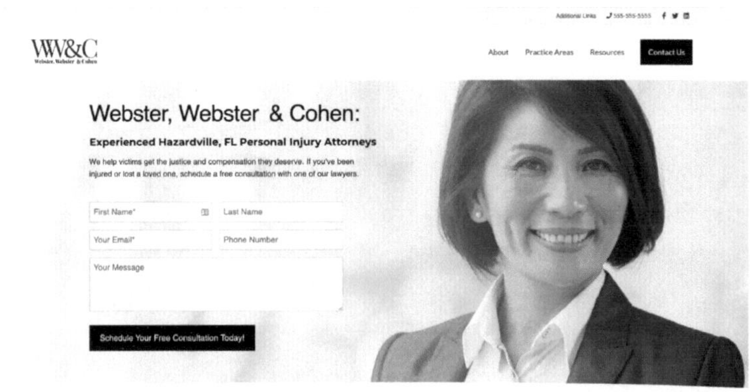

This type of high-level value proposition helps your potential clients accomplish the primary goal of the site: It makes Luke aware of what the firm is all about, describes how the firm can help Luke with his issue, and provides a way for him to move forward by scheduling a consultation.

Here are a few things you don't want potential clients to encounter as soon as they land on your home page:

- **A scrolling carousel of badges, seals, and awards.** These credentials may reinforce your expertise, but they don't directly explain how you can help a potential client, and they don't help potential clients progress toward contacting you.

- **A recent blog post.** While you want to promote the content you create, having an informational piece front and center doesn't explain how your law firm can help potential clients. And if the user clicks away from your home page to read a blog, they move further away from contacting your firm.

- **Information about how great your law firm is.** Testimonials reinforce your value proposition, and video testimonials can tell powerful stories that resonate with potential clients. But visitors need to know what you can do for them before they will become interested in the positive experiences of past clients.

- **A pop-up ad promoting your newsletter, an e-book, or another offer. Pop-up ads** can be effective, but only when they enhance the user experience on your website. If a potential client has just landed on your home page, you don't want to interrupt their progress toward your primary goal for them (scheduling a consultation) with a less valuable transaction that arrives via pop-up.

Supporting content pieces like the examples above can still help advance your primary goal, but these types of content should reside further down on your home page, **below the fold**. (Everything a visitor can see when they first arrive on a web page, without scrolling down, is considered **above the fold**.)

To improve the chances of visitors like Luke scheduling a consultation, the material above the fold should draw from the branding and positioning work we did in chapter 1, "Foundations: Your Brand," to highlight distinguishing factors of your law firm. Consider this: nearly all personal injury lawyers offer free consultations, so that information doesn't set your firm apart from competitors. If Luke has three law firm home pages in front of him, what will convince him to schedule a consultation with your firm?

Another factor to consider is your *ideal* client. Do certain types of clients or specific legal issues bring in more revenue? If so, can you focus your value proposition to target those specific types of clients and cases?

The answers to these questions will be different for each law firm. However, what will remain the same is that an audience-focused, goal-driven approach should guide all your website work and your overall digital marketing strategy.

As you generate and implement new ideas for your home page and other pages during planning, ask yourself this all-important question:

> Does this move my target audience closer to our primary business goal? If the answer is no, then rework your idea or table it for another time.

# Incorporating Imagery and Design

The overall look and feel of your site is the very first thing users will take in when they visit your home page. Compelling copy, strong headlines, videos—these all come after (and depend on) the user's initial glance over your site design.

Accordingly, your site needs a professional look and feel that speaks to your brand in an intuitive way and aligns with the expectations of your target audience. Your site's fundamental visual appeal depends primarily on two factors: design choices (like color palette and layout) and images. What constitutes good design can be subjective, but whether design is executed competently is not, so professionalism and polish are the key concerns here.

Your photography, meanwhile, should be high-resolution and attention grabbing (in an understated way—no used-car-lot ad gimmicks). Avoid **stock photography** if possible, and try to populate your site with authentic, professionally captured images that showcase your team, your office, and your location.

In addition, we always recommend featuring videos on your site, including your home page. The average web user prefers watching video over reading text, and video testimonials and FAQs can play a crucial role in reaching the many potential clients who refuse to wade through more than a sentence or two of copy.

# Planning: The Sitemap

Now that you know who your ideal client will be, and how your firm can differentiate itself from other firms, you need to create a **sitemap**. Your sitemap is a blueprint for your website.

Two primary types of sitemaps exist. The type you'll want to start with is a visual sitemap, which provides an easily readable outline of all the pages you're going to build on your website.

Here's an example of a simple visual sitemap:

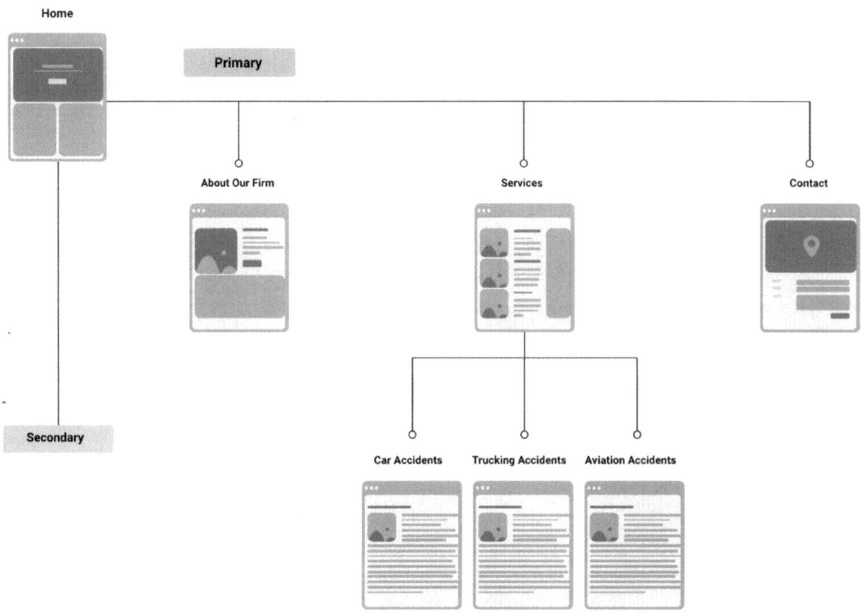


Your visual sitemap will help you plan the work involved in your website build or upgrade. It will tell you as follows:

- How many (and which) pages need to be built and designed.
- How many (and which) pages need to be written.
- How site users can find and navigate to a specific page.
- The **URL** structure of your site.

# Use Your Sitemap to Estimate Time and Costs

Based on several years of time-tracking data from people at our agency, we can help you approximate how much work is involved in creating a website. Use the table below to estimate the time investment for a very basic new or upgraded site:

| Task | Content Creation (Hours) | Design and Development (Hours) | Total (Hours) |
|---|---|---|---|
| Sitemap Creation (Visual and XML) | 2 | 2 | 4 |
| Initial site setup | 2 | 20 | 22 |
| Tools setup (Google Analytics, etc.) | 1 | 10 | 11 |
| New home page | 4 | 10 | 14 |
| New primary page | 4 | 8 | 12 |
| New secondary page | 4 | 6 | 10 |
| New tertiary page | 4 | 4 | 8 |
| Redirects (per 4 pages) | 0 | 1 | 1 |
| Existing page optimizations | 2 | 1 | 3 |
| Domain name hosting | Fixed: $2 per month and up | | |
| Managed website hosting | Fixed: $35 per month and up | | |

For Webster, Webster & Cohen to get their basic site off the ground, they would need to invest approximately 117 hours into the project, and they should plan on spending at least $40 per month to own their domain name and keep their site online.

Don't forget these estimates are based on tracked time from people who know what they are doing and have built many websites. If you've never spent time creating a website or working on one before, you should add more time to your estimate. How much more time depends on your comfort level with technology. If you're a tech-savvy person, you might add 50 percent more time to account for the hours you'll spend getting familiar with the platforms and tools. If you generally struggle with technology, you'll want to at least double the estimated time investment.

## Can't I Just Build a Free Site?

Definitely! The first website I built without knowing anything about websites was a free site, and it's still performing well (based on my own personal expectations) after almost ten years. However, my website is not a secure site. It's only a blog, and the pages all look the same (and I have very limited options for design customization). Not only do the pages look identical, but the site itself is visually generic and indistinguishable from thousands of other blogs. I don't own the **domain name** (and I have few options to customize the domain), and my site could go dark at any moment if the service I use goes out of business, changes their policies, or just decides that my site isn't worth hosting anymore.

A lot of free services can help you create and host a website, but most of them offer extremely limited options, and none of them are designed to enable long-term, sustainable website improvements.

If this is your first website and your business is in an early development phase, a free service may work just fine for you. Relying on a free site with limitations is better than having no website at all, and you can certainly build a free website that helps advance your primary business goals. Later, you can upgrade the site as your business and budget grow. However, you'll need to understand going in that you'll probably have to sacrifice security, reliability, and versatility by going with a free website. If you want your potential clients to trust you with sensitive information, showing them a no-frills website with questionable security features may not be the right way to start.

The good news is that you don't have to invest a small fortune to get a high-quality website. By budgeting only about $40 per month, you can open up a wide range of options that offer far more functionality and security. Here's what we recommend:

## Option 1: Do It Yourself

First, buy your domain name. GoDaddy is a popular domain name provider (https://www.godaddy.com/). NameCheap is another option (https://www.namecheap.com/). The important thing is that you own your domain and it reflects your brand, not another company's (in other words, you want "websterwebsterandcohen.com," not "webster.blogspot.com"). Owning your domain shouldn't cost you much more than $20 per year unless you're trying to buy an established URL. If someone already owns the domain name you want, you'll have to find another option or negotiate with the owner to try and secure the desired domain.

Once you own a domain name, you should use WPEngine (https://wpengine.com/) to get managed **web hosting**. Managed web hosting is when the web host not only hosts your domain but also takes care of various technical issues, like server operation and maintenance. Without managed hosting, fixing every technical issue falls to you. If you run into a problem you can't fix yourself—which is very likely unless you're an experienced web developer—then the hosting service will charge you a steep hourly rate for help.

For affordable managed hosting, WPEngine is a provider we recommend based on extensive firsthand experience. You can get their most basic plan for about $35 a month. This package will get you off the ground and give you options to scale up, and it also provides a great deal of customization so you can build something that doesn't look like every other site out there.

You can find cheaper web hosting options, but they probably won't manage your hosting for you. Plus, WPEngine offers 24/7 chat if you need help, and your site will be secured with an **SSL (Secure Sockets Layer) certificate**. An SSL certificate is a digital certificate that authenticates the identity of a website and encrypts information sent to the server. Having an SSL certificate makes your website more secure, and it also gives your site's URL an **https** designation, so visitors will know you've taken extra steps to secure their data.

You can also use all-in-one hosting and website creation services like Wix, Weebly, and Squarespace to create your site. Compared to WPEngine, these services have a much easier learning curve and require much less technical know-how. However, they also don't have the range of capabilities that WPEngine has, and the sites they create often look more like digital brochures than fully functional websites. Sites created by beginner-friendly platforms also don't import well into other platforms. If you decide you need more options and tools than Wix or Squarespace can provide, you'll most likely have to rebuild your website from scratch using WPEngine or another platform that has more functionality.

If you do decide to use a beginner-friendly platform, you don't have to go with that platform for hosting; you can still get your hosting through an independent service like GoDaddy and connect it to the web builder you've chosen. You may want to consider this option since it will keep you from putting all your eggs in one basket and tying up your domain name with a platform you may outgrow later on.

## Option 2: Work with a Developer or Marketing Partner

Many people assume that a developer or agency won't work with them unless it's to build a new website from scratch. However, that's not necessarily true. Even if you've already got a site built and don't want a new one yet, there are potential benefits to partnering with an agency.

For example, agencies can usually negotiate discounted rates or better service packages compared to what you'll find on your own. You may be able to get a cheaper hosting rate or better features just by reaching out to an agency and asking if they offer managed hosting or will host your site on their servers. And later, if you want to scale up your website, the agency should be able to help.

Many agencies will probably put a markup on their hosting, but if you have a candid conversation with them and outline exactly what you need (just the managed hosting while you handle everything else), you should be able to reach a mutually beneficial agreement. And if not, you can shop around or stick with the 100 percent do-it-yourself approach through WPEngine.

However, if you should remember one thing about working with an agency, it's this: do not let them (or anyone besides the principal stakeholder of your business) own your domain. When someone else owns your domain, they own your website and everything on it. If the partnership goes bad, they can hold your website hostage. You can always add domain managers from within or outside your organization, but make sure the domain ownership stays with you.

# Your Website's Most Important Functionality

Lead generation is the most important task your website has. During the process of planning and building your site, make sure to research and select tools that will allow you to capture lead information and respond to leads as quickly as possible. Many attorneys don't prioritize lead follow-up, and they believe responding within twenty-four hours is good enough. These two mistakes are probably why 71 percent of qualified leads never get pursued and the remaining 29 percent are only touched an average of 1.3 times.[1]

Here's the reality: just five minutes after initial contact, your chances of successfully contacting a lead drop by 90 percent. After thirty minutes, your chances are only 1 percent of what they were in the moments after the initial contact. And after twenty hours, every phone call you make actually *hurts* your chances of qualifying the lead.[2]

So, how can you get leads to reach out, and how can you connect with them right away when they do?

## Make Sure Your Physical Address Is Highly Visible

For most law firms, walk-ins are not a significant source of leads. However, it's crucial that you use a consistent address throughout all

1. https://www.forbes.com/sites/kenkrogue/2012/07/12/the-black-hole-that-executives-dont-know-about/#159fba1a38e3.

2. http://www7.insidesales.com/file.aspx/infographic_LeadResponseMgmt_4_.pdf?bb=01020000016725E4-C&f=3981-63736-614A6A5BCF14&3981_rm_id=168.20648206.7&mkt_tok=eyJpIjoiTnpkbU5UQm1ZVE5pTUdZeiIsInQiOi-JNRktzZzFTMWkwenpHR1g3dmJEck4zMnlmNmg1dFlEWVhJZndudFlvSDcxQmRmbkNqTk5YeXlKWTBWUGVrQTU1eHFRd3FOUlNVS2hhQ25CNE41Wk-dKdz09In0 percent3D.

your online listings (website, social media, business directories, and so on). That address should be in the standard USPS format:

Webster, Webster & Cohen
123 Fake St.
Hazardville, FL 10001

Also, you should always use the same brand name for your business (that is, decide whether it's Webster Law or Webster, Webster & Cohen and stick with your choice). Whether you get a lot of walk-ins or not, you're not going to be available in your office twenty-four hours a day, so you will want to make sure you have an alternative way for potential clients to contact you.

## Show Your Phone Number

Prominently displaying your primary office phone number is a great start. But will someone always be available to answer it? If not, consider a call center. Most centers allow you to provide your own call script and will only charge you for qualified leads. Similar to your address, make sure your phone number is the same throughout all your online listings. It should be in the standard format:

(800) XXX-XXXX

If you have a vanity number, make sure your numeric number is also prominently displayed. We have seen positive results with the following format:

(800) WEBSTER | (800) XXX-XXXX

And if you want more accurate ROI tracking for your digital marketing efforts, you may want to consider a **dedicated tracking phone number** for your website and other online listings. A dedicated tracking phone number is a unique phone number that is assigned to a specific marketing tool, like your website. When someone calls this tracking number, it forwards to your normal business phone number, but you'll collect data about where the person found your contact information.

Finally, make sure your phone number can receive (and respond to) text messages. Many potential clients, especially younger ones, prefer to communicate via text.

## Consider Using Online Chat

Phone calls can be intimidating for some people. For those who feel more comfortable with text, an online chat option can seem more approachable. And again, most chat services will charge a flat fee per chat or only charge for qualified leads.

## Use Online Forms

Forms are a crucial lead generation tool for any website. This is an example of a contact form from our agency's website:

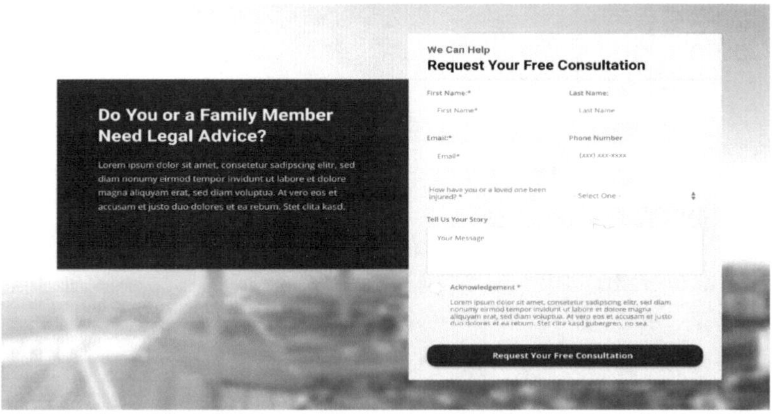

Here are a few important best practices to keep in mind for website forms:

- **Ask for only the information you need to fulfill the lead's request.** For example, if you're running a promotion such as a giveaway, you'll get a lot more people to sign up if you ask only for a name and email address. If someone is requesting a consultation, you'll probably need their name, email, and phone number. The general principle is that fewer fields mean more form-fills and more leads.

- **If someone fills out a form, they should get immediate confirmation that their information has been submitted.** People want to know they accomplished their goal. We recommend redirecting people to a thank-you page as soon as they complete a form. That thank-you page should tell them the information has been submitted, and it should outline what they can expect next (such as an email or call from your staff). We also recommend sending an immediate automated email when someone completes a form. It should include the same information as the thank-you page: confirmation of their action and what to expect next.

- **Forms need to notify you and/or your staff of the action a lead took on your site.** If someone requests a consultation, you need to know immediately so you can follow up with them as soon as possible.

Forms can also help you capture leads at different stages in their buyer's journey through the digital marketing funnel. Leads who walk in, call your office, or request a consultation are at the end of the buyer's journey; they're ready to discuss hiring you.

But what if someone is shopping around for attorneys? They're not likely to walk in, call your office, or request a consultation. Instead, they want more information about your firm or their legal issue without having to worry about getting harangued by phone calls and other outreach from your firm.

To cater to leads in the consideration stage of the buyer's journey, you can offer low-commitment, high-value options for potential clients. Use a form to let them download an e-book. Have an FAQs page on your site with a form to submit a question. Build a contact form that isn't about scheduling a consultation. These offerings give potential clients a chance to engage with your firm and have a positive experience *before* they're ready to hire you.

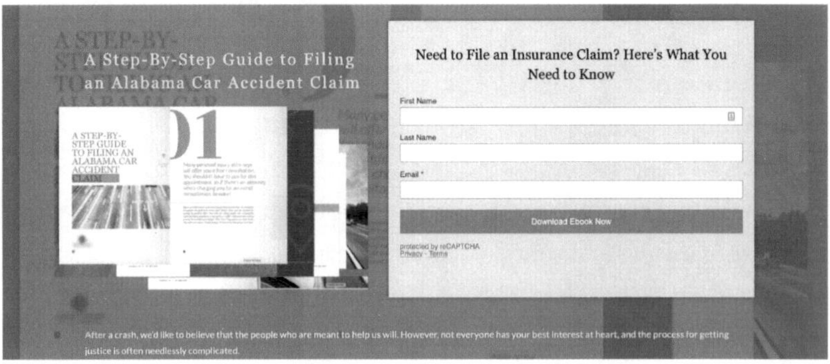

You should also consider building forms that appeal to leads in the earliest stage of the buyer's journey: the awareness phase. These leads are just learning about your firm, and they may even just be discovering they have a potential case.

One strategy for engaging with these early-stage leads is to let them sign up for a regular email newsletter. You could also provide a series of informational emails about your specific practice areas. You can offer giveaways for rideshare discounts, law firm swag, coffee, and other perks. These types of marketing campaigns help generate awareness about your firm and keep you in the forefront of people's minds until they (or people within their personal or professional network) have an issue that requires your help.

# Maintaining Your Marketing Database

No matter how leads come in, you need a reliable, consistent way to add them to your marketing database. Many attorneys have sophisticated case management software that helps them keep careful track of new and current clients—people who have completed the buyer's journey.

What most attorneys don't have is a similarly sophisticated tool that helps them keep careful track of *potential* clients. In marketing terms, this is known as a **customer relationship management** (**CRM**) system. At minimum, your CRM should keep track of who your leads are and how they've engaged with your firm.

Your marketing database doesn't need to be fancy. If you're just getting started or you don't have a lot of leads to keep track of, a simple spreadsheet is enough. Make each column a granular data point:

- First name
- Last name
- Email
- Phone number
- Street address
- City
- State
- ZIP code
- Lead **source** (web, referral, walk-in, etc.)
- Became a client?
- Attributable revenue
- Other notes

# Summary

Building your website is going to be a bigger project than you expect, but it's a long-term investment in your law firm. If you dedicate quality time to planning your core site's functionality, put your audience first throughout your project, and always keep your primary business goals in the front of your mind, you should end up with a site that can serve as a strong foundation for all your digital marketing efforts.

# Checklist for Building a New Website

- Identify your audience and primary goals (see chapter 1, "Foundations: Your Brand").
- Create a sitemap.
- Estimate time investment and costs.
- Purchase your domain.
- Sign up for managed hosting.
- Choose a website building platform (or hire an agency).
- Populate your site with your content (see chapter 6, "Plan and Maintain a Content Strategy").

# Additional Recommended Resources

- WPBeginner, available at: https://www.wpbeginner.com/
- Andy Williams, *WordPress for Beginners 2020: A Visual Step-by-Step Guide to Mastering WordPress* (Amazon.com Services, 2020).

# 5

# Upgrade and Optimize Your Website

Having a website is just the first step in successfully marketing your law firm online. If you have a simple, stripped-down website, you may reach a point where you need to scale up for the site to continue advancing your business goals. And even a robust, thoughtfully designed site can fall out of date given the ever-changing nature of digital technology and web users' expectations.

To make meaningful improvements to your website, you need to focus on two key goals, which are the same as the key goals we established in chapter 2, "Foundations: Your Audience," about building a website:

1. Provide a simple, reliable way for potential clients to contact you (and for you to add those contacts to a database).

2. Publish and promote relevant, compelling content that resonates with potential clients and gets noticed by search engines like Google.

Once again, the most important qualities of a good law firm website are that it's both *functional* and *findable*.

# How to Scale Up Your Website

Much like starting a new site, scaling up your existing website starts with a sitemap. As you plan improvements to your website and develop your larger marketing strategy, you'll probably need to add new pages to your site and modify your site's structure. For example, Webster, Webster & Cohen may want to expand their service offerings over time. This would require a shift from the simpler structure of their site launch, and it would take significantly more planning to execute properly. That planning still begins with a visual sitemap. First, let's look at the simple visual sitemap from chapter 4, "Build Your Core Website" and then compare it to an expanded sitemap with new pages.

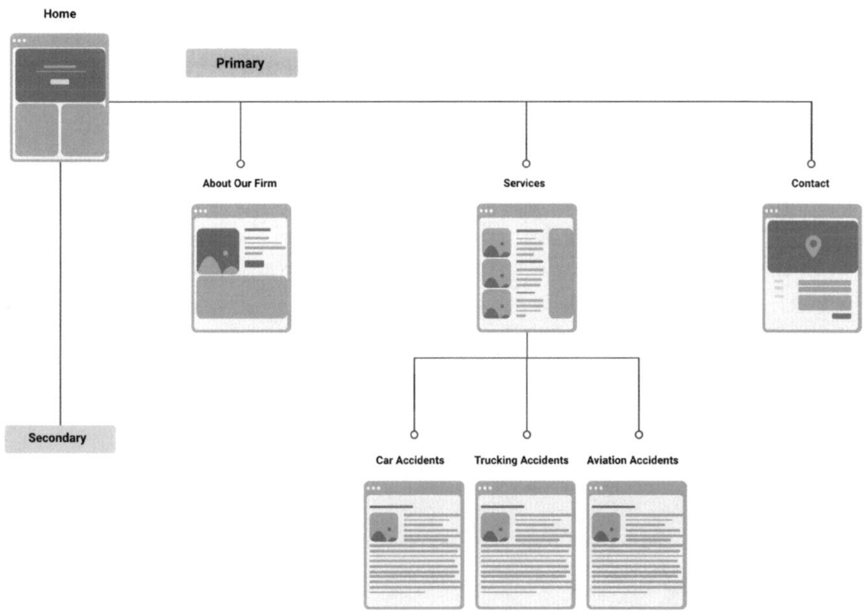

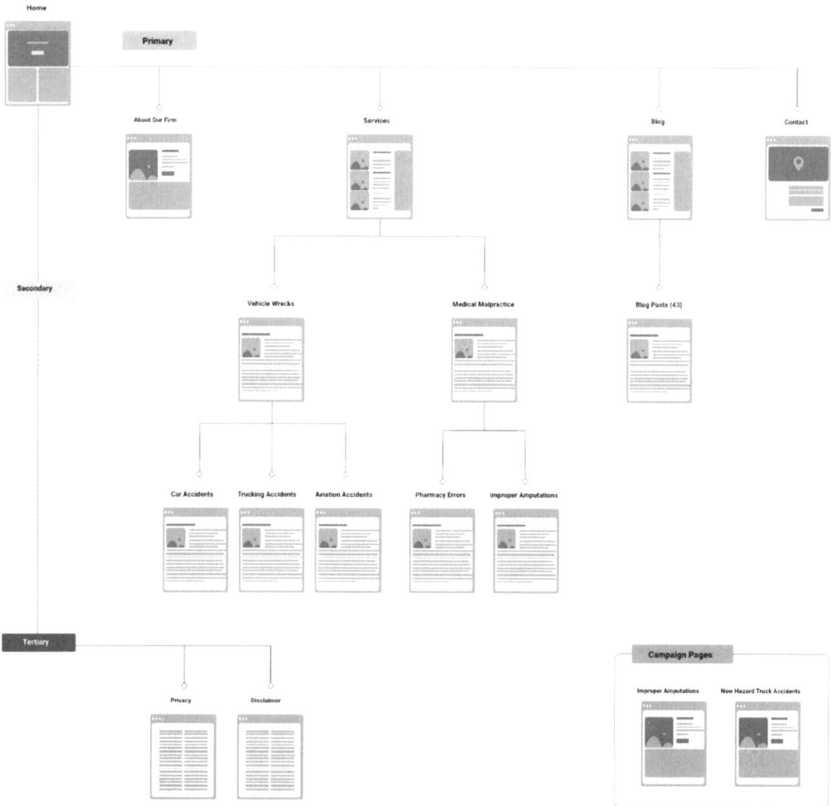


Note that some of the pages from before have moved down a tier. Previously, the "Aviation Accidents" page was a subpage of "Services." Now, it's a subpage of "Vehicle Wrecks." This should be reflected in the URL structure. Before, the "Aviation Accidents" page would have had a URL like this:

- https://websterwebsterandcohen.com/services/aviation-accidents

In the updated structure, it should have a URL like this:

- https://websterwebsterandcohen.com/services/vehicle-wrecks/aviation-accidents

Why worry about URLs at all? URLs have a clear effect on the user experience, and they can impact your search rankings. When you create pages, focus on building concise, descriptive URLs. In our "Aviation Accidents" URL, it's easy to see what the page is about and where it fits in the site's hierarchy:

- https://websterwebsterandcohen.com/services/vehicle-wrecks/aviation-accidents

This structured description tells users that aviation accidents are a type of vehicle wreck and that Webster, Webster & Cohen provides services related to them. You can also see that it's a secure site because it has an "https" prefix. Compare this to a URL that may be generated by a free website building service:

- http://websterwebsterandcohen.free.com/page/pageid=tk421

Yikes. From this, we can gather a couple insights:

1. First, it's not a secure site. The "http" prefix gives that away, and so will the browser we're using: it will say "not secure" instead of displaying a lock icon.

2. Second, Webster, Webster & Cohen doesn't own their domain.

3. Third, we are going to visit a page. But what is that page about? Is it even a safe web page to visit? The URL certainly doesn't inspire much trust.

However, updating URLs can cause complications. When a page gets a new URL, search engines regard it as a completely different page, even if it has the same content. So, let's presume your original page was ranking well in search engines. When you expand your site and move that content to a new page (.../vehicle-wrecks/aviation-accidents), two things will happen:

1. **Google will see the new page and consider that page just like any new page: a blank slate.** All the links and traffic that may have been boosting the old page's search performance are now erased.

2. **Google will see the new page as duplicate content.** Because Google already has a record of that exact content (or remarkably similar content) from your previous page, Google's algorithms will treat the new page as a copycat. At best, Google will ignore the new page and pretend it doesn't exist, which means it won't rank well. At worst, the search engine will penalize your site for using the same content in multiple places, which means all your pages will drop in rankings because of the **penalty**.

Taking down the old page (.../services/aviation-accidents) might help you avoid the second problem. However, if someone tries to navigate to the old URL (perhaps because they clicked a link on social media or had the old URL bookmarked), they will receive a "page not found" **404 error**. This is a frustrating experience for a user, and they will often abandon your website because of it.

The way to avoid these issues as you expand your site is to use a tool called a **redirect**. Redirects (specifically **301 redirects**) are small lines of code that tell browsers and search engines: "Hey, this page doesn't exist anymore. It has moved permanently to a new location. Please send people to that new page, and please give all the credit from the old page to the new page."

If you use 301 redirects effectively, between 90 percent and 99 percent of your **page authority** (the weight search engines give to a page to determine how well it ranks) will pass from your old page to your new page. Most importantly, by redirecting pages, you make sure your audience can find the information they're looking for instead of encountering 404 errors or not finding it in search engines at all.

Every time you plan to add or move pages on your site, you need to carefully review which ones will get moved and redirected. Using redirects appropriately will ensure that you will preserve all the hard work you put into your site as you continue to improve and expand it. In most cases, you can set up redirects within your web hosting platform.

Besides your overall site architecture and your URL structure, there are a few other essentials you should consider as you build new pages on your site, and they relate to search engine optimization (SEO).

## What Is SEO?

Search engine optimization (SEO), as we introduced in chapter 3, "Foundations: Tools and Tactics," is the practice of adjusting your website, web pages, and other website strategies so your website will rank higher in search engine results. Leading businesses care a lot about SEO because ranking higher in search can create a drastic increase in web traffic, which in turn can yield leads and customers.

When it comes to ranking in search results, many companies have a "page one or bust" attitude, and it's easy to see why: results on page one get more than 95 percent of all the clicks on Google, and the first five results on page one get more than 67 percent.[1]

But there's more to SEO than just elbowing your way into the first page. Having an optimized website won't get you into the map section of search results (also known as the *three-pack*, Google tends to show about three local results with a click-through option for "more businesses"), for example.

1. Madeline Jacobson, "How Far Down the Search Engine Results Page Will Most People Go?" *Leverage Marketing Blog*, https://www.theleverageway.com/blog/how-far-down-the-search-engine-results-page-will-most-people-go.

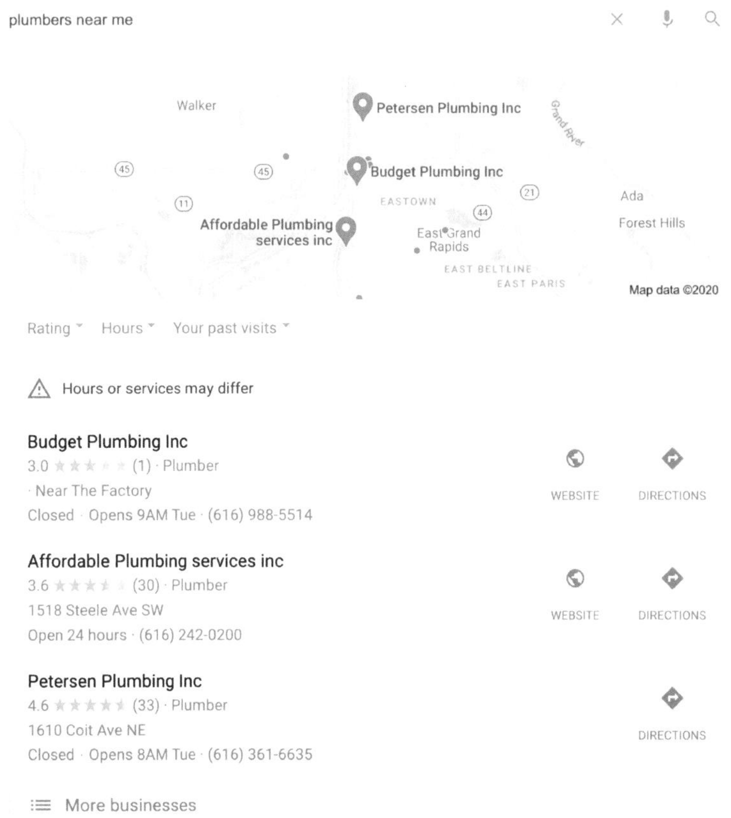


To get your site in the three-pack, you'll need to create a verified local listing with Google, gather a certain number of positive reviews, make sure your contact information is consistent across all your channels, and more.

Having a search-optimized site also won't get you in the top paid results in search engines (the ones labeled as ads, which appear before organic results in a standard search engine results page). Getting your website to appear in the paid results requires running paid search ads, and trying to compete in this area for many law-related search terms is shockingly expensive. Every year, at least seventy-five of the one hundred most expensive paid advertising terms relate to the legal industry.

And unfortunately, even having a great site full of search-optimized content still might not get you on the first page of Google for your most-desired keywords. The competition over premiere keywords, especially in lucrative practice areas like personal injury law, is tooth and nail. If someone is promising you first-page results, you need to find someone else to help you with your site, because that's not a guarantee anyone can make.

But don't lose hope. There's still plenty you can do to attract traffic to your website and generate leads, even on a budget.

## Rethinking Keywords

**Keyword** is one of those marketing terms that everyone has heard but few people really understand. Keywords used to be much more important for SEO than they are now. In the early days of SEO, you would use a keywords tag to tell Google what each of your web pages was about. The words you tagged had a 1:1 correlation to what your page ranked for. If you put down "personal injury lawyer" as a **meta keyword**, Google believed your page was about that, even if it was really about auto repair.

However, companies abused this system flagrantly, and Google stopped using keyword tags as a ranking signal over a decade ago. Today, hundreds of factors determine how any given page ranks, as well as what **keywords** it ranks for.

Over time, technology has become increasingly adept at understanding human language. When you type the term "car accident attorney" into Google, you will see ten organic results plus a few paid ones. If you type in "car wreck lawyer," you'll see almost the exact results. If you type in "auto crash attorney," you'll see extremely similar results once again. From our own independent research into keywords within the legal industry, we know that, on average, synonymous searches like the ones above will have 81 percent similar results.

We used to think of those different terms as distinct keywords, but Google doesn't see them that way anymore. Thanks to advancements in natural language processing, Google is smart enough to know that "car accident," "car crash," "car wreck," "vehicle accident," "vehicle crash," "auto accident," "auto wreck," and so on, are synonyms. Google also knows that "lawyer" and "attorney" are the same thing.

So, achieving high rankings for one keyword can bring an incredible amount of related traffic from similar keywords. However, as synonyms have gotten bundled together, ranking on the first page of Google has become increasingly more competitive and difficult. You can't corner the market on ranking for a slightly obscure wording like "car collision" simply because other firms forgot to target it; firms that rank well for "car crash" will rank just as well (or close to it) for "car collision."

By focusing on obvious keywords and their many slight variations, many law firms are ignoring where most of their site traffic actually comes from: **long-tail keywords**. Compared to simple, obvious keywords (which we could also call short-tail keywords), long-tail keywords tend to be longer and more specific.

- **Short-tail keyword:** car accident

- **Long-tail keyword:** back pain after car accident

If you look at the most popular searches online (which consist of mostly simple keywords), the top ten thousand most searched terms on the internet account for just 18.5 percent of web traffic. The other 81.5 percent of web traffic comes from long-tail keywords.[2]

Another benefit of long-tail keywords is that fewer companies target them using paid search ads. Even if your page ranks number one for a keyword organically, that page still can't compete with paid ads, which

2. Neil Patel, "11 Reasons You Need to Focus on Long-Tail Keywords for SEO," www.neilpatel.com (blog), https://neilpatel.com/blog/long-tail-keywords-seo.

always appear first. However, if there are no paid ads for a keyword—almost impossible for highly competitive keywords but very much possible for long-tail keywords—then organic results can appear on the page first. So, while your competitors are spending huge amounts on paid advertising and praying those expensive clicks turn into leads, you can publish content based around long-tail keywords to build a solid foundation of steady traffic for a fraction of the cost.

## Optimizing Your Website for Long-Tail Keywords

So, how do you build a base of content around these relatively unpredictable long-tail keywords? The answer involves putting yourself in your potential client's shoes.

Consider the question of why people use search engines at all. The answer is that they usually get results they find relevant. If search engines like Google stopped serving up content people found helpful, people would stop using them. Google knows this better than anyone, so they work constantly to refine and improve their search algorithms.

In the past, Google's algorithms were much less sophisticated than they are today, and marketers found loopholes they could use to make low-quality pages rank much higher than they deserved. Today, potential loopholes still exist, but they're much smaller, and Google is always working to close them. And when you create a page based around exploiting an oversight in Google's algorithm, you're left with nothing when Google eventually fixes that oversight.

Rather than try to jump between constantly closing loopholes, the way to create a website that ranks well in Google, Bing, and other search engines is much simpler: create content that your potential clients will find helpful and informative, and then make sure search engines can find and **index** that content. Here are a few tips, and note also that we go into this topic in more depth in chapter 6, "Plan and Maintain a Content Strategy."

## 1. Work to Understand Your Target Audience

Examine your past clients who brought lucrative cases. By looking at common factors among these clients, you can create detailed marketing personas (which we discussed in chapter 2, "Foundations: Your Audience") that can guide decisions about your content, including your blog's editorial calendar and the primary content on your home page and practice area pages. You can also perform market research and use the data to create personas if you don't have past clients to draw from or want to expand your target audience beyond the types of clients you're used to.

## 2. Use Your Personas to Create a Plan for Your Content

You can hire outside writers to create your website content or write it yourself, but either way, you'll want to use your marketing personas as the starting point for all writing and editing. Think about the people your personas represent and try to create content that addresses their questions, speaks to their needs, and explains exactly how you can help them. Don't forget that every page and blog article needs prominent calls to action (CTAs) that tell the potential client what you want them to do: call our firm, fill out this form, email our office.

No matter how proud you are of your credentials and bona fides, remember that your website content isn't about you—it's about your audience, and their needs always come first. Resist any urges to write copy that trumpets your achievements or extols your many virtues.

Draw from the personas we discussed in chapter 2, "Foundations: Your Audience," and when writing pages, consider the following questions:

- What do your ideal clients want to know about?
- What should they know that could help them, even if they don't hire you?
- What are they anxious about, and how can you help?
- What information could help them hire the best attorney for their case, regardless of who that is?

## 3. Make Sure Search Engines Can Find Your Content

Some people assume that Google searches every page on the web, but that's not true. You need to take proactive steps to make sure search engines like Google can find your site.

### Google Search Console

First, start by creating an account with **Google Search Console** (https://search.google.com/search-console) and then adding your website. Google will ask you to verify your website through one of several methods; adding an **HTML** tag to your home page is usually the simplest way. Google will provide all the instructions for you to do this.

Once your site is registered in Google Search Console, Google will ask you to submit a sitemap in a file format known as **XML**. This might sound technical, but it's fairly easy. If you created your website through a service like WordPress or Squarespace, then you should have free tools available that can help you create a sitemap. You can also create a sitemap using tools like Screaming Frog SEO Spider, which will generate a sitemap for free as long as your website includes fewer than three hundred pages or so.

Once you've uploaded your **XML sitemap**, Google will crawl and index the pages on your site, and you can check to make sure Google is seeing all the pages you want. If not, you may need to double-check the XML sitemap and make sure it's accurate.

## Your robots.txt File

If Google isn't seeing any of your pages, you may need to delete something called your **robots.txt** file. A robots.txt file is a tiny little text file that tells search engine bots what pages they should pay attention to on your site—and which one they should ignore. You shouldn't have to worry about robots.txt if you used a template-based, beginner-friendly website builder like Wix or Squarespace, or even if you used WPEngine as we recommended in the previous chapter. However, it can be an issue on some older sites or with some custom web builds.

Depending on which web builder you used or who built your website, your web host might set your robots.txt file by default to tell search engines to ignore *all* your pages. This is helpful when you're building a site because it will make sure your site doesn't show up in search engine results when it's only half-finished. However, you need to turn off this functionality when you're done with your site since now you *want* your site to show up in Google. The easiest way to do so is simply delete the robots.txt file. If you need to do this, just do a Google search for how to accomplish this task with your website building platform.

# Low-Investment, High-Return Web Page Optimizations

As you build and update core website pages, you'll need to pay special attention to the following SEO features:

- **title tag**
- **meta description**
- H1 tag
- H2 tag(s)
- **image alt tags**

It's easier to point out these SEO elements than to describe them (with the exception of image alt tags, which we'll describe shortly), so here's what these elements look like in a Google search results page and on your site:

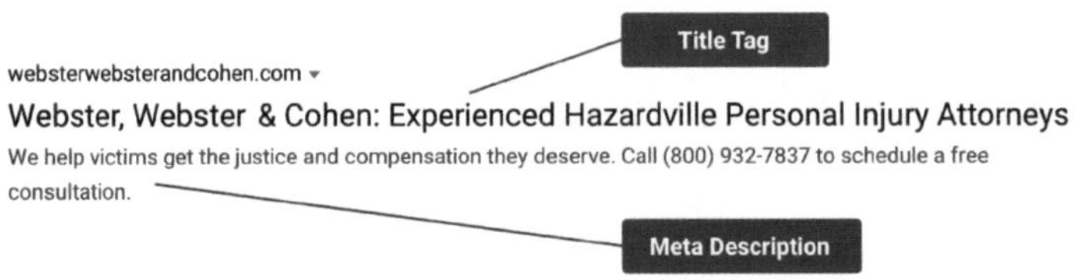

Note that the **H1 tag** is the same as the title tag—that's intentional. We'll explain why that's a good idea in a minute.

As far as we know (since Google doesn't share every detail about how their search algorithms work), Google reads your title tag, H1 tag, and H2 tags to help determine what your page is about and rank it in searches accordingly. The meta description doesn't matter at all for rankings, but the text from your meta description will appear in search engine results (sometimes).

To get the best results out of your core website content, you need to use these elements strategically. Here are some tips for improving the on-page SEO elements for your web pages.

## Title Tag

Google displays only the first sixty-five characters or so of your title tag in search engine results. So, you'll want to either keep your title tag around sixty characters (just to be safe) or put the essential information in your title first. Keep in mind that Google reads the entire title and considers all the words for SEO purposes, so it's okay to have a longer title tag—just make sure that the first sixty characters or so make sense on their own since that's all search users will see.

However, even though you can make your title tag as long as you want, cramming dozens of potential keywords in your title tag won't help you. (That's one of those loopholes Google closed long ago.) So, never create an overlong title tag that reads poorly just so you can stuff in more keywords. Instead, use a core keyword or two to create a title that succinctly describes what your page is about and sounds inviting to potential clients.

## Meta Description

Google cuts off your meta description after about 155 characters, so you'll want to keep it short and to the point. This is especially true since more people use mobile than desktop devices, and you have even less space in mobile search results.

Note that words from your meta description that match (or are synonyms of) words in a searcher's keyword will show up bolded in the search results page. Also, if your meta description doesn't include any of the keywords the searcher used, Google may pull from whatever section of your page does contain those keywords to create its own meta description on the fly. Don't take it personally—Google is just trying to show the search user that your page contains information that's relevant to their search.

So, don't try to write a sales pitch into your meta description. Not only will that turn off potential clients, but since it won't match with any potential search terms, Google will probably ignore your sales-y meta description and never display it. Instead, just write a short and helpful description of your page that gives users a preview of what they'll find when they get there.

## H1 Tag

As we mentioned earlier, the primary headline on your page, your H1 (heading 1) tag should closely match your title tag. If people click on your title tag in search and land on a page with a headline that's completely different, they're going to feel confused. They may mistakenly think they clicked on the wrong web page, or they may even think you've lied about the content of your web page. When a web user thinks they wound up at the wrong page or, even worse, thinks you've pulled a bait and switch on them, you can bet they'll leave the page as quickly as possible.

However, that doesn't mean you can never do anything except copy and paste your title tag and use it as your H1. If you had to cut down your desired title tag for a blog article because it was longer than sixty characters, you may be able to use your original full title as your H1 as long as it's not too different from your title tag. You can also add things like a subtitle to your H1 to describe the content in more depth.

Some marketers are starting to put multiple H1 tags on a page because they think Google will give the keywords in those tags higher importance and thus rank the page higher for those keywords. That could be true right now (remember that no one outside of Google knows exactly how Google's algorithms work), so this tactic might provide a temporary boost, but remember that Google is constantly improving their algorithm and closing loopholes. If they notice the H1 tag is becoming a poor signal of what a page is about, they'll demote its importance as a ranking factor and send shortsighted marketers scrambling for another, even less effective exploit.

## H2 Tags

During law school, you probably embraced outlining. Your ability to break complicated concepts down into outline form also comes into play when you're creating web content. Your H2 tags operate like the top-level Roman numerals in an outline. Each major section should have a heading marked with an H2 tag. When you reach another major section, you'll mark that section's heading with another H2 tag.

So, what do H3 and H4 tags do? They provide additional structure to your content, just like the letters and Arabic numerals do in an outline. Let's say your piece has three major sections, but one of those sections is broken up into even smaller subsections that need their own headings. You would mark those headings with an H3 tag. If one of those sections marked by an H3 needed to be broken up into still smaller sections, you would mark the headings on those smaller sections with H4 tags. You can do this all the way down to H6, although your piece would have to be very long and in-depth to warrant sub-sub-sub-sub-subheadings. (At our agency, we rarely use tags lower than H3.)

Google assigns a bit more weight to heading tags compared to plain paragraph copy, so it makes sense to use some of your desired keywords and keyword variations in your H2 and H3 tags. Just don't overdo it and compromise readability, because conveying helpful information for the users who actually visit your pages is still the most important function of heading tags.

## Image Alt Tags

When people who are blind or who have vision impairments use the internet, they do so with screen readers that read aloud the content of web pages. When these screen readers run into an image, they describe the content of the image using the image's alt tag, which you can specify while building the page. So, for an example, an image of a man fishing off a dock at sunset would have an alt tag that says—can you guess it?—"image of a man fishing off a dock at sunset."

Image alt tags are important to make your site accessible for people with disabilities, but they serve another purpose too. Search engine robots also can't view images and process the content like we can, so they also turn to alt tags. Using alt tags that reinforce the content of your page and your desired keywords—for example, writing "injured victim with bandages and crutch after a car crash" instead of "person with bandages and crutch"—can help give search engines extra cues as to what your page is primarily about, which can in turn help the page rank higher for relevant keywords.

## Summary

When it comes to web development and optimizing your web pages for search performance and conversions, there are countless nuances you can focus on. (For example, just changing the color of a button on your site can impact how many people click on it.) There's always room for testing and improving a website, but if you can nail the foundational SEO elements on your web pages, you'll be in great shape for ranking well in search and attracting new clients from the web.

# Checklist for Upgrading and Optimizing Your Site

- Build new pages as needed.
- Create redirects when deleting pages.
- Review site content to make sure it's user focused and keyword friendly (see chapter 6, "Plan and Maintain a Content Strategy").
- Create a Google Search Console account and upload your sitemap.
- Audit site pages to make sure on-page SEO elements are in place:
    - » title tags
    - » meta descriptions
    - » H1 tags
    - » H2 tags (and additional H# tags, for very long and in-depth content)
    - » image alt tags

# 6

# Plan and Maintain a Content Strategy

Many lawyers assume that creating content is the easy part of their digital marketing strategy. After all, they're subject matter experts and have specialized training in the arts of legal research and writing! However, if your blog and website content sounds like an amicus brief, it's unlikely to attract your ideal clients. You need to approach your digital content like a marketer—not a lawyer.

Outstanding website content attracts, engages, and educates your current and prospective clients in addition to increasing your site traffic, raising its authority, and providing other important SEO benefits. That means you need to regularly publish well-written content that speaks to your clients, not your peers.

As you begin planning your law firm's content strategy, you will need to focus on three key tasks:

1. Developing ideas and scheduling them in an editorial calendar.

2. Building a clear editorial process.

3. Assessing your content's performance.

In this chapter, we'll focus on the first and most crucial phase of content strategy: regularly writing and publishing great articles for your website.

# What Is Content Marketing?

Content marketing is more than writing information and articles for your website. It is a comprehensive strategic process that helps you reach your community, engage with your readers, and convert them into clients. Typically, content marketing involves research, writing, editing, publishing, and promoting original and meaningful information.

When your law firm invests in content marketing, it can provide a remarkable ROI year after year. Each new article will increase the number of keywords your site will naturally rank for and provide more material for your audience to engage with when they visit your site. If you're creating great marketing materials, you'll see steady improvements in site traffic, search rankings, and lead generation.

Ideally, your content will not only educate readers but also build trust and encourage conversion. Suppose someone finds one of your articles through a Google search. When they visit your page, they should gain valuable insight into their problems and find themselves exploring your website, subscribing to your newsletter, and submitting contact forms.

Typically, this means you need to supplement your content with forms, calls to action, links to related pages, images, and other design features that increase engagement and shareability. You can also develop infographics, white papers, videos, interviews, quizzes, surveys, e-books, podcasts, or other types of content that demonstrate your expertise and improve your visibility in search engines.

If you do all of this correctly, your efforts should increase your law firm's visibility online and position you as a trusted source of information and legal services.

# It's Not Easy to Make a Search Engine's First Page

You're a good writer and a subject matter expert, so writing high-quality content will be easy, right? Think again. There are millions of legal websites on the internet. Roughly ten of these websites will appear on the first page for any given search.

As we discussed in chapter 3, "Foundations: Tools and Tactics," you're better off building your content around high-value long-tail keywords, like "when should I consult with a truck wreck lawyer," rather than the highly competitive, overly general ones like "injury lawyer." However, many of these long-tail keywords still garner a lot of attention. For example, 274 million websites rank for "how do i file a personal injury lawsuit."[1] The ten web pages that appear on Google's first page are the very select few.

To reach the first page for your most coveted keywords, you're going to need a well-built and respected website with great content. This is a work-intensive process, and it's best to split tasks between several writers and editors. Depending on your circumstances, they may include your law firm's partners, associate attorneys, paralegals, or your marketing partner's staff.

1. Google search, March 23, 2020.

# What Makes Content Great?

As an attorney, your most valuable asset is your knowledge and expertise. To attract the right clients, you'll need content that appeals to both the search engines and your key demographics. It should be well written, approachable, and dense.

You've seen keyword-loaded blogs and web pages that jam terms into the most awkward of places. These websites encourage you to "Schedule Your Free 18-Wheeler Crash Settlement Consultation with Our Boston, MA Commercial Vehicle Lawyers and TBI Attorneys!" Although the page does not include a substantive discussion of either brain injuries or federal trucking regulations, it lists every imaginable keyword and wedges geographic locations into every header.

In the past, these ham-handed tactics sometimes worked. Thankfully, search algorithms are now sophisticated enough to identify this poorly written content as low-value spam.

Today, you'll need content that is typo-free, rich in information, and directly targeted at your ideal clients. Following are some of the key priorities you should include:

## Expressing Your Law Firm's Unique Value

Every lawyer and law firm has a value proposition. You may be a technical expert, focus on a specific population's needs, or have a reputation for your trial advocacy. Don't shy away from what makes your firm great!

You also want your content to closely align with your skill sets and value. If you're proud of your firm's client experience, make sure your content's voice reflects your in-person demeanor. Or, if you're known for your scientific approach to prelitigation investigations, share your success stories and insight online in a way that emphasizes your expertise.

For example, suppose Webster, Webster & Cohen's clients love their hands-on approach and personalized client experience. On their "About the Firm" page, the firm may note:

> The injury lawyers at Webster, Webster & Cohen know that your case and priorities are unique. That's why we spend time with our clients, getting to know them, their stories, and how someone's negligence changed their life forever. When you work with us, you'll be treated like family, not a number.

## Targeting Your Ideal Clients' Needs

While it's important to educate your community about legal issues, the ultimate goal of your content is conversion, turning your readers into clients and referral sources. If your content does not appeal to your ideal clients or address their pain points, you're wasting your time.

Ask yourself:

- What pressing issues are important to the community we serve?
- Are we providing meaningful information and insight?
- Does our blog or page use language that our key demographics will understand?

For example, we try to create blog content at an eighth- or ninth-grade level for most law firms—otherwise the subject matter may be too technical. For more information and resources, refer back to our discussion of readability in chapter 1, "Foundations: Your Brand." For example, suppose Webster, Webster & Cohen is trying to target bicycle accident victims and they decide to write a blog about bicycle helmets. Its bike injury expert writes a blog entitled "Bicycle Helmets and CPSC Noncompliance."

While this title makes perfect sense to the biking injury lawyer, it's unlikely that many laypeople would click on the article. First, they probably don't know that the CPSC is a federal consumer products watchdog. Second, even if they have some basic knowledge about cycling helmet certifications, the title isn't very enticing.

Luckily, Webster, Webster & Cohen's editor realizes that the blog's title won't speak to their ideal clients. They change the title to "Who Is Financially Responsible for Defective or Unsafe Bicycle Helmets?" and break the issue down in simple, understandable terms.

## Demonstrating Your Expertise and Knowledge

While search engines typically prefer long-form content, their algorithms don't equate word count and quality. Instead, they give priority to resources that are rich in content and analysis. This doesn't mean your blogs should resemble appellate briefs or law review articles. Rather, they should translate complex legal issues into plain English, distilling their key concepts and requirements.

For example, consider the following sentence:

> After a car crash, plaintiffs need to promptly assess both their first- and third-party claims, provide notice, and submit a settlement demand.

Do your clients know what a first-party claim is? Are they searching for this term? In our experience, it's unlikely that even your most sophisticated leads are looking for a "first-party claim lawyer."

Instead, it would be better to provide a more comprehensive, plain English analysis that defines important terms.

> After a car crash, you'll need to identify all of the insurance policies that cover your claim, including:
>
> - **Liability insurance:** all drivers in our state must purchase auto insurance that steps in when they injure someone in a wreck.
> - **Uninsured and Underinsured Motorist Coverage (UM/UIM):** you may have this optional coverage as part of your auto insurance policy, which steps in when the at-fault driver lacks insurance or after a hit-and-run.
> - **Personal Injury Protection (PIP):** another type of optional coverage that will cover your medical bills and lost income, no matter who caused the accident.
>
> It's not easy to identify each and every insurance policy that covers your accident. To ensure that you get the compensation you deserve, it's best to consult with an injury lawyer early on.
>
> When you meet with one of our attorneys, they will help you identify all of the responsible parties, which may include the driver, their employer, and others. Then they'll investigate your claims, compile your medical bills, calculate your lost income and other damages, and demand fair compensation from the insurance company.

We believe that this second approach offers two significant advantages. First, a deep dive into content naturally boosts your number of long-tail keywords and organic search ranking. Second, the ability and willingness to explain difficult legal concepts to your readers demonstrates your expertise and can build trust and goodwill.

## Creating Original Content

Sometimes, lawyers are tempted to "borrow" content from a reliable source. However, if you're simply cutting and pasting content from another site, it will damage your organic ranking. Search engines can easily identify plagiarism—and pages with copied content will never rank well.

# Creating a Content Marketing Plan

A well-built content marketing strategy is rarely thrown together on an ad hoc basis. If you're inconsistent in your approach and don't set a clear definition for success, you'll have a hard time determining whether your marketing investment is paying off.

Your plan doesn't need to be a highly technical document. However, it should set attainable goals and identify your marketing tactics.

## Setting Goals

You need to outline the overall goals and objectives of your content marketing efforts. For most law firms, your primary goal will be increasing the number of qualified leads and clients you obtain through the website.

You may also set secondary, performance-based goals. For example, your law firm may aim to double its number of website visitors within twelve months. Or you may want to reduce your **bounce rate**, the number of people who visit your site and immediately leave, by 25 percent. If you're brand new to legal marketing, your goal may simply involve sticking to your blogging schedule.

## Defining Your Content Strategy

For most law firms, their content strategy focuses on creating and promoting articles and blogs. We have found that if you consistently post a minimum of two high-quality monthly blogs, you're going to see a positive impact. While this may sound easy, it takes organization and preparation.

How many times have you sat down to write an article or blog, and you're struck with a case of writer's block? Or you quickly fumble for a topic, and the resulting article is a dud? To avoid these problems, your law firm should introduce systems that set you up for success. That includes setting clear timelines and standard operating procedures for each step in your content development process.

Now, we'll outline a proven editorial process for creating digital content.

# Step 1: Research Your Potential Topics

You may be fascinated by the nuances of your state's joinder rules. However, that doesn't mean that your ideal clients are searching for information on that topic. As you start to build your editorial calendar, which sets out the blog topics you plan to cover each month, you will want to research popular and trending keywords as well as your audience's interests.

You should always be on the lookout for potential topics, and you'll be surprised where you find them. Sometimes, other lawyers bring them up. Other times, you'll learn about new developments at a seminar or conference. They'll even pop up while you're researching other blogs.

Keep a blogging ideas notepad on your desk or smartphone. When inspiration hits you, write your idea down.

If you don't have a trove of ideas at the ready, you can do some preliminary research to develop a topic. Here are some places to look for ideas:

## Your Favorite News Sources and Resources

You're probably already tracking news in your area of expertise. When you're scanning your local newspaper, the *New England Journal of Medicine,* your state bar journal, or the FDA's latest round of recalls, keep an eye out for topics that may also interest your clients.

While it's tempting to rehash interesting news or a cutting-edge study, look for stories that you can put your own spin on or provide a new level of insight for. For example, rather than just report on a fatal drunk driving crash in your community, craft a blog that uses the story as a springboard for a more detailed discussion of your state's wrongful death and drunk driving laws, and the possibility of punitive damages in such a case.

Ideally, you should spend about 20 percent of the piece summarizing the news, 70 percent discussing the central issue, and 10 percent covering how you and your firm can help individuals who are struggling with that central issue.

## Your Competitors' Content

Competitive research is a great way to get inspiration for your own blogs. As you research blog topics, look at the top-ranking articles on the issue—both from your law firm's competitors and from directory sites like FindLaw. However, you should never copy their content verbatim. As mentioned above, the search engines strongly discourage plagiarism.

To ensure that your content is original, look for gaps in your competitors' content. For example, suppose your top competitor has a blog called "4 Questions You Should Ask a Car Accident Lawyer Before You Hire Them." You like the topic and click on the link. Their blog's body looks like this:

Before you hire a lawyer, ask them these four questions:

1. How long have you been practicing?
2. Will you handle my claim or will a junior associate be my attorney?
3. How often do you handle car accident cases?
4. Have you ever represented someone with injuries similar to mine?

If they can't answer these questions, keep looking.

Call us today for a free consultation. We're ready to answer these questions and more!

That's it: 74 words! Your law firm definitely can do better than that. You call your version of this blog "A Car Accident Victim's Guide to Hiring a Lawyer." You not only list a series of questions, but also outline the kind of answers the crash victim should be looking for. For example:

***Do You Have Experience with Cases That Are Similar to Mine?***

At Webster, Webster & Cohen, we know that every car accident claim is different. However, that doesn't mean that you shouldn't learn from experience. There's a significant learning curve for some types of cases, like spinal cord or traumatic brain injuries (TBIs). If your lawyer already has relationships with respected experts and can easily interpret your complex medical records, it's a significant advantage. Don't be shy about asking your lawyer about their experience and familiarity with your type of claim.

If they've never handled a claim like yours or can't answer your questions to your satisfaction, it's a good idea to get a second opinion, since you want to build your attorney-client relationship on a strong foundation of trust.

Then you list a series of five other questions and important considerations, explaining how an experienced and trustworthy lawyer should answer them. Without a doubt, your blog's content is going to rank for more keywords and resonate with your ideal clients when compared to your competitor's puff piece.

## Your Current and Former Clients

Your current and former clients are invaluable as sources for content ideas. Ask them what they wish they would have known before calling you, what they would like to learn more about, and what they are currently struggling with.

For example, we work with a law firm that published a detailed blog about the settlement process, based on their clients' questions. After several years, it still is consistently one of their best-ranking articles, bringing in hundreds of visitors each month.

You can also ask your staff about the challenges your clients face, what questions your team answers over and over again, and what resources they could use to help educate clients. These topics can serve to both attract new audiences to your website and save your staff time and energy. Rather than having to write (and rewrite) the same email to new clients in the future, they can point to an article on your site or send a templated email.

## Legal Trends and Emerging Causes of Action

The law is constantly evolving, and traditional metrics like search volume can't always help you identify potentially lucrative or important areas of developing law. This is especially true if you focus on mass torts, intellectual property, or patent law. If you identify an issue that your clients need to know about, take some initiative and explain the information to your readers in plain English.

# Step 2: Create an Editorial Calendar

No matter where you get your topics from, they are only rough ideas until you build them into a detailed editorial calendar. This calendar serves several purposes:

- Setting publication deadlines for each topic.
- Reducing writer's block by providing approved topics to your writers.
- Ensuring that all of your blogs and content meet your high standards and align with your overall marketing strategy.
- Connecting your writers with high-quality resources and research.

Ideally, you should create quarterly editorial calendars that provide your writers and editors with three essential elements: a working title, a framework for the blog, and reference materials.

Our editorial calendars typically look like this:

| | |
|---|---|
| June<br>Blog 1 | **Working Title:**<br>How Do I Prove Someone Was Texting While Driving?<br>• Discuss ways a lawyer can prove that an at-fault driver was texting at the time of a crash.<br>• Emphasize that victims need to act quickly to preserve the driver's electronic data and other evidence.<br>• Note Webster, Webster & Cohen's long history of success handling cases against distracted drivers.<br>**References:**<br>https://www.nhtsa.gov/risky-driving/distracted-driving<br>https://www.cdc.gov/motorvehiclesafety/distracted_driving/index.html |

<table>
<tr><td>June<br>Blog 2</td><td>Working Title:<br>5 Things You Need to Know about Drowsy Driving and Truck Wrecks<ul><li>According to the Large Truck Causation Study, at least 12 percent of truck crashes are due to fatigue, falling asleep at the wheel, and nonperformance.</li><li>Educate readers about the FMCSA's hours of service rules.</li><li>Explain how many trucks have advanced technology (like telematics) that tracks drivers' behavior.</li><li>Outline why victims need to quickly preserve logbooks, black boxes, and other evidence.</li><li>Direct readers to Webster, Webster & Cohen for help and more information.</li></ul>References:<br>https://www.fmcsa.dot.gov/regulations/hours-of-service<br>https://www.fmcsa.dot.gov/safety/research-and-analysis/large-truck-crash-causation-study-analysis-brief</td></tr>
<tr><td>June<br>Client Story</td><td>Working Title:<br>Rebuilding After a TBI: Cathy's Story<ul><li>Introduce readers to Cathy and Ed Client. Ed suffered a TBI after a trucker failed to yield the right of way.</li><li>Explain how Webster, Webster & Cohen helped the couple get the answers and help they needed.</li></ul>References:<br>Cathy and Ed Client testimonial video<br>Mediation_summary.doc<br>Final_settlement_agreement.pdf<br>Note:<br>The clients signed a confidentiality agreement, and we cannot name the trucking company or divulge their settlement amount.</td></tr>
</table>

Now, let's explore each section of the editorial calendar in more detail.

## Working Title

A **working title** is just that, a jumping-off place for your writers. It can help them identify the key purpose of the blog and your intended audience. However, since working titles frequently become final titles, don't just jot down "A blog about the risks of distracted driving." Instead, craft a title that is optimized for search engines, like "5 Ways to Prove a Distracted Driver Caused Your Accident." Ideally, it should be about sixty to seventy characters and should speak directly to your ideal clients' concerns and interests.

## The Blog's Rationale or Purpose

Your editorial calendar should guide the writer through the basic issues the article will discuss. It should answer the "so what?" question: you're writing about an editorial process—so what? Why should I care? What can I do with this information?

This description is crucial for writers, whether that's you or your staff. You're building your editorial calendar in advance and should not assume that you or anyone else will recall your thought process later on. You should also highlight potential stumbling blocks within the piece. For example, if there's a recent change in the law, mention the need to address the new statute or legal precedent. Having a well-developed description and outline will streamline the research and writing process.

## Sources and Reference Materials

Reference materials are the foundation for each writing task. While you don't need to provide an annotated bibliography or an exhaustive resource list, you should give your writers a solid starting point. Your sources may include important cases, statutes, regulations, law review notes or legal analysis, academic research, data, and sample blogs on the same topic. When possible, include primary sources, rather than articles that simply summarize their findings.

This may seem like a lot to do before you've even started writing, but investing in the earliest stage of your ideas will save you time and energy throughout the rest of the writing process. Once you've completed a few editorial calendars, it could take as little as thirty to forty-five minutes to build each blog topic.

Finally, as you're creating your editorial calendar, keep the scope of each project in mind. It should take an average of four to eight hours to write and edit an eight-hundred-word blog post. More complex projects like e-books and white papers will take much longer. However, if your blog topics deserve a treatise, take some time and refine them.

# Step 3: Project Management

Now that you have an approved editorial calendar, you need to address the logistics of content development. Many lawyers and law firms' in-house marketing projects stall because there isn't a clearly defined process, people don't understand their marketing roles, and there aren't firm deadlines.

Before you start developing content, it's a good idea to do the following:

- Break each blog's creation into discrete tasks, such as writing, editing, and posting.
- Assign each task to someone on your team.

- Set clear deadlines for each task, giving everyone sufficient time to properly complete the work.

- Create a system of accountability that balances your need for on-time completion and high-quality content.

If your law firm already uses project management software, such as Asana, Basecamp, or Microsoft Planner, you can build your marketing projects within these tools. However, smaller firms and sole practitioners can set tasks and deadlines in their email and calendar systems.

# Step 4: Research and Writing

While legal marketing strategy may not be within your wheelhouse yet, you're probably an adept researcher. Once your editorial calendar is set and you've assigned writers, editors, and due dates, you can delve into the subject matter and build your content. As you write, keep the following priorities in mind.

## Target Your Personas

You spent a lot of time identifying who your ideal clients are. Make sure that your content directly speaks to at least one of your law firm's personas. For example, you should use language that your clients will understand and provide information that sparks their interest.

## Create Dense, Meaningful Content

While longer content typically performs better than short content, we're not big fans of mandatory word counts. Instead, you should focus on writing rich, dense content that comprehensively answers your readers' questions and provides them with meaningful advice. Depending on the topic, you may be able to do that in seven hundred words. Other times, your content might merit a three-part series of fifteen-hundred-word blogs.

## Follow Your Bar Association's Marketing Guidelines

Every state bar association has legal advertising rules—and they apply to your website and blog content. You should never make misleading statements, guarantee success, or imply that you're a certified specialist when you are not.

## Edit and Proofread Your Work

While your editorial process should always include a detailed round of editing, the writer should always perform a careful once-over before completing their task. In addition to looking for typos, the writer should consider whether they adequately addressed the topic and review the content's legal accuracy.

# Step 5: Editing

Editing is more than proofreading and spellchecking an article or web page. While you may use software that scans for errors and plagiarism, these **applications** cannot fully edit your work. Instead, your editors should carefully review the following for each piece of content:

- Typographical and grammatical errors.
- Structure and readability.
- Legal and factual accuracy.
- Violations of your state bar association's advertising rules.
- On-page search engine optimization, including internal links.

Importantly, editing should always be done by someone other than the writer. It's best to have at least two sets of eyes on everything you publish; if the topic is particularly challenging, add a final review by your law firm's subject matter expert.

It's also best to use a multistep process. Your editing tasks should involve these steps:

1. Reading through the content, assessing its general flow and accuracy.
2. Restructuring the content to make it more readable and digestible.
3. Correcting any legal or factual inconsistencies in the content.
4. Improving headings and calls to action for SEO purposes.
5. Reviewing the revised content for typographical and grammatical errors.
6. Taking a break.
7. Performing a final review.

You might pause here and wonder about that break. We've found that stepping away from a piece of content, even for a brief time, can freshen your eyes and mind, helping you catch and correct those last few errors.

While editors should trust their writers, they also need a healthy level of skepticism. If the writer's assertion or analysis seems inaccurate, always go back and confirm or corroborate it. If necessary, editors should add content and analysis that fleshes out an article.

Consider your writers' word choices as well. If they used language that exceeds your clients' level of sophistication, simplify it. However, also consider the content's keywords. If you're not using the right keywords, many of your ideal clients won't find your content.

For example, internet users in different locations often use different search terms. We were recently working on a blog about truck accidents in Mississippi. Our writer was debating whether to refer to the wreck as a "semitruck accident," "18-wheeler accident," or "tractor-trailer accident." The writer visited Google Trends, a free service that tracks the popularity of keywords, and discovered that while the majority of states prefer "semitruck," people in Mississippi tend to use the term "18-wheeler" in web searches.

## Step 6: Publishing and Sharing Your Content Online

Now that you have well-written content that speaks directly to your ideal clients, you need to share it with them. To do so, you will need to properly publish your content online, using your website's **dashboard**. (Whether you use WPEngine, Squarespace, or another platform, you'll have access to a dashboard that helps you build and publish your blogs and web pages. For more information about these platforms, refer back to chapters 4 and 5.)

Typically, you will cut and paste your content on the portal, adding header tags, images, and links. Once you hit the "publish" button, it should be live on your website. However, if you make a mistake, don't panic. You almost always can go back in and revise your content.

Once your content is live, it should start drawing in new visitors, improving your keyword and page rankings, and funneling more ideal clients toward your law firm. However, you can accelerate this process by sharing your content via your social media channels and email newsletter. (We will discuss social media and newsletters in more detail later on in chapters 7 and 8.)

## Step 7: Assess Your Content's Performance

However, your work isn't done just because you've released your content in the wild. Now it's time to revisit those goals you set early on. Is your content keeping people on your website, or is your bounce rate increasing? What topics seem to resonate most with your readers? Do you see an increase in **form fills** or phone calls from a specific page?

Periodically, take a candid look at your content. If a page isn't performing well and you see room for improvement, consider revising it. If you notice an uptick in interest in a specific topic, look for complementary blog topics for your editorial calendar. We will discuss data analytics in more detail in chapter 16, "Going Beyond the Basics: Analytics."

# Summary

Without a content marketing strategy, your website will have a hard time connecting with readers and converting them into clients. While your strategy should evolve over time, it should always be client-centered, rich in information, and engaging. Preparation and planning are also essential, and a clear editorial calendar can help your law firm reach its content marketing goals.

As you start building your law firm's content strategy, aim for quarterly editorial calendars that include at least two blogs per month.

# Checklist for Building a Content Marketing Strategy

- Create an editorial calendar.
- Set deadlines and assign tasks to your team.
- Research the topic and write your content.
- Edit and revise your content.
- Publish it online and share the content with your readers.
- Evaluate your content's performance and revise your strategies.

# 7

# Engage Your Followers on Social Media

In the past, many law firms were reluctant to use social media. There was (and sometimes still is) a misperception in the legal industry that people are looking for cat videos on Facebook, not legal advice. In reality, social media has become so deeply embedded in our lives that it's often one of the first places people go to for news and information.

There are real challenges associated with law firms' social media marketing. However, when you implement legal social media best practices and take the time to post engaging content, you can significantly build awareness, nurture leads and referral sources, and convert followers into clients.

According to the 2017 ABA Legal Technology Survey Report, 77 percent of lawyers reported that their firm has some type of social media presence.[1] However, simply having a LinkedIn profile doesn't mean you have an effective or meaningful social media strategy. In this chapter, we'll explain the importance of social media and how to harness it.

# An Overview of Social Media Platforms

While Facebook may immediately come to mind, there are many social media platforms that can boost **brand awareness** and engagement. Rather than focus on a single platform, we find it best to consider your ideal clients' behaviors, needs, and preferences—and then implement a comprehensive, multiplatform strategy.

Different platforms serve different purposes. To create a strong social media strategy, you need to understand the most popular platforms' target audiences and core functions.

## Facebook

Facebook is the world's most used social media site. Lawyers frequently scoff at Facebook, arguing that it's only for sharing cute pictures of your grandkids and political rants. In reality, it's a powerful network that reaches more than 2.4 billion people per month.[2] Seventy-four percent of Facebook users connect to it daily, and more

1. Allison Shields, "2017 Social Media and Blogging," *ABA TechReport 2020* (American Bar Association: 2017) www.americanbar.org/groups/law_practice/publications/techreport/2017/social_media_blogging.

2. Facebook, *Facebook Q1 2019 Results* (2019) https://s21.q4cdn.com/399680738/files/doc_financials/2019/Q1/Q1-2019-Earnings-Presentation.pdf.

than 50 percent are on Facebook more than once a day.[3] And while we love those adorable pictures as much as the next person, a lot of real business also happens on Facebook.

In 2019, 69 percent of Americans used Facebook according to a Pew Research Center Survey. Furthermore, 43 percent of adults get their news from the social media giant.[4] Globally, there are more than 140 million businesses on Facebook today.[5] They post organically on their profiles, publish ads, and engage with the followers.

## YouTube

YouTube is the internet's video streaming behemoth. Almost 2 billion people log into YouTube each month, and the platform reaches more eighteen- to forty-nine-year-olds than any broadcast or cable television network.[6] It's also the second largest search engine after its owner, Google, and the second most popular social media platform after Facebook. Even if searching YouTube for legal information may not be your first inclination, many people are doing just that.

Right now, you may be thinking, "I'm not going to make silly YouTube videos!" However, the platform isn't just for kids—the majority of adults also visit YouTube channels.

---

3. A. Perrin and M. Anderson, "Share of U.S. Adults Using Social Media, including Facebook, is Mostly Unchanged Since 2018," *Fact Tank: News in the Numbers* (blog) *Pew Research Center* (2019, April 10) https://www.pewresearch.org/fact-tank/2019/04/10/share-of-u-s-adults-using-social-media-including-facebook-is-mostly-unchanged-since-2018.

4. *Id.*

5. Facebook, "Company Info" (2020) https://about.fb.com/company-info.

6. J. Solsman, "YouTube Crosses 2 Billion Viewers a Month," *CNet* (2019, May 2) https://www.cnet.com/news/youtube-crosses-2-billion-viewers-a-month/; "The Way People Are Watching Video in the Living Room Is Changing: Here's How" *Think With Google* (2019, April) https://www.thinkwithgoogle.com/advertising-channels/video/video-streaming-trends.

Consider making informational, how-to, and testimonial videos, which are perfectly suited for legal marketing. For example, you could publish videos discussing common personal injuries, such as TBIs, and your results. Or you could suggest tips for people attending depositions or independent medical examinations. While some law firms opt to work with a videographer or a marketing agency, it's also possible to film your own videos. For more information, see chapter 10, "Use Visual Content to Hold Attention."

## LinkedIn

LinkedIn is a professional social network with over 610 million members. About 40 percent of LinkedIn users check the site daily.[7] The platform is for more than job searching. It is the internet's premier business-to-business forum where Fortune 500 companies, executives, and corporate decision-makers look for insight and information.

While LinkedIn is typically seen as a **B2B** site, that doesn't mean that trial lawyers should disregard it. Consider this: many professionals go to LinkedIn, rather than a corporate or law firm website, to get biographical information about people they'd like to work with. If you don't have a thorough and conversion-focused LinkedIn profile, they may pass you by when they need to talk to a lawyer.

Furthermore, LinkedIn is a great place to foster referrals. If you're already connected with your legal peers, consider sharing posts and information that demonstrate your thought leadership and expertise. If your LinkedIn connections start viewing you as a foremost authority on your legal practice, you're more likely to get referrals from them.

7. A. Perrin and M. Anderson, "Share of U.S. Adults Using Social Media, including Facebook, is Mostly Unchanged Since 2018."

## Google My Business

**Google My Business** (GMB) may not seem like a traditional social media platform, but it's an essential part of your digital marketing plan. Google My Business, previously known as Google Places, provides information about your business hours, location, services, and customer reviews—all from a Google search engine results page. You can also post pictures of your office and share blog posts and other content.

According to a 2019 study, the average business gets about one thousand GMB views per month.[8] Many of these are searches for a business's general services or products, not its name. Notably, the legal industry had one of the highest rates of these so-called "discovery searches;" about 92 percent of legal Google My Business views are people searching for general information rather than a specific law firm.

If your firm is very small or does not have a physical office, you may face some challenges using Google My Business. Its guidelines clearly favor firms and companies that welcome clients and customers into their space, and prohibits the posting P.O. boxes and off-site mailbox addresses on your listing.

However, there is an exception for "service area businesses," which could include law firms that offer their clients in-home appointments. You will need to designate the geographic area that you serve, and you will still need to confirm your physical mailing address with Google. (The company will typically send you a verification postcard to your mailing address that includes a confirmation code.)

If your physical office is a shared or coworking space, be prepared to jump through some extra hoops, like taking pictures of your signage or office space before Google My Business approves your listing.

---

8. Rosie Murphy, "Google My Business Insights Study" *BrightLocal,* July 15, 2019, https://www.brightlocal.com/research/google-my-business-insights-study.

## Twitter

Sometimes called a micro-blogging site, Twitter lets you share your thoughts in 280 characters. In 2019, the website reported that it had 152 million daily users.[9] About 24 percent of American adults use Twitter—and this number is growing.[10]

Most people head to Twitter to get news and entertainment. If your law firm or lawyers are using the platform, you should focus on developing legal issues, your unique perspective, and law firm updates. Even though Twitter is known for its casual (and sometimes inflammatory) tone, make sure your firm's handles align with your brand guidelines.

## Legal Industry–Specific Platforms: Avvo and Martindale

You're probably familiar with Avvo and Martindale. Both companies rank attorneys, but using different metrics. Martindale's peer-reviewed rating system is well known to most lawyers since it predates the internet. The company asks other lawyers to anonymously rank their peers on a variety of metrics, including legal knowledge and experience. Today, clients can also post their own reviews on Martindale's website.

Avvo is a more recent player in legal social media. The website's algorithm ranks lawyers based on their online information and information contained in their Avvo profile. Clients and peers can also post reviews on Avvo—and there is a Q&A function where lawyers can respond to readers' legal questions.

While I recommend completing your Avvo and Martindale profiles, they don't need to be the focus of your social media strategy. People are

9. Twitter, *Q4 and Fiscal Year 2019 Letter to Shareholders*, February 6, 2020, https://s22.q4cdn.com/826641620/files/doc_financials/2019/q4/Q4-2019-Shareholder-Letter.pdf.

10. A. Perrin and M. Anderson, "Share of U.S. Adults Using Social Media, including Facebook, is Mostly Unchanged Since 2018."

more likely to turn to the bigger platforms first, since they are more reliant on Facebook, LinkedIn, and YouTube.

## Does My Law Firm Need a Social Media Policy?

In short, yes. Every law firm should have clear guidelines about what should be posted on its social media pages and rules about its employees' conduct on social media. If you have consistently enforced rules that everyone understands, you hopefully will avoid unwanted attention due to inappropriate posting.

However, that doesn't mean you need a one-hundred-page social media policy that outlines every single potential activity your team does online. First, it's impractical. Second, it's nearly impossible to manage or maintain, considering the variety and rapid evolution of social media platforms.

Consider this: if you had crafted a detailed social media policy in 2006, it would mention Facebook, YouTube, and **MySpace**. **Instagram**, LinkedIn, **Snapchat**, Twitter, **Pinterest**, and TikTok didn't exist yet. Today, there are countless social media platforms that cater to a wide variety of demographics and interests. You just can't create a policy that addresses them all.

Instead, it's a good idea to set clear, but general, expectations about your employees' social media activities. Here are some you might include:

- A reminder that simply because you delete a post doesn't mean it disappears. The internet has an uncomfortably long memory.

- A policy that says employees should keep their personal profiles as private as possible.

- A clear statement that all posts should align with your law firm's code of conduct and expectations of professionalism.

- Well-defined and consistently enforced disciplinary policies for inappropriate or damaging posts made by employees on either their professional or private pages.

It's a good idea to establish clear limits and expectations. Some law firms even suggest that their teams create professional social media profiles, like "Sarah Webster, Esq." that they use for any work-related posting and commentary. That way, there's less of a risk that the line between personal and professional content gets blurred.

## Confidentiality and Social Media

While social media can give people more insight into the amazing work your law firm does and the people who work there, you must always be aware of the risks of social media. Confidentiality and attorney–client privilege should be at the forefront of your mind every time you work on a social media post.

Here are some general confidentiality and privacy best practices:

- Never post a picture of someone without their consent or the consent of their legal guardian.

- Do not provide any information about a client's case, even if you do not give their name, without their express permission.

- Never contact someone who is already represented on social media.

## ABA Formal Opinion 480: What You Need to Know

In 2018, the American Bar Association (ABA) issued Formal Opinion 480, "Confidentiality Obligations for Lawyer Blogging and Other Public Commentary." It addresses the ethical implications of publishing anything about your clients or success stories—and opines that you should get informed consent before posting any type of disclosure about a client on social media or your website.

Formal Opinion 480 broadly interprets Model Rule 1.6, which states:

> A lawyer shall not reveal information relating to the representation of a client unless the client gives informed consent, the disclosure is impliedly authorized in order to carry out the representation, or the disclosure is [otherwise] permitted.

This rule applies to more than privileged information; it covers anything relating to your representation of the client, including war stories and shoptalk. Furthermore, even if this information becomes part of the public record, the ABA says you still must get informed consent. This means that just because there is a public court order or a news story outlining the information, a lawyer should not disclose it online or elsewhere without their client's informed consent.

It's not uncommon for law firms to post or share stories about their successes or day-to-day experiences. However, if someone could reasonably ascertain the identity of your client or you're sharing specific information about their case, you should almost always obtain consent before doing so.

For example, you won't violate Formal Opinion 480 by posting something like this:

> Presenting at an AAJ seminar this week! I'm excited to share my knowledge with my peers and new insight into the modern mass tort practice.

However, you may run afoul of the opinion if you post this:

> About to start a major TBI trial. Here's hoping the jury agrees to punitive damages! #websterwebsterandcohen #truckwrecklawyer

Even though you do not name your client, you've provided enough information that someone could reasonably ascertain who you are discussing. To avoid an ethical violation, you should ask your client for approval before sharing this message with your followers.

# Implementing Social Media Best Practices

As a lawyer, social media can seem intimidating and ethically complicated. You may worry about your team's social media activity and clients' privacy and wonder what you should write about. To market your law firm effectively, it's best to be proactive when it comes to social media.

## Claim All of Your Social Media Profiles

To protect your law firm, it's best to claim your Google My Business, Avvo, and other platform-generated profiles. First, they are sometimes inaccurate. When a social media platform creates a law firm's profile, a person isn't crafting it by hand. Instead, it uses software to search the internet for information to populate your profile.

Unfortunately, a single piece of inaccurate information can create havoc. For example, we worked with a business litigation firm whose platform-generated Google My Business profile reported that it worked out of a trailer park. The profile even provided images of the trailer park for prospective clients—and likely deterred some individuals from contacting the firm. (We quickly corrected the error.)

Second, claiming the profile lets you flesh out its information and make it consistent with your brand. You'll also be able to track and monitor reviews that are posted on the site. This gives you greater control over your online presence, helps you communicate with existing and prospective clients, and may even improve your online visibility.

### How Do I Claim or Create Social Media Profiles?

While the process of claiming or creating a social media profile varies from site to site, there are several common steps.

- **Open an account:** You'll need to create an account associated with the platform. This typically involves inputting your name, email address, and other contact information. You should also set clear guidelines on how to handle and store passwords. If the employee who is responsible for your social media leaves the firm, you may suddenly become locked out of your profiles. To avoid this issue, consider using password management software (like LastPass) and linking your profiles to a shared email account, like "info@websterwebstercohen.com."

- **Link your profiles to your account:** If your law firm already has profiles, many social media networks will make you verify that you're really part of the firm. This typically involves a two-step process where the platform will either call you at the phone number listed on your profile or mail a numeric code to the listed address.

- **Customize your profile:** Once you have control of your profiles, you should update their information, link them to your website, and make them consistent with your brand guidelines.

## Build a Social Media Plan

Sometimes, it may seem like social media is spontaneous and off the cuff. However, it's best to actually have a thoughtful and comprehensive social media plan. When you post on one of your profiles, you want your followers to see you as a leader, as an engaged community member, and as approachable. If you're truly shooting one-liners off the hip, it's easy to make mistakes that alienate the people you want to reach.

So, how do you avoid gaffes and make sure that your firm is posting consistent and high-quality content? Create a social media calendar that aligns with your overarching editorial calendar and brand guidelines.

For example, suppose you decide to post a quick Facebook message about your beloved legal assistant's retirement. They have worked for your law firm for thirty-five years, and they've become an essential part of your brand. Over the last few weeks, you've been joking with them about their retirement plans—and you decide to share your humor with your social media followers.

On Facebook, you post a picture of your assistant, Photoshopped into a nursing home scene. The comment says:

> Now that senility is kicking in, it's time for Pat to call it quits. We're sad to see you go! #sorrynotsorry.

The calls and comments start flooding in. Some of your clients are worried that Pat has been struggling mentally, compromising their cases. Others are angered that you made light of Pat's age, perceived disability, or years of service. You spend hours apologizing and explaining your inside joke. Unfortunately, the damage to your brand is already done—and you look like a jerk.

Now, suppose you had a social media posting calendar. On your monthly calendar, you schedule a "Pat's retiring!" post. Because you planned the post in advance, you have time to think about how you can best encapsulate their decades of tireless service in a funny but sentimental post.

> After thirty-five years of wrangling the lawyers at Webster, Webster & Cohen, Pat has had enough. Before she departs at the end of the month, please share your appreciation and favorite Pat stories below!

You attach a hilariously dated image of Pat sporting a 1970s era haircut and a powder-blue pantsuit. Your clients and followers deluge your site with **likes**, well wishes, and fond memories. To make things even better, the post encourages a dozen people to follow your Facebook profile and subscribe to your newsletter.

## Building Your Social Media Calendar

When you're building your social media posting schedule, it should typically follow the rule of thirds, where each of the following represents a third of your content:

- Directly engages with your followers, such as encouraging comments.
- Promotes your law firm and its services.
- Is from third-party sources, such as news articles or community partner.

It should also align with your overarching content calendar, sharing blogs, and discussing topics that you're addressing on your website.

When you're looking for potential social media topics, you can always get inspiration from your top competitors' social media profiles. Look to see what content resonates with their followers and use it as inspiration. If their users love FAQ videos about your practice area, it's likely that similar content will resonate on your site too.

## Consider Your Ideal Clients or Marketing Personas

Remember those client personas you created early on in your marketing strategy? It's time to take another look at them. Your client demographics can help you build social media content that will engage them and nurture your relationships. For example, if your clientele is primarily millennial professionals and executives, you may favor LinkedIn over Facebook.

Here are some general trends about social media users, according to a series of 2018 and 2019 Pew Research Center surveys:

- 50 percent of people with a college degree use LinkedIn.
- Rural populations are slightly less likely to use social media.
- 85 percent of people between the ages of thirty and forty-nine are on YouTube, and 91 percent of those ages eighteen to twenty-nine are on the platform.
- Individuals with income of $75,000 or more have increased use of all social media sites.
- 78 percent of people between the ages of eighteen and twenty-four use Snapchat.

# What Should I Post?

Now that we've outlined a lot of prohibitions, it's time to focus on what you *should* be posting!

## Personal Interest Stories and Pictures

Let's be honest, lawyers and law firms have a reputation for being serious, stodgy, and (occasionally) impersonal. Many people just can't see past your suits, fancy diplomas, and courtroom demeanor. Social media gives you a chance to humanize your brand and provide a more genuine and approachable perspective.

You'll be surprised how much traction your posts about your team's birthdays, personal milestones, and achievements will get. The same goes for candid pictures of your team working and spending time together.

## Promote Events and Community Projects

If you're like many lawyers, you went to law school to help people, and your commitment to service probably continues to this day. If your law firm supports local causes, sponsors community events, and gives back to the disadvantaged, promote these events on social media and share pictures and stories afterward.

For example, suppose you schedule a time where your entire team volunteers for a local animal shelter. You spend a couple of hours walking dogs, performing chores, and preparing for one of their major fundraising events. You take tons of pictures of your team, both hard at work and playing with adorable puppies.

Then you post your best pictures online, tagging the animal rescue group, and encouraging others to donate or attend their upcoming fundraiser. Think about who might share that post: your team, the shelter, your collective followers, people who like cute dogs. Suddenly, a lot of people are seeing your team doing good in the community—fostering a sense of goodwill and awareness.

## Videos

Videos are incredibly effective marketing tools and typically are a good marketing investment. Consider the following facts:

- 78 percent of people watch online videos every week, and 55 percent watch them daily.[11]

11. A. Collins and M. Conley, "The Ultimate Guide to Video Marketing," *HubSpot* (2019) https://blog.hubspot.com/marketing/video-marketing?__hstc=4273004.6dca435f45a79c9564fcaa51da776d0c.1547689825317.1547689825317.1547696706583.2&__hssc=4273004.1.1547696706583&__hsfp=2440387509.

- 72 percent of people prefer learning about a product or service through a video.

- Social media posts that include videos get 48 percent more views.

- People are more likely to share your post if it includes a video.

While a glossy, professional video is great, you don't always need to have that level of production value. A livestream of a press conference or presentation can be just as effective.

However, it's best to follow these basic guidelines:

- **Keep your message concise:** Many people will stop watching a video after thirty seconds. To ensure that your message delivers its full impact, make sure you convey your message quickly and relay the most important information in the first few seconds.

- **Use visual imagery:** Some 85 percent of Facebook users watch videos without sound. If your key messages aren't conveyed visually, they may lose their impact. You can also use auto-caption tools on most platforms, but you should always proof your video captions before publishing a video, since the software is imperfect.

- **Mobile-friendly:** About 75 percent of online videos stream on mobile devices. You should always test your videos on a small screen, try to keep your videos' load times short, and use graphics that will pop on a small screen.

## Share Your Website Content

If you're publishing high-quality blogs on your website, make sure you're also sharing them on your social media profiles. While social media shares and likes may not improve your organic search ranking, they will increase the number of people who see and engage with your content.

## Should I Respond to Negative Comments and Reviews?

Today's consumers rely on social media for much of their information. According to BIA/Kelsey, 97 percent of consumers use online reviews to evaluate local businesses—and are less likely to use your services if you have negative reviews.[12]

Whether you like it or not, your ideal clients are evaluating your online reviews, your number of followers, and the quality of your posts before they decide to call your office. They're also turning to social media when they want to share their positive or negative opinions about your services. In other words, social media can make or break your law firm.

However, you should never simply delete a negative comment or review unless it contains profanity or confidential information. It may be tempting to simply erase the negativity, but that can encourage even more vitriol and unwanted trolling.

# Caution about Social Media Contests and Giveaways

Many law firms and businesses try to increase their likes and follows through contests, giveaways, and promotions. Typically, the law firm asks people to like their profile, make a comment, share a post, tag someone, or otherwise engage with their social media pages. Then it

12. BIA/Kelsey, "Nearly All Consumers (97 percent) Now Use Online Media to Shop Locally, According to BIA/Kelsey and ConStat," *PRNewsWire*, March 10, 2010, https://www.prnewswire.com/news-releases/nearly-all-consumers-97-now-use-online-media-to-shop-locally-according-to-biakelsey-and-constat-87221242.html.

randomly selects one follower and gives them something of value, like tickets to a sporting event or a gift card.

While this may sound like an easy and fun way to boost your number of followers, at least one state bar association has indicated that these tactics violate the Rules of Professional Conduct. In 2019, the North Carolina Bar Association issued an ethics opinion indicating that today, a like or a follow is essentially a recommendation or endorsement of a law firm.

Notably, the opinion did not ban all contests, only those that try to boost likes, comments, follows, shares, and engagement on social media. The bar association determined that because potential clients may use a law firm's number of likes, comments, and followers to evaluate their reputation, attorneys cannot offer incentives to build up these metrics.

It's unclear how many states will follow North Carolina's example. However, as people become increasingly reliant on social media for their decision-making, lawyers should be cognizant of its power. And before you post that "likes" giveaway for an iPad, it's a good idea to check your state bar ethics rules and opinions.

# Summary

Law firms need to embrace the power of social media. You can use your profiles to connect with leads, clients, and referral sources, and build your brand awareness. However, you'll need to build a comprehensive strategy that resonates with viewers and aligns with your bar association's advertising rules.

To do this, you'll need to claim your social media profiles, schedule regular posts that educate, inform, and entertain your followers, and take time to respond to comments and questions. Additionally, if it's permitted under your state bar's rules of professional responsibility, you should also encourage satisfied clients to post reviews.

As you build your social media strategy, it's best to create a social media calendar that gives you time to create thoughtful and well-written content.

# Checklist for Social Media Marketing

- Create a law firm social media policy.
- Claim all of your social media profiles.
- Create a social media calendar.
- Create engaging content and assets.
- Post your content on your social media pages.
- Respond, when appropriate, to your followers.
- Evaluate your content's performance and revise your strategies.

# 8

# Email Newsletters That Engage Your Followers

Do you remember when law firms mailed out physical newsletters? Lawyers spent a lot of time and money designing, printing, and shipping them out to their client lists. While it was a work-intensive process, many firms thought that it was a wise investment because their newsletter helped reinforce their expertise and connection to their clients. Today, you can get the same impact with a cost- and time-efficient email newsletter.

Email newsletters are sent to a list of subscribers on a consistent, often monthly, basis. They are a remarkably effective way to stay at the top of your clients' and followers' minds, providing a no-pressure source of information about your area of practice and your law firm.

We've found that email newsletters, when done properly, nurture leads, turn clients into law firm ambassadors, and encourage referrals from other professionals. In this chapter, we'll outline the essentials of your email newsletter and discuss best practices.

# Why Do I Need an Email Newsletter?

In the marketing world, we like to talk about **touchpoints** or the places where your potential clients interact with your law firm's brand. They include your website, social media, face-to-face interactions, and other communications. Every time you engage with your followers, you have an opportunity to build trust, demonstrate your knowledge, and reaffirm your law firm's brand. An email newsletter is one of these touchpoints.

Let's go back to your marketing personas. If you're like most law firms, your personas may include people in various stages of the buyer's journey or with varying objectives. For example:

- A person who is early on in their buyer's or client's journey and just looking for information about their problems.

- A potential client who is less likely to engage with you on social media, but would still like to receive up-to-date information from your firm.

- A family member of a potential client who wants to help them find a solution to their issues.

- A lawyer or other professional who occasionally needs to refer people to someone with your expertise.

For these people, an email newsletter is ideal. Unlike a phone call or in-person consultation, there's no pressure to retain you. However, it provides them with the information they need, helps them get to know you and your law firm, and builds up trust and brand awareness. When they're ready to engage with a lawyer directly, they will be more likely to call your office because they've started to build a relationship with you through your newsletter.

However, email newsletters are also powerful marketing tools for existing and past clients. A monthly newsletter helps maintain your connection to your clients, educating them about their legal issues and reminding them of your law firm's value. When you're at the top of your clients' minds, they're more likely to call you with their current legal questions or refer a friend or neighbor.

## How to Build an Effective Email Newsletter

Before you start sending out newsletters, it's best to build a comprehensive email marketing strategy. Our email inboxes are increasingly filled with spam and marketing messages. To catch your subscribers' attention, you need a plan.

As you craft your email newsletter strategy, you should focus on the following:

- Creating an easy-to-read newsletter that entices subscribers to click and explore your content.
- Building a robust and engaged subscriber list.
- Making your monthly newsletter build as simple as possible.
- Ensuring that you comply with anti-spam laws.

Next, we'll outline the steps you'll need to take to achieve these goals.

## Step 1: Build Your Newsletter's Infrastructure

Your law firm's email newsletter isn't just a compilation of legal updates and other content. Your newsletter's infrastructure is made of software, design, and legal compliance. It should deliver insight into your subscribers' habits and be easy to use. To do this, you'll need the right software platform and a well-designed template.

### Use Email Automation Software

An email newsletter may sound like a lot of work, and that used to be true. Thankfully, there are many programs available that can streamline the process and make your newsletter an even more powerful marketing tool. The first step toward creating your newsletter is selecting an **email automation** system, like SharpSpring, Constant Contact, or Mailchimp.

These systems, once implemented, make sending out and tracking your email newsletter's performance much easier. These applications automate your email marketing, letting you send messages to your entire database of subscribers and clients with the push of a button.

To a varying degree, email automation systems also provide you with data about your subscribers' engagement. For example, some platforms not only tell you how frequently people open your email newsletters but also help you track their website usage. You can tell what pages they read and how frequently they visit your sites. This information can help you personalize your interactions with them.

For example, suppose Cathy Client subscribes to your newsletter. When your system inputs her email into its database, you realize that she has consistently visited blogs about traumatic brain injuries, post-traumatic stress disorder, and intoxicated driving. After three months of visiting your website and reading your newsletter, Cathy calls you. Because you have an idea of what her questions involve and are aware that she (or someone she loves) may struggle emotionally, you can provide a better client experience from day one.

If you're not sure which email automation platform is best for you, or you don't want to manage its day-to-day operations, consider partnering with a respected digital marketing partner. Ideally, you want to find an agency that has a certification from your preferred software system. It should also educate you about all of your options, train you in the essentials of your chosen platform, and empower you to make educated decisions about your newsletter and other digital marketing strategies. If an agency isn't willing to guide you through every step of the process, you should continue your search for the right marketing partner.

## Design an Easy-to-Read Newsletter Template

Most email software systems provide customizable templates, and it's fine to use one of them. Email newsletters don't need to include flashy animation or intricate design elements—they just need to be easy to read. We've found that minimal email templates work as well (if not better) than design-heavy ones.

Ideally, your template should contain the following:

- A **header** with your newsletter's title and, if you wish, a brief message from the law firm.

- Enough white space, or blank space, between your newsletter items, making them easier to read.

- A color scheme and feel that is consistent with your brand guidelines.

- A **footer** that provides your law firm's contact information and a link to unsubscribe.

Here's an example of a poorly built newsletter:

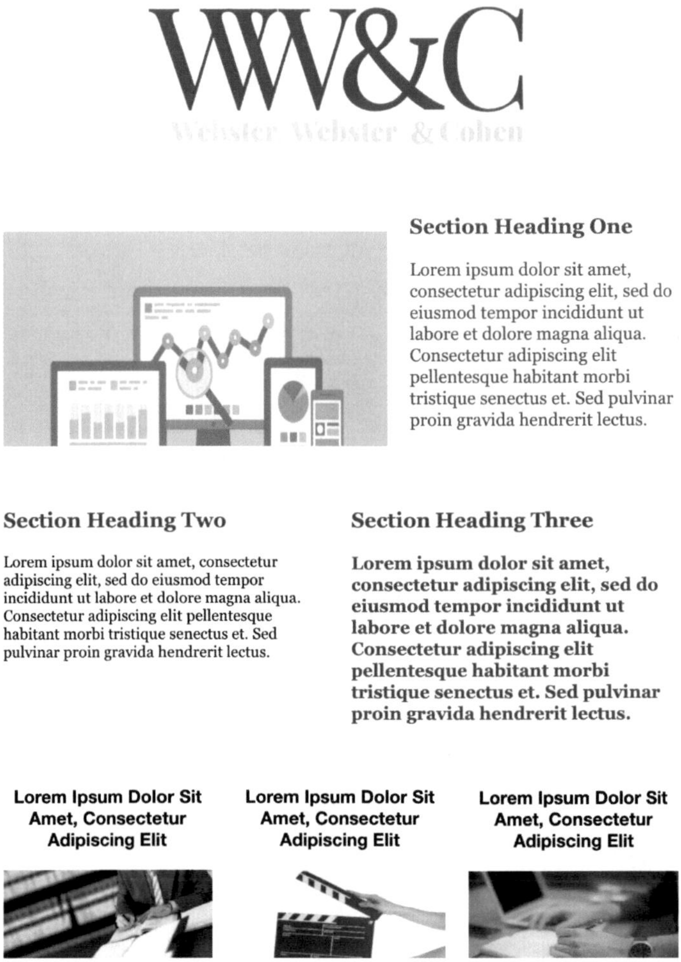
WW&C
Webster Webster & Cohen

**Section Heading One**

Lorem ipsum dolor sit amet, consectetur adipiscing elit, sed do eiusmod tempor incididunt ut labore et dolore magna aliqua. Consectetur adipiscing elit pellentesque habitant morbi tristique senectus et. Sed pulvinar proin gravida hendrerit lectus.

**Section Heading Two**

Lorem ipsum dolor sit amet, consectetur adipiscing elit, sed do eiusmod tempor incididunt ut labore et dolore magna aliqua. Consectetur adipiscing elit pellentesque habitant morbi tristique senectus et. Sed pulvinar proin gravida hendrerit lectus.

**Section Heading Three**

**Lorem ipsum dolor sit amet, consectetur adipiscing elit, sed do eiusmod tempor incididunt ut labore et dolore magna aliqua. Consectetur adipiscing elit pellentesque habitant morbi tristique senectus et. Sed pulvinar proin gravida hendrerit lectus.**

**Lorem Ipsum Dolor Sit Amet, Consectetur Adipiscing Elit**

**Lorem Ipsum Dolor Sit Amet, Consectetur Adipiscing Elit**

**Lorem Ipsum Dolor Sit Amet, Consectetur Adipiscing Elit**

What's wrong with it? First, it's hard to read due to its compact style and flashy color scheme. Second, there aren't any calls to action or links that encourage readers to continue their journey or contact the firm.

Here's a better newsletter template:

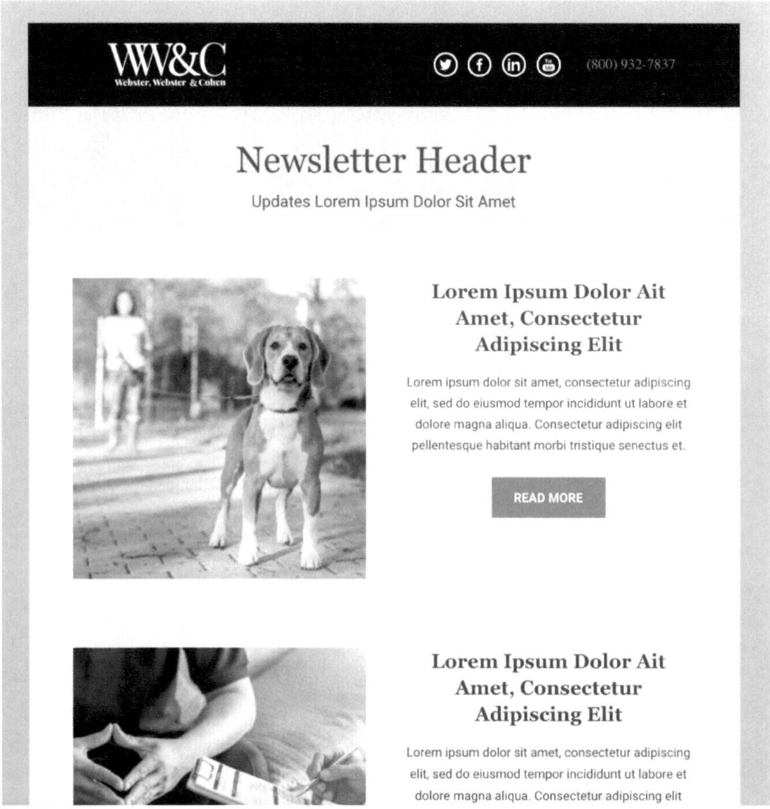


Here, the layout is clean and contains a lot of white space, making it easy to read. There are **blurbs,** or short synopses of each blog that aim to entice readers to click, and plenty of calls to action.

It is also essential that your template is mobile-friendly. Today, a majority of people read their email on their phones and other mobile devices. If your subscribers can't quickly skim your newsletter on their devices, you're losing out on marketing opportunities.

### Include an Option to Unsubscribe

Federal laws prohibit businesses from spamming email recipients. To comply with CAN-SPAM (Controlling the Assault of Non-Solicited Pornography and Marketing) and other legal requirements, your newsletter should always include these:

- An obvious and simple way to unsubscribe to your newsletter.
- Your physical or mailing address.
- Content that is accurate and does not mislead readers.

This information is typically included in the email's footer, a distinct block in the message that may also include additional information about your law firm, such as social media links and your phone number.

While you never want anyone to unsubscribe from your **email list**, you must honor these requests. Typically, you should remove someone from your email list within ten business days of getting their unsubscribe request.

## Step 2: Create an Email Content Strategy

Once you have a software system and a template, you can start building your first newsletter. Typically, this involves the following steps.

### Don't Ignore Your Subject Lines and Sender

In addition to the body of your newsletter, which contains your content, it has other parts. Before you open an email, your inbox tells you who it's from, provides a subject line, and may give a **preheader** that provides a little more information about the email.

- **Sender name:** Since most people won't open an email from someone they don't know, you want a sender name that is recognizable. Typically, your newsletter should be sent on behalf of your founding partner or the law firm.

- **Subject line:** This line of text identifies the purpose of your email. At our agency, we've compared the performance of newsletters with specific titles, like "5 Ways to Strengthen Your Injury Claim and More from Webster, Webster & Cohen" to generic titles like "News and Updates from Webster, Webster & Cohen." Surprisingly, the generic newsletter titles perform better. If possible, try to keep your subject line between forty and sixty characters.

- **Preheader:** The preheader is a short section of text that follows your subject line. It should summarize your newsletter in less than one hundred characters. However, you don't need to update your preheader each month. Instead, you can create a preheader you use again and again, like "News and legal insight from your friends at Webster, Webster & Cohen."

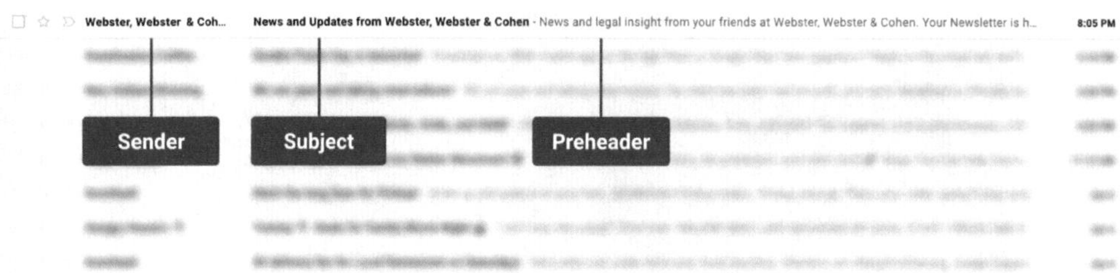


While subject lines and senders may seem unimportant, most of us would quickly delete an email from someone we didn't know that simply said "Newsletter." As you start to build your newsletter, take a little time to create a subject line and preheader that will encourage people to open your email.

## Include Your Blogs and Articles

While it's tempting to use your newsletter primarily for self-promotion, it's best to focus on information rather than sales tactics. If someone has subscribed to your newsletter, they're already interested in your services. Instead of a hard sell, they want information about your practice areas and law firm's culture.

Your high-quality, informative blogs are the foundation for your newsletter content. Every month, you should be producing at least two blog posts that speak directly to your ideal and current clients' needs and concerns. You should include these blogs and other high-performing content to your monthly newsletter. (To learn more about the content development process, refer to chapter 6, "Plan and Maintain a Content Strategy.")

Typically, you don't want to include the entire text of your blog in the newsletter itself. Instead, readers should see the blog's title, a related image, a blurb or summary, and a "Read More" or "Learn More" button that links to the full story.

This way, you're encouraging newsletter subscribers to explore related articles, download e-books and other resources, and request a consultation. The more you can get your followers and subscribers to engage with all of your website, the more likely they are to convert into clients.

## Deliver Office News and Personnel Updates

In addition to blogs, many law firms include updates about their staff, professional development, and office happenings. This type of content provides a human face to your law firm and gives you a chance to celebrate your successes. Your personal interest newsletter content may include as follows:

- Staff and attorney profiles.
- Stories about your office celebrations, such as birthdays, employment anniversaries, and graduations.
- Calendars highlighting your team's speaking events.
- Highlights of your law firm's continuing education activities.
- Your community outreach and volunteer activities.
- News coverage of your law firm.

Whether it's images from a holiday dinner, tales from a team-building event, or a lawyer's baby announcement, this information will help your subscribers see beyond your courtroom demeanor.

These stories don't have to be long. For example, suppose Andy, one of the paralegals at Webster, Webster & Cohen, is celebrating his fifth anniversary with the law firm. The firm's newsletter may include a picture of Andy and say:

We can't believe Andy Ayudante has already been part of the Webster, Webster & Cohen team for five years! We deeply appreciate Andy's hard work, amazing research skills, and wicked sense of humor. He's our office prankster, and he always keeps us on our toes. Congratulations, Andy!

## Implement a Multistep Editing Process

When there's a typo on a website, you or your marketing partner can easily edit your content in real time. However, you don't have that ability with an email—once you hit "send," there's no chance to fix your mistakes. Your subscribers may not bother to open an email entitled "February Newsletter" that is sent in March. A link in your newsletter that sends readers to the wrong blog content may cause frustration and disengagement.

While everyone makes mistakes, we suggest using a multistep editing and proofreading process before you send out each and every newsletter.

First, multiple people should review your draft newsletter. We've found that having multiple sets of eyes on an email helps reduce the likelihood of sending an error-laden newsletter out.

Second, make sure that your review team always confirms that your newsletter contains the following:

- The correct subject line and preheader.
- Well-written content that is free of typographical and grammatical errors.
- Links that send readers to the correct pages on your website.
- Images that are consistent with your law firm's brand.

- Consistent fonts and colors.
- No obvious design issues, such as oversized images or misaligned text.

If you identify any errors, correct them before you send out the final newsletter.

## The Importance of Project Management

Email newsletters require commitment, and it's easy to lose track of each step of your monthly process without a project management system. To do so, you should break your newsletter into discrete tasks:

- Writing personal interest stories.
- Selecting blogs for each newsletter.
- Building the newsletter in your template.
- Reviewing the draft's content and design.
- Implementing edits to the newsletter.
- Sending the newsletter to subscribers.

As mentioned in other chapters, if you already have software like Asana, Basecamp, or Microsoft Planner, you should build projects and tasks for your team within these systems.

If you don't use project management software, add tasks with hard deadlines to the responsible team members' calendars and track their progress. Otherwise, your monthly newsletter may become a quarterly (or nonexistent) one.

# Creating an Email Subscriber List

Unless you have a subscriber list, your email marketing strategies are for naught. Subscribers are the people who receive your newsletter due to an existing relationship with your firm or their interest in your services. Every email address is an opportunity to communicate with a lead or potential referral source, so take your list-building seriously.

Your first source of subscribers should be your existing and past clients and referral sources. If you have their emails, you can input them into your software platform's database. These individuals may already get email from your office, so a newsletter won't be an unwanted surprise.

Second, when you interact with someone online or over the phone, get their email address. You can add these individuals, who have shown interest in your law firm to your subscriber list.

Third, you need to add "subscribe" calls to action to your website. Typically, you will add a **widget**, or an embeddable website application that does a single task, to your site, which allows people to quickly sign up for your newsletter. You may implement your subscription widget in a variety of locations: a sidebar, at the top of your blog page, or even in a pop-up window.

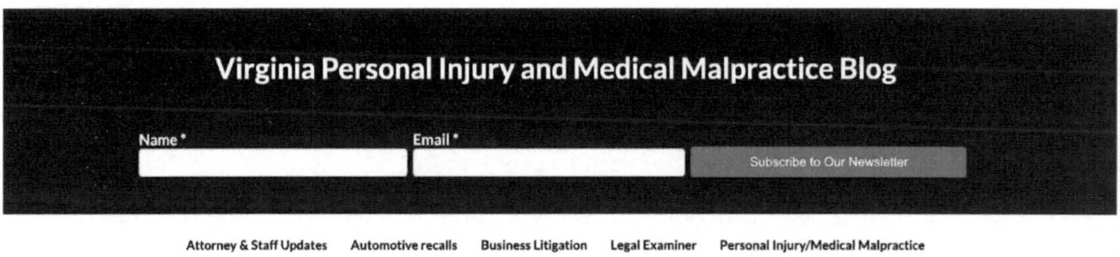


Once someone signs up for your newsletter through your subscription widget, it should trigger a thank-you email from your email automation system. This email doesn't have to be long, but it should confirm that the individual is now on your email list, that they'll regularly receive your newsletter, and that they can unsubscribe at any time.

## Should I Buy a List of Leads for My Newsletter?

No. When you're building your email newsletter subscriber base, it's never a good idea to buy a list.

First, it's legally dubious. CAN-SPAM bans the sale or purchase of email lists, although renting them is legal. If you're found in violation of the act, your law firm could face up to $42,530 for each improper email you sent out.

Second, it's a bad investment. The people on that purchased list probably aren't aware of your law firm and may not need your services. They probably won't open your email and may quickly mark it as spam. And even if they do open your newsletter, it may simply be to unsubscribe.

Finally, if those unwanted emails from your law firm are too sales-driven and personalized, your state bar association may consider them an improper solicitation.

# When Should I Send My Email Newsletter?

Newsletter subscribers should know whether they're getting a weekly, monthly, or quarterly newsletter—and you need to meet their expectations. Before you promise a twice a month newsletter loaded with detailed legal analysis, ask yourself a few critical questions:

- Do you have enough capacity within your law firm to build these newsletters?

- Does your editorial calendar provide sufficient content to fill each newsletter?

- Does your proposed schedule reflect your marketing personas' needs and preferences?

If your answer is no to any of these questions, you should reduce the frequency of your emails. For most law firms, a monthly newsletter makes sense.

Additionally, you should consider the time and date of when you plan to send your newsletter. Many studies and surveys suggest that people are more likely to open your emails on Tuesdays and Thursdays at either the beginning or end of the day (before 8:00 a.m. or after 4:00 p.m.).

## Tracking Your Newsletter's Performance

Like any marketing program, you should always analyze your newsletter's performance. Your software platform should provide you with analytics and data, such as these:

- **Open rates:** how frequently subscribers open your email newsletter. Typically, newsletters have about an 18 percent open rate.

- **Click-through rates** (CTA): the number of people who click on a link in your newsletter. Most links in a legal newsletter get about a 2.4 percent click-through rate.

- **Sharing rates:** how frequently your subscribers hit a share or forward button on your newsletter.

- **Hard bounces:** the number of emails in your list that are invalid, resulting in a returned newsletter.

- **Unsubscribe rate:** how frequently people opt out of your newsletter.

These key performance indicators (KPIs) can help you build a better newsletter and content strategy. In many platforms, you can not only see who opened your email newsletter but also which links they clicked on and the number of times they read your email. This can help identify your leads' interests and engagement.

If something is working well, build on that success. For example, suppose your subscribers clicked on the link for a blog entitled "7 Surprising Facts about Car Crashes and TBIs" at double your average rate. In your next editorial calendar, you may want to publish both a list-based blog and a traumatic brain injury article to see whether the structure or the topic is what led to the increased traffic. Then you can use this data to make even more improvements.

If your newsletter isn't performing well, don't do a complete overhaul all at once. Instead, change one element at a time and see if your subscribers' engagement increases. That way, you can determine which tactics work best with your subscribers. For example, you may want to reassess your content, the subject line, and the timing of your newsletter.

You can also send reengagement emails to subscribers that lose interest in your newsletter. This email reminds them of your newsletter's value and encourages them to revisit it.

# Checklist for Email Newsletters

- Choose an email automation software platform.
- Design your email templates.
- Build your email content, including an editorial process.
- Create your subscriber lists.
- Send your newsletter to subscribers.
- Track your newsletter's performance and revise your strategies.

# 9

# Nurture Leads with Email Automation

Email newsletters are great, but there's more to email marketing than a monthly rundown of law firm updates and new blog articles. **Email automation** lets you automatically send targeted content to leads without constant monitoring and data entry. Instead, when someone downloads a resource or fills out a form, automation software sends an immediate response to them without anyone in your office having to hit "send." This initial email can be automatically followed up by other lead-nurturing or educational content, further strengthening your relationship with each lead.

If you're looking for ways to increase your conversion rates without using more time and resources, you need to explore automated email campaigns.

# Clients Expect Quick and Seamless Communications

Potential clients are exploring your website and social media profiles right now. If they decide to click your "Schedule a Consultation" button, what happens? In a nonautomated environment, someone on your team needs to open their message, read it, and respond. This can quickly become burdensome and work intensive, leading to slower response times.

Unfortunately, leads don't wait forever. According to *Harvard Business Review*, if your firm responds to a lead within an hour, you are seven times more likely to make a meaningful connection than someone who responds within two hours.[1] If you wait twenty-four hours or more to respond, you are sixty times less likely to connect with the lead.

The average business's response time is forty-two hours.

Today's legal consumers are savvier and have higher expectations than past generations. Social media, online chat functions, and targeted marketing make us expect almost instantaneous service, transparency, and a personalized client experience. That means that more leads are willing to lawyer shop until they find the perfect fit.

# What Is Email Automation?

Email automation can help eliminate unwanted delays in your lead nurturing processes. When a potential client clicks a button or engages with your website, their activity automatically triggers a templated

1. James Oldroyd, Kristina McElheran, and David Elkington, "The Short Life of Online Sales Leads" *Harvard Business Review* (March, 2011), https://hbr.org/2011/03/the-short-life-of-online-sales-leads.

email message (or a series of messages). While these initial messages aren't a substitute for one-on-one interaction with a lead, they give you a little more time to react and help build trust and brand awareness.

For example, suppose Cathy Client stumbles on a Webster, Webster & Cohen blog about mild TBIs. Her husband was recently in a truck wreck and has been struggling with debilitating headaches, blurred vision, and mood swings. She continues to explore the website and decides to download an e-book entitled *The Essential Guide to Truck Accident Claims.*

As soon as she clicks the "Download" button, an email automation system shoots off a thank-you email that includes a link to the e-book. The email also advises Cathy that she's also subscribed to the Webster, Webster & Cohen newsletter—and that she can unsubscribe if she wishes.

The next day, Cathy gets another email from Sarah Webster, the founder of the firm. It says:

Dear Cathy:

We hope you found our truck accident e-book interesting and informative! While the lawyers at Webster, Webster & Cohen tried to include all the basic information that a crash survivor would need, nothing compares to personalized advice. If you have any questions or need assistance, don't hesitate to reach out.

You can always schedule a free consultation by calling our office or visiting our website. I know that truck wrecks can be overwhelming, and we'd love to help you understand your legal options.

If you're not ready to chat yet, I understand. In the meantime, consider following us on social media. That way, you can stay up to date on legal developments that may impact you and the ones you love.

Sincerely,
Sarah Webster, Esq.

Cathy isn't sure she needs a lawyer yet. So, she reads the e-book and saves the email, "just in case." Several days later, Sarah Webster sends her another message.

Dear Cathy:

Did you know that many insurance companies rush their adjusters and investigators to the scene of a truck wreck—trying to shape the narrative in their favor. To fight back, victims need to do three things:

1. Preserve evidence: You may be surprised to find out that truck drivers have to keep detailed logs about their hours on the road and other activities. However, if you don't act quickly to preserve these records, the trucker and their employer can destroy them.
2. Get the truck's black box data: Many modern trucks have sophisticated sensors that track their every move. Again, this data can be essential to your claims—if you can get your hands on it.
3. Get the medical care you need: Complicated injuries, like TBIs and spine injuries, need prompt attention from specialists. If you're struggling with pain or other issues, see a doctor ASAP. Plus, their records may strengthen your legal claims.

I founded Webster, Webster & Cohen because I believe that truck wreck victims deserve the same kind of high-quality representation that big business gets. I'm proud that we've helped thousands of people get fair compensation for their injuries. To learn more about their stories, you can visit our website.

If you need personalized advice about a truck wreck, call my office. We'll schedule a free, no-pressure consultation for you.

Sincerely,
Sarah Webster, Esq.

Impressed, Cathy and her husband decide to request an appointment. Shortly after getting off the phone, she gets a confirmation email with directions to Webster, Webster & Cohen. In the days preceding their consultation, Cathy gets three more emails, one that includes a list of "New Client FAQs," another that discusses the firm's approach to injury claims and its client experience, and a third with suggestions about how to prepare for their appointment. The clients head to their first meeting with their new lawyer feeling confident about their choice to retain the firm.

Every single one of those emails was automated. However, the communications felt authentic and personal. Just as importantly, they were prompt and built trust.

# How Does Email Automation Work?

While the Webster, Webster & Cohen team created all of those thoughtful emails, they were supported by powerful software. There are numerous email automation platforms available, including SharpSpring, Mailchimp, and HubSpot. These software platforms let you build templated emails, identify triggering events, and use data analytics to better understand your potential clients.

Once you've selected a software package, your email automation process will typically follow the following steps to create a campaign.

## 1. Identify Your Campaign's Purpose

Even though email automation starts with a templated message, it's not a one-size-fits-all approach. Instead, you should create different email campaigns that target different populations.

Generally speaking, most automated email campaigns are **drip campaigns.** These campaigns build or maintain interest and awareness by consistently sending messages to your leads, clients, and referral sources that relate to their interests and concerns. However, your campaign's message and purpose will vary.

- **Lead nurturing:** Sometimes, prospective clients aren't ready to schedule an appointment or sign a retainer. However, that doesn't mean that you should ignore them. We suggest crafting a campaign of low-pressure emails that educate recipients about important legal issues, tell them about your law firm, and offer easy ways to reengage when they're ready.

- **New client:** Hiring a lawyer is a momentous decision. Help solidify your relationship with your new clients by answering common questions, providing practical advice, and sending reminders to them.

- **Segmented messaging:** Your followers and clients include a diverse group of people. You can tailor specific campaigns to reflect different persona's interests. (We'll go into more detail about this later.)

## 2. Create Your Email Content

Now that you've identified the purpose of your email campaign, you need to create the individual emails. First, you'll create an outline of the topics you want to address. For example, Webster, Webster & Cohen's new-client campaign might include the following:

- A welcome email.

- An introduction to Webster, Webster & Cohen.

- An overview of injury claim procedures and terminology.

- New-client FAQs.

- Worksheets that help a client compile information about their damages.
- The importance of consistent medical treatment.
- A reminder to update the firm about their medical treatment and other issues.

When you're outlining your email topics, consider your clients' and your leads' journeys, their core concerns, and ways you can alleviate their worries and provide meaningful education.

## Make Your Emails Personal

When you're creating individual emails, you want to make them personal, informative, and digestible. You should write in the first and second person. Instead of noting, "Many truck wreck victims have questions about their rights," say, "I'm sure you have a lot of questions about truck wrecks and your legal rights." This conversational tone is more likely to resonate with your readers.

You can also include custom fields and tags in your emails, which let your automation platform automatically personalize the content for each reader. For example, the prompt [first name] may tell your software to input each individual reader's first name into the email, providing a more individualized experience to each lead. In your email content, you would write:

*Dear [first name], thank you for downloading our e-book!*

But when Cathy Client submits a form, she sees:

*Dear Cathy, thank you for downloading our e-book!*

Research suggests that increasingly, consumers expect this kind of personalized experience—and prefer brands (including legal brands) that customize marketing messages to their specific needs and circumstances.

## Focus on Education and Building Trust

Finally, instead of creating fear or pushing your services, ask questions, provide information, and encourage discourse. For example, an email about insurance company tactics may look like this:

> Dear [first name]:
>
> I hope you're doing well. Over my career, I've dealt with countless insurance adjusters, and I've learned a lot about their tactics. Whether your adjuster is pleasant or combative, their job is to get your case closed as quickly as possible.
>
> Here are some common insurance company tactics to look out for:
>
> - **Recorded statements:** They may pressure you to make a recorded statement about your crash, hoping that you'll make damaging statements or minimize your injuries.
> - **Quick settlement offers:** The adjuster rarely (if ever) will offer you their full settlement authority right away. Don't accept that first offer.
> - **Independent medical exams:** While you need to attend the appointment, this exam is more about building a case against you than valid medical analysis.
> - **Discouraging legal counsel:** Sometimes, adjusters discourage you from talking to a lawyer, arguing that it will just slow down the process and cost you money. However, they're hoping that you won't discover your claim's real value and legal rights.

For more information about insurance company tactics, you can check out this helpful blog article.

Do you have questions about an insurance adjuster? I'm happy to answer them and help you build a response plan. Send me an email or give me a call at any time!

Sincerely,
Sarah Webster, Esq.

You'll notice that this email doesn't push a consultation or hype the law firm's contingency fee structure. Instead, it delivers concise information that may help a lead during the early stages of their accident claim. Then, at the end, the lawyer reaches out and asks a question, subtly encouraging conversion.

## 3. Build Your Emails

Once you have your content, you'll use a template in your automation system to create the actual emails. These templates are reusable files that provide the framework for your emails. Rather than build every campaign from scratch, you can use a template—and then customize it with images, logos, and content that align with your law firm's brand.

You can store customized templates on your email automation platform and use them as a framework for each individual email in a campaign. This will give all of your messaging a consistent fit and feel—building and reaffirming your brand every time they're sent.

However, customizing a template is only the first step of your email build. While each platform's workflow varies, here's what you'll typically need to do:

- Create a campaign folder that includes each of its emails.

- Add content, images, and links to your email.
- Designate each email's triggering event (more on this in just a moment).
- Proof and test your emails internally.
- Launch the campaign.

Because each platform has its idiosyncrasies, make sure you familiarize yourself with its basic operations before you get too far into the process. If you become overwhelmed, consider speaking with a marketing agency that has a certification in your email automation system.

## 4. Create an Automation Schedule

As part of building each email, you'll need to designate a triggering event for each email. While the triggering event for the first email in a campaign may seem obvious—a lead clicks on a call to action and provides their contact information—you may wonder when to send subsequent messages.

This is supposed to be a drip campaign; you don't want to flood them with multiple emails each day. Typically, it's a good idea to send an email every two to three days. If your campaign will go on for longer than a week or two, consider a weekly email schedule.

## 5. Integrate and Track the Campaign's Performance

Once you've released your email automation into the wild, you'll need to monitor its performance. Using the data analytics tools on your platform, you can assess these activities:

- Which emails are most frequently opened.

- Which emails, links, and calls to action get the best click-through rates.

- Which messages have the highest conversion rates.

- What the unsubscribe rates are.

Additionally, you can track a specific lead's engagement. This information can help you gauge their interest and tailor their experience to their exact interests and needs.

Typically, this involves integrating your email automation system with your case management or **customer relationship management (CRM)** software. These applications help you track leads and clients at every step of their journey. (We'll discuss CRM software in more detail in chapter 15, "Practical Client Acquisition Strategies.")

## Encourage Conversion with Data from Your Automation Platform

While email marketing is appealing because it's effective and scalable, there are also other benefits. Many automation platforms can give you powerful insight into your leads' behavior on your website, especially if they're integrated with your client and lead management systems. Once a lead provides your law firm with an email address and your system puts it into the automation platform, the software may be able to link the address to their past and ongoing website activity.

This can help you identify a lead's biggest interests. For example, when Webster, Webster & Cohen looks at Cathy Client's history, they'll notice that she started her client journey by clicking on a TBI blog and that she's read an article about drowsy commercial drivers twice. When Cathy calls to schedule a consultation for her husband, the intake clerk connects them with the firm's top TBI litigator and they block extra time for the interview.

This kind of personalization can help you tailor your clients' experiences and provide better service. However, that doesn't mean you should make assumptions about your leads' stories or needs; ask them open-ended questions and let them tell their stories. Plus, too much personalization through tracking and data analytics can feel creepy and invasive.

## Segment Your Leads for a Bigger Impact

Your email list probably contains a wide variety of contacts: current and former clients, leads, professionals that refer cases to you, and others. For many of these populations, their only connection is that they're familiar with your law firm.

While general emails, like an email blast about a record-breaking settlement, may appeal to everyone, it's sometimes better to send narrower segments communications that target their specific needs or interests.

Let's go back to Cathy Client's initial interaction with Webster, Webster & Cohen. When Cathy downloaded a truck wreck e-book, she triggered a campaign focusing on truck accidents. Rather than giving her generic information about personal injury claims, the law firm could demonstrate their knowledge of the specific area of law that Cathy needed help with.

This detailed list segmentation can help you convert more leads into clients and personalize your clients' experience. Don't be afraid to create individualized campaigns and content for your law firm's diverse audiences.

So, how do you segment an email list? You can do some of it manually, like when a lead converts into a client. However, some email segmentation can be done automatically within the system. For example, individuals who download an e-book or infographic on a specific topic (like truck wrecks) can be automatically segmented into a truck-accident group of messages. Meanwhile, someone who requests a TBI survivor's guide would be segmented differently and get head injury-specific messaging.

# Automation Can Make Your Marketing Efforts Scalable

If you're like many law firms, you don't have an in-house marketing manager. Instead, your administrative staff wear a lot of hats; they're assisting clients, ordering medical records, cutting checks, and trying to keep up with your editorial calendar. If the law firm suddenly intensifies its marketing campaigns, you have a legitimate concern that the added work will end in a mutiny.

Email automation can relieve some of that stress because it's scalable. Whether two or two hundred people trigger an email campaign, the system should reliably send out your scheduled messages.

Furthermore, your staff may be able to streamline many of its processes using email automation, for example, to handle tasks such as these:

- Answer new clients' frequently asked questions, which may reduce phone call volumes.

- Request updated information, such as medical histories.

- Remind clients of important appointments or court dates.

- Send email blasts that notify clients and followers of important legal developments, law firm news, or changes in your office hours.

- Send personalized happy-birthday or other messages.

Rather than reduce their productivity, email automation may simplify your communications, improve the client experience, and ensure a consistent, on-brand message.

## Checklist for Email Automation

- Select an email automation platform.

- Build email campaigns that target your ideal clients and nurture leads.

- Create content for the campaigns.

- Build individual emails within the campaign.

- Set triggering events for each email.

- Implement your email campaign.

- Evaluate the campaign's performance and revise your strategies.

- Use data from your email automation to improve your client experience.

# 10

# Use Visual Content to Hold Attention

Humans are visual creatures by nature. Our earliest recorded communications as a species weren't sentences of prose—they were pictures drawn on cave walls. And we instinctively remember pictures much more readily than words: it's called the picture superiority effect. In one remarkable study from the early 1970s, participants showed they could remember more than two thousand pictures with at least 90 percent accuracy in recognition tests over a period of several days.[1]

So, it's no surprise that audiences want to see visual content online. Content with strong images and visual design elements outperforms text-based content on every metric you can imagine: traffic, time spent on page, conversions, social media likes, and shares. And web users trust visual content more too. In a 2003 study that asked twenty-five

1. Lionel Standing, Jerry Conezio, and Ralph Norman Haber, "Perception and Memory for Pictures: Single-Trial Learning of 2,500 Visual Stimuli," *Psychonomic Science* 19 (1970), https://doi.org/10.3758/BF03337426.

hundred participants to evaluate the credibility of websites they saw, the overall visual design of a site was the factor participants mentioned most when asked what influenced their perception of whether a website was trustworthy.[2]

Among the primary types of visual content that digital marketers use, video content is by far the most popular with web users and the most important to incorporate into your marketing efforts. We'll devote most of this chapter to the ins and outs of video marketing, both because of its relative importance and because you can feasibly produce video marketing content yourself.

Later in the chapter, we'll also touch on other types of visual content like e-books, infographics, and your website photography. While these types of content can deliver significant return on your investment, they're challenging to create without extensive formal training or professional experience in graphic design, so you'll probably need to hire an agency or at least an experienced freelance designer to execute them. Given that, we'll mostly focus on how these content types work within your overall digital marketing strategy rather than how to build them.

## Why Video Marketing?

I'm a voracious reader, and many lawyers I've met are big readers too. Online videos often irritate me—I hate when I can only get certain content like an interesting news item in video form, because I know I would be able to read it much faster. Maybe you feel the same and don't think video is the way to go for informative content.

---

2. B.J. Fogg et. al., "How do Users Evaluate the Credibility of Web Sites?: a Study with Over 2,500 Participants" (DUX '03: Proceedings of the 2003 Conference on Designing for User Experiences, June 2003), https://dl.acm.org/doi/10.1145/997078.997097.

Guess what? You and I are in the minority—the vast minority. Most digital marketing experts believe video is the future of online advertising, and for good reason: video is *huge*.

In 2017, a white paper from the IT company Cisco found that video traffic made up 69 percent of all global consumer internet traffic.[3] Cisco projected this figure to reach 82 percent by 2022. And numerous digital marketing studies have repeatedly shown that websites with video attract more visitors and keep those visitors on the site longer compared to websites that don't have video.

In the past, maybe you wondered whether you could afford to produce videos for your law firm. Based on the current popularity of video and the medium's projected future growth, you should really ask: Can I afford *not* to produce videos as part of my law firm's marketing efforts? Can I turn away 69 percent (soon to be 82 percent) of my audience at the door and expect to receive the best return on my marketing investment? The answer is no.

But today, producing video content that engages users doesn't mean shelling out for slickly produced television ads with high production values and expensive lighting rigs. In fact, that's exactly the kind of video content most web users *don't* want to engage with. If you watch videos from some of the most popular personalities on YouTube, you'll have to sit through a few seconds of one of those high-gloss traditional ads before you can click "skip" and get to the real content. Often, this content amounts to someone setting up a stationary iPhone or consumer-grade camera in their bedroom and talking directly to their audience. And audiences love these types of videos because they feel intimate, authentic, and inviting—more like a conversation with a friend than watching an ad.

The simplicity of this content doesn't necessarily mean it's easy to produce. Many of the top YouTube personalities work very hard on their content despite the low production values. But their work

---

3. Cisco, *Cisco Annual Internet Report (2018–2023) White Paper*, March 9, 2020, https://www.cisco.com/c/en/us/solutions/collateral/service-provider/visual-networking-index-vni/white-paper-c11-741490.html.

gives the lie to the notion that you need a film crew, Hollywood-grade lighting, and a camera that costs as much as a new Jeep to create online video content that generates engagement and revenue.

# What Kind of Videos Should I Create?

So, if web users don't want to watch traditional television-style ads, what do they want? Based on our experience working with many different types of law firms, some of the most successful types of video content include the following.

## Frequently Asked Questions (FAQ) Videos

Most new clients who have a legal issue have lots of questions, and many lawyers hear the same questions time and again. Creating videos that anticipate and answer potential clients' initial questions is a great way to get them familiar with you, build their trust, and start them down the path toward getting in touch.

## Video Blogs (vlogs)

Lots of people don't like to read, especially at length. Turning some of your blog articles into short videos can widen the potential audience for your content without requiring much extra work on your part. YouTube has lots of video tutorials that can show you how to make a video blog with zero budget. Even with the bare minimum of equipment (an iPhone and a miniature tripod or stand), you can film yourself talking through the topic and then use free beginner-level video editing software to overlay text, insert images, and add cuts, all of which keep the video from looking stale and static.

The topics of your video blogs can overlap with your written blogs (some people prefer to read and others prefer to watch, so redundancy is okay), or they can cover entirely different topics. The best approach is probably a blend where you try out some new topics via video but also adapt some of your most popular written blogs into video format.

## Client Testimonials

People trust people they can relate to, and most people don't relate to lawyers. But if they're looking for a lawyer, they will relate to lawyers' clients since those clients probably had similar issues and challenges to what they're experiencing now. Seeing your clients on video and hearing them talk about their positive experiences gives your potential clients confidence that what you do works and that they'll wind up better off for retaining your services.

Client testimonials will probably be the most challenging type of video to shoot if you don't have experience. With most of the other video types, you could hold a smartphone selfie-style and get people to watch if your content interests them enough. However, your clients probably won't feel comfortable appearing on camera in such an off-the-cuff way, so you'll probably have to assemble something that more resembles a professional video shoot if you want convincing testimonials. So, you may want to consider hiring a marketing agency or video production firm to shoot your testimonials if you're inexperienced, even if you handle the rest of your video content yourself. Here are some examples of questions you might want to ask the client:

- What problem did you have that made you look for a lawyer?

- How did your problem affect your life?
- What made our firm stand out to you?
- How did you feel when you first met with your attorney?
- What was your biggest concern about working with a lawyer, and how did we help put that worry to rest?
- What did you like most about working with us?
- If your best friend asked you what working with our firm was like, what would you say?
- What was your life like before you worked with our firm? Is it better now because you worked with us? If yes, how so?
- What surprised you most about working with our firm?
- Anything else you want people to know about us or about you? (Always give people one final chance to speak their mind; you never know what profound things they might say! If you don't get anything useful, you can just delete the material later.)

## Office Tours and Staff Profiles

Who wants a video tour of a law firm or a video meet-and-greet with a law firm receptionist? Boring, right? You might be surprised how many potential clients sign up. Visiting a lawyer's office for the first time is an intimidating prospect for many people, and turning that office into a familiar space by exploring it online first and seeing your welcoming team can take the anxiety out of a free consultation appointment.

# Shooting Video Content

We can't teach you every detail of how to shoot and edit video content in this chapter—it's outside the scope of the book and would probably make for a slim volume all on its own. But we will provide some entry-level tips and direct you to some resources that can help you learn more.

The best way to get a feel for what your videos should look like is to head to YouTube, browse around, watch some videos from popular personalities, and take note of the choices they made: location, lighting, cuts and edits, style of speech. You should also search some legal topics and watch some videos from law firms who are getting lots of views, but don't get too hung up on imitating what your direct competitors are doing. You'll never find your own style and stand out from the online crowd by aping the law firm across town. Besides, most law firms stay about five or six years behind the leading edge with their digital marketing tactics, so copying something another law firm did a year or two ago is like jumping onto a conga line when the song's already fading out.

## Location

Shooting video is like real estate: it's all about location, location, location. A well-chosen location will make your job easy, and an unfavorable one will make your life hell. You need to consider three factors when choosing a location: sound, light, and background.

Sound is the single most important characteristic of your location. You can adjust the lighting and background in a room quite easily, but fixing a noisy room with lots of echo will prove much harder. Background clatter can kill the conversational vibe of your video and annoy your audience, so make sure not to shoot in a noisy area or when a road crew is operating a jackhammer on the street outside. If your office doesn't have a good spot, try checking your home for a suitable spot. Rooms that have lots of furniture and soft carpet tend to create the best environments for recording sound, which is why many famous YouTubers record in their bedrooms.

The lighting in your location is much easier to adjust than its acoustic character: often, bringing in a lamp or two from another room is enough to even out imperfect lighting. Just watch out for locations that let in lots of natural light that you can't control, like a giant picture window with no shades. Natural light can be a wonderful thing, but too much can make it impossible to shoot video on a sunny day.

From a visual standpoint, try to choose a background that's free from any clutter or mess, but include a few objects of visual interest in the frame, like bookshelves, lamps, and paintings. Again, watch successful YouTubers, and you'll see that most of them avoid distracting and cluttered backgrounds, but they rarely record in front of blank walls either.

## Camera

Today, most new smartphones and tablets can shoot professional-quality video, especially with a few accessories, so you don't need to worry about your camera setup too much. However, we'll go over the three primary camera options just so you know what's available.

1. **Smartphone or tablet:** You probably already own one of these devices, and they're light and easy to transport. If you have no prior experience with the other options, it makes sense to start with your phone. Learn to use it, see what kind of results you can get, and if you feel like your phone is holding you back (hint: it probably isn't unless you're going for a studio-quality production), you can explore the other options.

   However, smartphones and tablets do come with a few inherent limitations. The zoom function on most smartphone cameras is terrible, so you should avoid using it altogether. This is far from a deal breaker—just learn to position your camera to get the shot you want in the first place, without relying on a zoom.

More problematic is the microphone on your smartphone or tablet. It might get you usable audio in a very quiet room at a close distance, so it's worth taking a shot with the built-in mic. However, you may find you need to pick up an additional microphone to get audio of acceptable quality. Fortunately, external microphones are available for most smartphones. These small mics plug right into existing jacks on the phone and can clip onto your shirt or jacket for easy placement, and most of them are quite affordable. So, upgrading the built-in microphone is as simple as placing a quick Amazon order and plugging your new mic in.

2. **Digital single-lens reflex (DSLR) camera:** DSLR cameras are the choice of most professional still photographers (think of the ubiquitous black cameras you see photographers use at concerts or sports games, the ones built like tiny tanks). Almost all DSLRs sold today shoot video in addition to taking still pictures, and the ones from reputable brands like Canon and Nikon do it quite well.

   A DSLR camera will give you the most flexibility to adjust how your video looks by adjusting settings like color saturation and sharpness. (You can adjust these elements with an editing program too, but the best results usually come from tweaking them before shooting rather than after.) Also, the zoom function on the lenses of these cameras works much better than the zoom on a smartphone camera.

   Despite the advantages, DSLR cameras have lots of drawbacks. DSLRs have a very high learning curve, so expect to spend a lot of time with your nose buried in the user's manual and then even more time practicing before you're ready to shoot. A good DSLR camera won't come cheap, and you may find that additional accessories like a variety of lenses, lens filters, and other doodads are necessary to get quality results—all of which adds to the price tag and complexity of your video setup.

3. **Dedicated video camera:** Camcorder-style video cameras have many of the same drawbacks as DSLRs. Video cameras are complex, and they require lots of practice to use. Like DSLRs, video cameras have a high "doodad factor"—you'll probably find you need to shell out for and lug around a whole kit of accessories just to shoot in everyday situations. And video cameras tend to carry even higher price tags than DSLRs of comparable quality, so they're probably the least budget-friendly option.

   Video cameras offer similar benefits to DSLRs when compared to smartphones. When compared to DSLRs, dedicated video cameras use an ergonomic design that makes holding the camera and shooting video feel a bit more natural. However, if you're placing the camera on a tripod and using it to film yourself, this advantage is totally moot.

The type of camera you use shouldn't make or break your video content. We've already seen music videos from A-list pop stars and photography exhibits at world-class museums that were shot on smartphones and tablets, so if you have a newer smartphone from a major name like Samsung, Google, or iPhone, you probably have everything you need on the camera front to get started.

## Lighting

If you've managed to find a quiet space with good acoustics (again, carpet and soft furniture are good; rooms with hard floors and lots of empty space are bad) and soft lighting, you shouldn't need to worry too much about lighting and audio. When you film yourself, watch out for harsh lighting that makes you look washed-out or places shadows on your face.

Usually, bright overhead lights with white-colored bulbs are bad (fluorescents are about the worst) while lamps with warmer-colored (meaning slightly yellow) bulbs work best. Often, a combination of multiple light sources works best, like overhead lights plus a desk lamp to remove shadows from your face. Depending on the time of day and the location of your space, natural light coming in through the windows might provide everything you need.

## Preparation

The most popular video bloggers on YouTube work hard to make it look like they're not working hard. These personalities carefully design their content to make it look like they hit record when the mood strikes and then let their muse guide them. In reality, they spend unseen and untold hours planning their shoots and rehearsing their on-camera presence.

You'll need to prepare too if you want to seem natural on camera. Every time you film, you need to know what you want to say, who your target audience is, and why your message should interest them. Depending on how comfortable you feel improvising on camera, you may want to write out every word you want to say, or you may want to create an outline and let yourself talk through it in a semi-spontaneous fashion.

There's no one-size-fits-all approach, so you'll need to figure out what works for you, but you should never press record without any notes or advance planning and let yourself ramble into the camera. Expect every video to require multiple takes, and don't get frustrated if you mess up.

I haven't often appeared on camera, but I do record a **podcast** for our agency, and I know from experience that many people (including myself at first) experience a vague, creeping anxiety when they realize they're being recorded, even if no one else will ever see or hear the results. So, don't worry if you feel self-conscious or uncomfortable on camera—it's normal. The cure is simple: keep practicing, preparing, and filming yourself, and you'll feel a little more natural and confident every time.

## Editing

Orson Welles once said: "The notion of directing a film is the invention of critics; the whole eloquence of cinema is achieved in the editing room."[4] No one, whether they're an elite Hollywood director or a bedroom vlogger, shoots perfect video that's ready for the world as soon as the recording stops. Everyone who succeeds with video shoots more footage than they need, usually across multiple takes, and then uses editing tools to cut away the excess and stitch together a finished product.

We can't provide a guide to video editing in the space allotted in this chapter: it's too big of a topic, and it would send us straight down a rabbit hole. But the good news is that while video editing can be an extremely technical process, the popularity of YouTube has given rise to dozens of user-friendly, affordable video editing tools aimed squarely at beginners. Check out some of the resources at the end of this chapter for help with video editing.

# Keys to Video Marketing Success

Even the best videos will languish in obscurity if you don't promote them, and even videos with thousands or millions of views will fail to generate revenue if you don't integrate them into your larger marketing strategy. Here are some tips to get compelling results from your video content:

4. Originally published in *Cahiers du Cinéma*, No. 84 (June, 1958) a translated and annotated version appears as "An Interview with Orson Welles," trans. Sally Shafto, *Senses of Cinema* 46 (May, 2008), http://sensesofcinema.com/2008/the-new-wave-remembered-focus-on-charles-bitsch/orson-welles-bazin-bitsch.

## Maintain a Consistent Video Publishing Schedule

We've discussed the importance of a consistent publishing schedule for content in previous chapters, and it's no less true for video. You may not have a million YouTube subscribers, but don't let that make you think no one cares how often you post. Web users prefer newer content over old, and they're more likely to watch and follow videos from law firms and attorneys who produce a steady stream of content.

Just like with your video content, you'll need to create an editorial calendar. The process works much the same as we described in Chapter 6, "Plan and Maintain a Content Strategy," although as we'll discuss next, your video content generally won't go into as much depth on a subject as written blog content.

## Keep Your Videos Brief

How long should your videos be? The most accurate answer is "as long as they need to be"—emphasis on *need.* Stick to the most important points of your topic, don't go off on tangents or side topics, and explain everything in enough detail so as not to mislead or omit critical information.

Most web marketers believe that the ideal length for a YouTube video is two minutes or less. According to a 2019 study from the video marketing company, Vidyard, 73 percent of all business videos on the web are two minutes or less in length.[5] However, there's no need to be prescriptive; don't stretch out a video when you've already said everything you need to say, and don't cut vital info just to trim a video down from two minutes and fourteen seconds. Just keep in mind that if you make a video that's five or six minutes in length, only a very small percentage of users will watch until the end.

5. Vidyard, *The 2019 Vidyard Video Benchmark Report* (2019), https://www.vidyard.com/business-video-benchmarks.

## Focus on Educating Viewers

The worst thing you can do is try to bury the information the viewer wants behind explicit advertising messages. So, if you're creating a video that provides tips about how to strengthen a personal injury case, *do not* start the video with a twenty-second pitch about how great your firm is before you move on to the content the user wants. No one will sit through your pitch, and no one will watch your content, either. There's too much content available for users online, and you have no leverage that can force users to sit through content they don't care about. Instead, get to the point and then finish your video with a compelling call to action (CTA).

## Include a Clear Call to Action

Shooting and editing a video can involve so many different considerations that it's easy to get swept up and forget the *why* behind what you're doing: you want this video to get you clients! The call to action (CTA) is the part of your video that helps you accomplish this. You need to close every video with a clear message that tells the potential client what you want them to do next.

Ideally, that next step is to pick up the phone and schedule a consultation. In practice, you probably need more than one CTA since not every potential client will feel ready to call you after watching a single video. For those clients who still want to learn more before connecting, direct them to other resources. If you have in-depth resources like e-books and infographics (which we'll discuss shortly) that tend to move potential clients further down the funnel, your closing CTA provides an opportunity to draw attention to those. If not, encourage viewers to visit your blog and sign up for your newsletter and subscribe to your YouTube channel. You can also point them directly to another video they may find helpful.

## Treat Video as Part of a Holistic Marketing Strategy

Finally, don't forget to share your videos and incorporate them into other marketing strategies. Share your videos aggressively on social media, provide links in your blog posts to videos that discuss related topics, embed a video or two on your home page, and create a video library page on your website that houses all your videos. You should also embed relevant videos on your landing pages for paid search campaigns; you'll learn more about these types of landing pages in chapter 13, "Paid Advertising: Pay per Click."

To help get your internal wheels turning, we've shot and edited a few short videos for the fictional law firm of Webster, Webster & Cohen. To view them, visit the following URL: https://lafleur.marketing/trial-guides-videos.

# Infographics

An infographic is what you'd get if you waved a magic wand and transformed a blog article into a Disney film. Infographics usually still contain a fair amount of text, but they weave lots and lots of colorful images around that text. They often represent statistics and prominent bits of information in charts, graphs, or clever illustrations. Some companies even publish interactive infographics that allow users to click on or drag elements to reveal information, respond to questions, or otherwise affect the images in front of them.

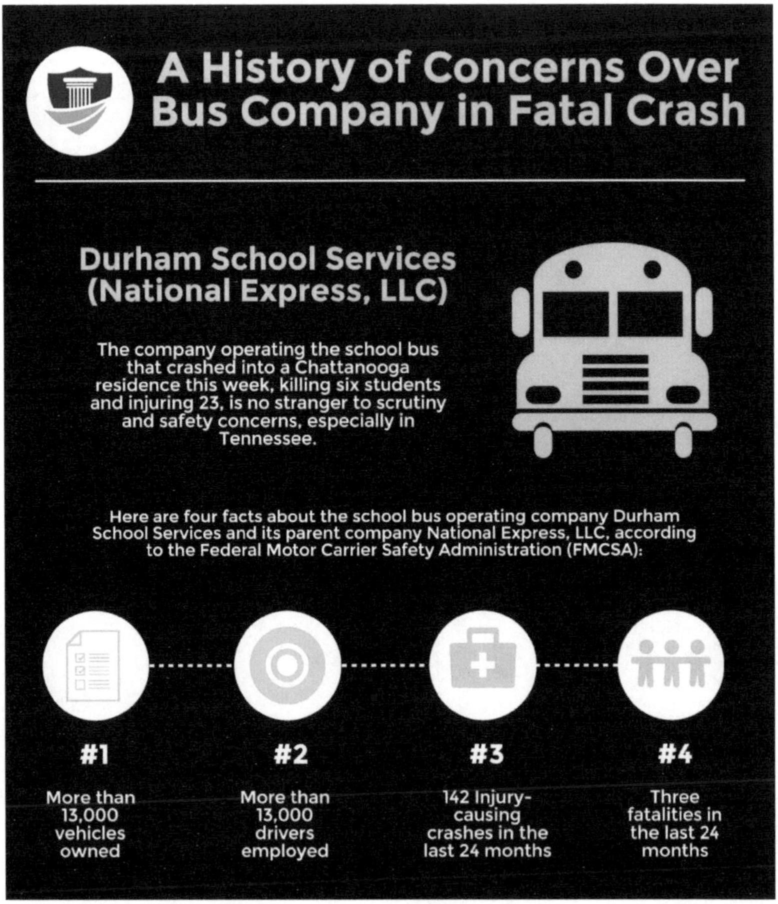


Most topics that make for interesting blog articles work well as infographics too. Blog articles that include a lot of statistics or figures become much more engaging to readers when those numbers come alive as colorful graphs and illustrations. Infographics can keep your blog from seeming monotonous, make even dry topics seem fascinating, and pique the interest of potential clients who wouldn't otherwise click on a blog article. And infographics tend to perform especially well on social media, where the colorful illustrations show up in previews and often attract extra likes and shares.

Some online web services like Venngage and Piktochart allow you to create infographics from templates at very affordable rates. Most of these services have enough customization options to make your infographics reasonably distinctive, so if you think you have an eye for design, feel free to experiment with these tools. If you find the results underwhelming, then hiring a graphic designer is your other option.

In terms of strategy, professionally designed infographics require you to put a lot of eggs in one basket; you could probably publish at least five or six blog articles for the cost required to publish one infographic. Even infographics created using free tools will take significant time to create, especially as you're teaching yourself how to use these tools. So, you probably shouldn't worry about infographics until you have a blog marketing strategy in place that's delivering tangible results (meaning web traffic and leads).

Once you've proven that you can come up with topics that interest potential clients and turn them into content that delivers traffic and leads, you can take the next step and experiment with infographics. Rather than spending the resources on a topic that may or may not perform, consider taking one of your blog articles that receives the most traffic or ranks highest in search for a desirable term and repurposing it as an infographic.

If you're not sure how to tell which blog articles are performing best, we'll cover that information in chapter 16, "Going Beyond the Basics: Analytics."

## E-books

If you're a Kindle lover, you probably think of an e-book as something you download before vacation and read by the fire or at the beach. But for digital marketers, e-books (also called digital white papers) serve an important function by providing an opportunity to showcase expertise and offer content potential clients can sink their teeth into.

Generally, an e-book is much longer than a blog article, but much shorter than an actual digital novel. It's an in-depth treatment of a topic that usually includes a number of chapters or subsections. For example, the topic for an article on your blog might be "How Does Property Division Work in an Ohio Divorce?" Meanwhile, the topic for an e-book might be "The Definitive Guide to Ohio Divorce." The e-book would then include a chapter on every legal issue related to divorce: separation and filing, communications, spousal support, child custody, property division, and so on.

E-books help bridge the gap between an engagement and a conversion. Many potential clients who engage with your firm by visiting your website won't feel ready to get in touch for quite some time. They'll flit around in your orbit like fireflies for days or weeks, bookmarking your website and coming back now and then, but never quite taking the next steps to become a lead. An e-book can provide the enticement these users need to provide contact information, at which point your automated email campaigns and newsletters can kick in and make sure these users stay engaged until they're ready to reach out. E-books also appeal to research-oriented folks like myself who want to read all about the legal aspects of their case and develop their knowledge as much as possible before they show up before a consultation.

You may be wondering: Why would I give away all my expertise in an e-book? What if a potential client reads my e-book and decides they can handle their case on their own? The answer is that reading one e-book does not an attorney make, and the types of curious and detail-oriented potential clients who crave e-books will either know this intuitively or figure it out quickly as they read. You can never cover all the intricacies and possibilities of a complex legal matter in a brief e-book. So, the potential client will most likely end up with a long list of follow-up questions based on their unique circumstances, and scheduling a consultation with you is now their fast-track to getting those questions answered.

Some companies also publish much longer infographics that are more like image-heavy e-books. These infographics function much the same way as e-books for strategy purposes; you can ask users to provide an email address in exchange for a free download.

If creating an infographic is like wading into the shallow end of investing in content, developing an e-book is a full-on header off the diving board. You should consider creating an e-book only if you're seeing traction from your existing blog marketing strategy. You can collect and weave together information you've published in relevant blog posts to create e-book content, but don't just copy and paste a stack of blog articles together—you need to treat an e-book as a standalone and unique piece of content, so it will require a significant amount of planning and writing.

E-books also need to look visually appealing, so you'll need to work with a graphic designer who can design a cover, format the book in professional software like Adobe InDesign, and add features like pull quotes and illustrations to break up the pages. You can also try to work with the free e-book templates that companies like HubSpot offer, but given the time required to create the content for an e-book and the valuable commodity you want to ask for in return for your e-book (potential clients' contact information), investing in a unique visual design created by a professional is probably the best choice here.

## Summary

Creating visual content like videos, infographics, and e-books isn't easy work, but it builds a level of trust and engagement that no other digital marketing tactics can achieve. If you can take the plunge and permanently incorporate visual content into your digital marketing strategy, you'll find that the returns justify the investment and hard work, and you'll quickly pull away from competitors who don't understand or properly value the unique and powerful spell that images and design cast over an audience.

# Visual Content Checklist

- FAQs (Video)
- Client testimonials (video)
- Staff profiles (video)
- Video blogs (video)
- Infographics
- E-books

# Additional Recommended Resources

- Gretchen Siegchrist, "Before You Begin Video Editing: Choose the Right Equipment and Software for Your First Movie," *Lifewire* (December, 2019), https://www.lifewire.com/introduction-to-video-editing-1081794.
- Buildscale, Inc. "Chapter Three: Video Production," https://www.vidyard.com/video-production-guide/shooting-video.
- Adorama Camera, Inc. "Video Editing Tips for Beginners" (August, 2018), https://www.adorama.com/alc/video-editing-tips-for-beginners.

- Chris Atkinson, "Basic Video Editing Tips—The YouTube Advertiser Playbook: Part 3" Tubular Insights & Tubular Labs, Inc. (May, 2012), https://tubularinsights.com/video-editing-zyoutube-advertiser-playbook.

- Steve Stockman, *How to Shoot Video That Doesn't Suck: Advice to Make Any Amateur Look Like a Pro* (New York: Workman Publishing Company, 2011).

- Michael Clarke, *Video Marketing in 2019 Made (Stupidly) Easy* (Punk Rock Marketing, 2018).

- Aaron Goold, *The Video Editing Handbook: Simple Strategies for Editing Effective Video* (2017).

# 11

# Networking and Creating Brand Ambassadors

If you have a group of reliable referral sources, you already understand the power of brand ambassadorship. It is remarkable how word of mouth can boost your practice and help you attract your ideal clients. Today, you can build your reputation through more than word of mouth, using online reviews, social media, and testimonials.

Modern legal consumers are more sophisticated than their predecessors. They're looking for more than a well-built website, since they view branded messaging with a healthy dose of skepticism. Instead of taking your statements at face value, modern legal consumers will vet your law firm's credentials using their personal connections, research, and online reviews.

If you're not building a strong online reputation and fostering a network of brand ambassadors, you may lose out on valuable leads and cases. In this chapter, we discuss the importance of networking, thought leadership, and how brand ambassadors can give your marketing efforts additional traction.

# Why Should Lawyers Network?

We get it. We've all been at those awkward networking events where you get pinned in a corner by a professional who wants to push their services or tell puffed-up war stories. You're stuck, nodding absent-mindedly, sipping your complimentary beverage, and desperately planning your escape strategy. Thankfully, we're not talking about that kind of networking here.

As a lawyer, you probably realize the power of referrals and endorsements from other professionals and past clients. If a lead gets your name from their neurosurgeon, another attorney, or a trusted community member, you automatically gain credibility and trust.

Your network of referral sources is invaluable. However, many lawyers neglect their biggest fans, assuming that they'll always be there. Unfortunately, most people aren't as committed to their favorite brands as past generations, and you need to stay at the top of their minds.

# Why Do Reviews and Referrals Matter to Law Firms?

In this world of celebrity endorsements and social media influencers, you might think that people have become jaded to reviews and recommendations. However, the opposite is true. According to a 2015 Avvo survey of roughly nine hundred legal consumers, 96 percent said that reviews played a role in their decision to hire a lawyer. A remarkable 49 percent said that reviews were "very important" to their decision-making process.[1]

1. Nika Kabiri, "Sink or swim: How to adapt to the New Legal Consumer," Avvo (2016), https://www.martindale-avvo.com/wp-content/uploads/how_to_adapt_to_the_new_legal_consumer_avvo_whitepaper_2016.pdf.

So why do people think that reviews are so important? Because people don't trust you to tell them the complete truth. In 2018, Jack Morton, a global branding agency, surveyed six thousand consumers in three countries. It found that 41 percent of American millennials assume that businesses will not live up to their brand image and want consumers to believe that they're something they are not.[2]

However, your potential clients do think that reviewers (including people they've never met) will provide them with the real story. Academics and marketers refer to the power of a referral or review as an example of **social proof.** Most, if not all humans, want affirmation of their choices from others. This psychological phenomenon is often triggered when people are unsure how to act in an uncertain situation—such as during a legal claim. Innately, they turn to those around them for information, assuming that other people have additional knowledge and insight.

Now, let's explore how you can nurture and build your social proof and bolster your referral network.

## What Is a Brand Ambassador?

A brand ambassador has fully bought into your law firm's mission and posts favorable reviews, recommends your services, and engages with your firm's social media profiles. They are a powerful resource that can help you find, nurture, and convert leads. While anyone can become a brand ambassador, they often come from these relationships:

- current and past clients
- employees, both past and present

2. Jack Morton, "The Experience Brand Index," *Jack Blog* (blog), September 19, 2018, http://www.jackmorton.com/blog/experience-brand-index.

- other lawyers
- physicians and medical providers
- nonprofit organizations' staff
- financial advisors
- friends, family, and other loved ones

The goal is to keep your law firm at the forefront of these people's minds, so that when the opportunity arises, they suggest your services.

For example, Webster, Webster & Cohen helps Cathy Client get a six-figure settlement for her husband, who was in a truck wreck. After they close the case, she continues to get email newsletters and other communications from the firm. They even send her an (automated) happy birthday email each year!

She consistently likes Webster, Webster & Cohen's Facebook posts and shares them with her friends. When her neighbor is injured in a car-motorcycle crash, Cathy provides the family with several ready-made dinners and her lawyer's business card. She raves about their experience with the law firm and encourages the victim to schedule a consultation—even offering to drive them to the appointment. Cathy is a Webster, Webster & Cohen brand ambassador.

Here's a less traditional example of a brand ambassador. One of attorney Sarah Webster's clients wins a disability nonprofit organization's Advocate of the Year award for his work with other spinal cord injury survivors. To celebrate his achievement, Sarah attends the gala.

At the party, she starts chatting with Tim Handup, the nonprofit's job coach. He mentions that many of his clients don't understand the Americans with Disabilities Act (ADA) and their legal rights. Sarah offers to run a free workshop for them and provides the organization with Webster, Webster & Cohen's ADA Accommodation Checklist. After the workshop, Tim and Sarah have coffee and discuss the community's needs. In follow-up, Sarah sends him a personal note and signs him up for the firm's newsletter.

Whenever one of Tim's clients runs into ADA issues, he gives them a copy of the law firm's checklist. He also starts telling them to call Sarah when they run into serious problems, touting her connection to his organization and willingness to educate disabled workers. Tim is also a Webster, Webster & Cohen brand ambassador.

## Relationship Building: The Key to Referrals

When you connect with a potential referral source, what do you do? Squirrel their business card in your Rolodex? Connect with them on LinkedIn? Send them a personal note? Invite them out for coffee to learn more about their needs and goals? Add their email address to a segmented list?

When you build personal connections with potential brand ambassadors, they are more likely to champion your law firm. You may not buy every referral source a latte, but it certainly makes sense to build their awareness of your firm and send them personalized content. Just like with lead nurturing, a steady (but not overwhelming) drip of high-quality, targeted information can build trust and lead to more referrals and opportunities to engage with the community.

# Email Segmentation and Networking

As we discussed in chapter 9, "Nurture Leads with Email Automation," email segmentation and automation can help you send personalized messages to specific audiences. Professionals that refer clients to you may have different interests and priorities than your leads and clients. When you place them into segmented email lists, you can seamlessly deliver targeted messages to their in-boxes.

For example, suppose Webster, Webster & Cohen gets a groundbreaking decision about an undocumented employee's right to workers' compensation benefits, and they want to send out a news blast. To get the most impact, they could tailor their emails' messaging to each individual audience:

- **Leads, clients, and laypeople:** "Even If You're Undocumented, Workers' Comp Must Cover Certain Bills," offered in both Spanish and English

- **Lawyers:** "Supreme Court: Workers' Comp Carrier Must Cover Undocumented Workers' Reasonable and Necessary Medical Care"

- **Doctors:** "How to Get Your Undocumented Patients' Bills Paid by a Workers' Comp Carrier"

Each email is carefully written to answer the targeted audience's questions and reflects their level of sophistication. Then the firm sends each one to its segmented email lists of lawyers, physicians, and legal consumers. They also issue a press release to their media contacts.

If you have not already done so, take some time to segment your email lists, dividing people by their interests and relationship to your law firm. If you need help with this nuanced process, consult with a marketing partner.

# LinkedIn: Take a Segmented Approach to Social Media

Many lawyers, especially those who do not serve businesses, fail to leverage the power of LinkedIn. While not every plaintiff is searching for lawyers on LinkedIn, it's a fantastic place to connect with other professionals and nurture these relationships.

As discussed in chapter 7, "Engage Your Followers on Social Media," LinkedIn is the foremost social media platform for business-to-business marketing and networking. While you may speak more directly to your clients and leads on Facebook or Twitter, consider doing the following through LinkedIn:

- Share your law firm's milestones, including important legal decisions, awards, speaking events, and anniversaries.

- Post blogs and commentary that demonstrate your thought leadership and expertise.

- Provide pointers and insights from your legal practice.

- Share insightful posts from your referral sources and other partners.

- Highlight your law firm's growth when you're hiring or expanding.

# Nurturing Brand Ambassadors

In the legal realm, it's very important to understand what you can and cannot do with respect to your brand ambassadors. Because most companies understand the power of reviews and recommendations, you've probably seen countless posts from social media influencers where they rave about a product, then wrap it up with "#ad." This and similar **hashtags** are an attempt to comply with state and federal truth in advertising laws.

While we don't suggest you hire a pop star to promote your legal services, you need to be aware of how the Rules of Professional Conduct, governmental regulations, and platform policies constrain the nurturing of brand ambassadors.

## Don't Violate Your State's Rules of Professional Conduct

As an attorney, you have an obligation to follow your state's rules of professional responsibility, and you should understand how your bar association approaches the topics of referrals and reviews.

While every state is different, here is what you typically should avoid:

- Paying referral or finders' fees to nonlawyers.
- Offering referral fees to other lawyers when prohibited by the Rules of Professional Conduct.
- Offering gifts or prizes for a referral.
- Pressuring or coercing clients or others to review your law firm.

However, other than these basic prohibitions, state bars have diverse perspectives on the nurturing of referral and review sources.

For example, some states allow you to offer incentives for posting a review, but you must designate it as a paid advertisement, which may negate its power. Others, such as North Carolina, are taking a hard stance on contests or giveaways triggered by liking a page or publishing a review on social media. Another group of states, including New York, limit reviews or testimonials from a client while a case is pending. To protect yourself, you should always check with your state bar or review its Rules of Professional Conduct before offering a program or incentive that encourages referrals or reviews.

## Review the FTC's Guides

In 2009, the Federal Trade Commission (FTC) issued revised rules about the use of endorsements and testimonials in ads. These rules acknowledge that it's becoming increasingly difficult for consumers to differentiate between paid advertising and unpaid reviews.
According to the FTC:

> Endorsements must reflect the honest opinions, findings, beliefs, or experience of the endorser. Furthermore, an endorser may not convey any express or implied representation that would be deceptive if made directly by the advertiser.[3]

Additionally, you must disclose any incentives or compensation you provide a reviewer, including discounts. If you do not disclose your relationship with an endorser, you both may face liability.

Many social media influencers get around this hurdle by including hashtags like "#ad" or "#sponsored" to their content. (Vague disclaimers, like "#collab" or "#ambassador" are insufficient.) If your

3. Federal Trade Commission, "Guides Concerning the Use of Endorsements and Testimonials in Advertising," https://www.ftc.gov/sites/default/files/attachments/press-releases/ftc-publishes-final-guides-governing-endorsements-testimonials/091005revisedendorsementguides.pdf.

bar association permits incentives for reviews, your clients and others should always note if they received a discount, items, or any form of compensation for their input.

## Double-Check Your Social Media Platforms' Policies

In addition to bar association guidelines and truth in advertising laws, you also need to consider each platform's stance on the solicitation of reviews. Google My Business, one of the premier platforms for online reviews, clearly prohibits mass solicitation of reviews and incentives for posting a review. If Google believes you've violated its rules, it may delete some (or all) of your positive reviews.

On the other hand, Avvo actively encourages law firms to solicit testimonials and ratings—even offering a system where you can send a mass email to up to fifty clients or lawyers, asking for their input.

## Create Systems That Encourage Favorable Reviews

Again, you must fully understand your state's Rules of Professional Conduct. Florida, a state that is notoriously strict about lawyer advertising, bars you from asking a client for an online review. While clients can go on their own to Google My Business or other platforms, Florida lawyers cannot ask or encourage them to do so. Not sure about your state's stance on testimonials and review nurturing? Check your Rules of Professional Conduct.

However, in most jurisdictions, you can encourage your clients to provide testimonials or reviews—as long they are not misleading or coerced. You can also make it easy for them to post reviews.

One of the simplest ways to streamline review posting is to send an automated email to the client at the end of their claim, thanking them for their trust and business. Then ask them to share their experience with others and provide them with links to your social media platforms.

For example, Webster, Webster & Cohen's referral email may look like this:

Dear [first name]:

It was an honor representing you in your injury claim. I know that it wasn't always an easy process, but you handled it with strength and dignity. If you ever have questions about your claim or need assistance, please call me or email me right away. We are always ready to help our clients, both old and new!

I hope you had a positive experience working with Webster, Webster & Cohen. If you would like to send me feedback or suggestions on how we can improve, you can contact me directly. You can also post your review on:

- Google My Business
- Facebook
- Avvo

We think that positive reviews and referrals from past clients are the best compliment you can give us!

If you have problems posting your review, you can always call my office for assistance. We know that everyone isn't comfortable with technology, and we can help! Again, thank you.

Your friend,
Sarah Webster, Esq.

If your clients need help posting reviews, it's okay to offer in-office assistance. However, you should never write a review for a client or pressure them into posting a favorable review. (We've seen other marketing professionals suggest that you ask your clients to post their reviews while you "finalize their settlement" or "cut their settlement check." However, some people may find this tactic coercive or pushy—and we discourage it.)

You can also use software, like BirdEye, to automatically send this request. Many of these review-generating and monitoring platforms also let you track your reviews and quickly identify negative feedback.

## Build Your Reputation through Thought Leadership

Another way to stay at the forefront of your brand ambassadors' minds is by exhibiting thought leadership. This may involve the following:

- Publishing your perspectives and insights in online and print periodicals.
- Publishing a podcast or appearing on a media outlet.
- Speaking at events, workshops, and webinars.
- Offering high-value resources, like e-books and white papers.

You should always promote these opportunities and projects on your website, through your newsletter, and via social media to ensure that your brand ambassadors know about them.

# Bad Reviews and Reputation Management

Bad reviews are inevitable. You'll have dissatisfied or frustrated clients that take to the internet and vent. Some of their complaints may be legitimate; others may be unfounded and inaccurate. So what do you do to combat them?

First of all, it's never a good idea to delete a negative review. This can escalate the situation, leading to even more negative feedback. Instead, it's best to quickly respond, show empathy, and continue the conversation offline.

And while you cannot erase bad reviews, you can create a more accurate picture of your services by encouraging satisfied clients to post stories about their positive experiences with your law firm.

# Do Badges and Awards Matter to Legal Consumers?

Law firms love **badges**, logos associated with an award, association, or honor they've received. Many lawyers proudly emblazon their home pages with all of their badges, hyping credentials ranging from "Martindale-Hubbell AV-rated" to "Coolest Places to Work." While these logos are omnipresent, do they actually build credibility with legal consumers?

Research suggests that most of these badges have little impact on a legal consumer's actual decision-making. An array of meaningless badges, like "Our City's Favorite Lawyer" and "Top Ten Local Lawyers" can actually reduce trust, not build it, since savvy legal consumers are innately skeptical of this kind of puffery.

Instead, they want to experience or hear about concrete examples of your law firm's performance and commitment. That's why people turn to online reviews—and why you want your brand ambassadors filling your Google My Business, Facebook, and other profiles with their amazing stories.

# Networking and Brand Ambassador Checklist

- Identify your potential referral sources and brand ambassadors.
- Create segmented email lists that target each ambassador audience (such as past clients, physicians, and other lawyers).
- Create email campaigns that speak to each audience.
- Use LinkedIn to connect and nurture professional referral sources.
- Take advantage of opportunities to show your thought leadership.
- Encourage brand ambassadors and satisfied clients to post online reviews, if permissible.
- Create emails and systems that make review posting easy, if permissible.
- Monitor and respond to your online reviews.

# 12

# Paid Advertising: Start with Social

## Using Social Media for Advertising

Paid advertising can build brand awareness and improve your law firm's visibility, but it's not for the faint of heart, especially in the legal industry. Among the top one hundred most expensive paid advertising keywords on the web, over 70 percent of them are related to legal topics. To compete in that space, you typically must have a minimum monthly budget of $1,500 for pay-per-click (PPC) advertising, and in many competitive markets, law firms are spending $25,000 to $50,000 per month on PPC ads!

Thankfully, there are other options. Small and medium-sized law firms that don't have the funds to compete with the large firms in the pay-per-click space should start in an environment that has lower risk and could have higher rewards: social media advertising. (And if you're intrigued by the power of PPC advertising, refer to chapter 13, "Paid Advertising: Pay per Click," and chapter 14, "Paid Advertising: Monitoring.")

From promoting a post to increase visibility or drive traffic to your website, to full campaigns that can target a potential client at any point in their journey, social media advertising can do it all with a relatively low commitment.

According to 2018 research by GlobalWebIndex, social networks have surpassed search engines as the go-to product research channel for Gen Z consumers, and the popularity of social networks continues to grow across all generations.[1] Whether you are trying to grow brand awareness or increase leads, social media is a place where people are doing their research, and paid advertising can help increase your visibility to potential clients.

In this chapter, we will discuss what you need to get started in paid social advertising, essentials for a successful campaign, and ways to track that success.

## Build a Strong Foundation for Your Social Media Ads

Before you start creating ads or calculating your budget, there are a few essentials that you need to make sure your campaigns can get off to the right start. Without these assets, you won't take advantage of social media's capabilities or use your budget to its full potential.

1. S. Lundberg, "The Biggest Social Media Trends to Know in 2019" *globalwebindex*, December 14, 2018, https://blog.globalwebindex.com/marketing/social-media-trends-2019.

## Optimize Your Social Media Profiles

When you advertise, traffic to your social media profiles should increase. An optimized social media profile will engage visitors, educate them about your law firm's brand, and encourage interaction. Whether you are advertising on Facebook, YouTube, Instagram, or LinkedIn, if your profiles and pages are not optimized with the most accurate and comprehensive information, you may lose potential leads because your profile does not accurately represent your firm or it is difficult to navigate.

To optimize your social media profiles, make the following tasks a habit:

- Update your profiles and profile photo.
- Provide accurate and up-to-date bio information.
- Post new content.

You can have the most compelling advertisement, but if someone gets to your profile and the most recent post is three years old, they will either think your law firm is out of business and the advertisement is spam—or that you're not interested in a high-quality client experience and engaging with the community. For more advice, refer to chapter 7, "Engage Your Followers on Social Media."

## Implement Tracking Pixels

Second, **tracking pixels** may be one of the most underutilized pieces of a social media ad campaign. A pixel is a piece of HTML or **JavaScript** code that creates a tiny graphic that most people cannot see. When you insert a tracking pixel into an ad or web page, it lets you collect data about the viewer's online activity. The pixel works by placing and triggering cookies, which are small pieces of data that websites and apps place on your device and then use to remember information about you and record your activity.

Essentially, the pixel acts as a bridge that connects a users' interaction with your social media ads to their behavior on your website. Without tracking pixels, you could see when someone clicked on your ad, and your website would separately record their activity once they arrived on the website, but you would have no way to connect the two. Thanks to the pixel, you can say, "Aha! This user clicked on my social media ad, and then here's what they did on my website after they clicked the ad."

Tracking pixels have many uses in social media advertising. You can create custom audiences of people who visit your website or interact with your social media channels (more on this later on). Pixels also let you attribute actions on your website, helping you identify how people get to your website or a form; this can provide a better understanding of your campaigns' performance.

You should install tracking pixels on your law firm's website as soon as possible—ideally during the website build. That way, your pixels can start tracking your website traffic from the very beginning, and when you decide to start advertising on social media, you will already have analytic data and will not have to wait for the traffic to populate. Each social platform has its own tracking pixel. It's a good idea to install all the major social media platform's pixels, even if you do not want to advertise on them right away. A preinstalled tracking pixel will streamline the process if you decide to start advertising later on.

## Create High-Quality Assets and Content

Lastly, you need quality assets to promote through your social media advertising. This may be a fifteen-second video about your law firm that helps increase your brand awareness or a downloadable e-book that appeals to a broad audience. Ideally, you want to get people into your system so you can follow up with them directly and engage with them through automated emails or a monthly newsletter.

Social media advertising is a conduit to move people down the marketing funnel, and what makes social media advertising unique is that you can reach people at every stage of their journey.

- At the awareness stage, you can promote a video sharing what makes your law firm different and what a potential client can expect when interacting with your law firm.

- At the consideration stage, you can promote an interesting blog article that shows your firm as a thought leader in the space and get the potential client to your website to learn more about your firm.

- At the conversion stage, you can get potential clients to reach out to you directly through a downloadable asset or a contact form.

Having those assets for each stage of the client's journey can help your social media advertising campaigns be successful and reach your law firm's business goals.

## Three Essential Questions about Your Campaign

Now that you have the pieces in places to make sure your social media campaigns are successful, you need to start thinking critically about your advertising campaigns. Each of these questions impacts every aspect of the social media advertising campaign, so if you do not answer them properly, it will greatly impact the overall success of your campaign.

## 1. What Is Your Campaign's Goal?

Before starting any advertising campaign, whether that be email marketing, pay-per-click ads, or social media advertising, you should identify its end goal. What do we want people to do because of this advertisement?

In social media advertising, you can have a wide variety of goals:

- Having someone watch three seconds of a brand awareness video so you can add them to a custom audience and retarget them with other advertisements.
- Getting people to engage with a top-performing social post to help increase its visibility.
- Promoting one of your downloadable assets to get a user's email and then follow up with them directly or add them to an automated drip campaign to keep them engaged.

Whatever that end goal is, it should be well defined before creating any campaigns or advertisements because that goal will impact who you are targeting and the ad you are creating.

## 2. Who Is Your Target Audience?

Next, you'll need to decide who you want to target in your advertising campaign. Your audience will guide every aspect of the campaign, so if you don't have a clearly defined persona upfront, your campaign will not be as successful as it could be.

When defining that target audience, you should outline the following:

- Their geographic location.

- Their demographic attributes, such as age and gender.

- Other aspects that make them unique, such as job titles, relationship status, interests, behaviors, or any other attributes that can be tracked by their social profiles or social media activities.

Once you define your target audience, it will help you choose the right social media channels for your advertising, what type of campaigns you are creating within those channels, and the look and feel of each advertisement.

## 3. What Is Your Budget?

Finally, you can start thinking about the amount you are willing to invest in social media advertising. This becomes much easier once you've answered those first two questions because most social media channels have forecasting tools to help guide you through your budget decision.

For example, suppose Webster, Webster & Cohen sets the following framework for a social media campaign about defective booster seats:

- Gain ten conversions per month.

- Target an audience of parents in a twenty-five-mile radius of their office.

When they use social media platforms' forecasting tools, they can accurately calculate an appropriate budget to reach those goals. When they input a budget into a forecasting tool, they'll see an estimated range of impressions or clicks they can expect, helping the law firm make an educated decision about their ad spend.

However, when you're setting a budget, don't forget to think about your return on investment (ROI). If Webster, Webster & Cohen's ten conversions are worth $100 each and they need to spend $2,000 per month on the campaign, they should probably either rethink their platform or the overall goal of the campaign.

# How to Build a Social Media Campaign

You've defined your audience, goals, and budget. Now it's time to create your social media campaigns! Let's dive into the details of an individual campaign.

## Select Your Platform

Since you've already defined your target audience, you'll have an easier time selecting a social media platform. As we discussed in chapter 7, "Engage Your Followers on Social Media," Facebook, LinkedIn, and other platforms all have their own distinct user base. If your law firm is looking to target business professionals, LinkedIn is where you want to be. Instagram may be a good option if you are promoting your community involvement with quality visuals. And if you want to reach a broad audience at a low investment, you should be advertising on Facebook.

However, if you do not already have a regular presence on a particular social media channel, you shouldn't invest your advertising dollars on that platform. Instead, take the time to build up your credibility and presence before you advertise.

The particular workflow to set up a social media campaign is different for each platform, but there are some basic components that you will need to create a successful campaign, and we will cover those next.

## Articulate an Objective

When you build a campaign, you need to explain your goals to the platform. Each platform has many different objectives to choose from, and your choice will impact who sees your ads, the bidding strategy for your campaign, and the type of advertisement you will create.

For example, Facebook has eleven different objectives within three overarching categories: Awareness, Consideration, and Conversion.

- **Awareness:** Your firm builds brand awareness through videos, images, and other content.

- **Consideration:** You reach people in the middle of their client journey, emphasizing your expertise and thought leadership. Objectives may focus on video views and increasing traffic to your website.

- **Conversion:** You encourage people to connect with your law firm by downloading an asset, filling out a form, or visiting your physical location.

## Identify Your Audience

Similar to the objectives, each social media platform has different capabilities in terms of audience. In LinkedIn, you can target people by their job title, company name, and job skills. In Facebook, you have broader capabilities and can target users by their relationship status or education or can use interest-based targeting that focuses on specific hobbies or activities.

You can also take advantage of your tracking pixel and create **custom audiences**. These custom audiences can be based on activity on your website or how people interact with your social media channels.

For example, suppose Webster, Webster & Cohen wants to move people from brand awareness to the consideration stage of their journey. They decide to create a custom audience of people who viewed a video on their social media channel. When these people visit Facebook, they see additional ads about the law firm's services.

If their goal is to move people from consideration to conversion, they might create a custom audience of anyone that visited Webster, Webster

& Cohen's website or, to get more targeting, anyone that has visited a particular practice area page on the site, such as their truck wreck page.

You can also create custom audiences using your existing client or email list, and the social media channel will match your current contacts to that person's social media profile. Then you can retarget these individuals with advertising to either get them reengaged or move them further down the funnel. To make sure this strategy is effective, your list must be particularly large. Facebook matches only 60 to 70 percent of your list, so your list must be robust enough to withstand this drop-off and still have a large enough audience that your budget remains effective.

Once you have those custom audiences, you can take them a step further and create **lookalike audiences** based on the people within each of those audiences. The social platforms use their algorithms to identify similarities among the people within your custom audiences and then to find people with similar demographics, interests, or behaviors and create an audience of those people.

## Design Your Ads

Creating a compelling and thought-provoking ad is the most important part of social media advertising. Today, there is so much noise that you need strong messaging and design to catch your ideal clients' attention, get them to stop scrolling, and then do the action that you want them to do. You don't want your ad to be wallpaper; you want it to be something that jumps off the screen.

Before you start finding images and writing copy, you should look back at those must-have questions about your business goals and audience. Now, ask yourself, "What is going to get that target audience to do the thing I want them to do to reach my goal?"

You'll have many ad styles to choose from to entice your readers:

- **Photo and graphic ads:** These include an image, a headline, a short body of text, and a call to action.

- **Video ads:** Viewers watch a brief video and see a headline.

- **Carousel ads:** These ads showcase a series of images or videos in a rotating "carousel" that users can browse; each image may have its own link.

- **Stories:** An image or video displays for a limited period of time on the platform.

If you want to promote your law firm's diverse practice areas, then carousel ads would be a good option. You may choose a video ad if you're highlighting a compelling client testimonial and want to grow awareness of your firm. A graphic ad could highlight your law firm's historical data or the timeline of a top case.

## Create Content That Aligns with the Platform's Standards

Once you have nailed down the type of ad you are going to run, then the focus turns to the messaging. Each platform has different specifications for the placement of your message on the ad and also the character limits. Your ad's structure will depend on the objective, audience, and platform that you choose. However, your ads will typically include these components:

- **Headline:** A relatively brief statement that grabs your readers' attention.

- **Image or video:** High-quality images or video that specifically target your audience and express your brand identity.

- **Call to action:** A specific action that you want your reader to do, such as "Learn More" or "Sign Up."

The main focus of your messaging should speak directly to the user and your ad's desired outcome. Also, make sure your messaging is consistent with your overall brand. If someone sees an ad on Facebook, clicks on it, and goes to a landing page with completely different messaging and tone, it could discourage the user from moving forward and converting.

Always include a call to action. You should never make the user guess what you want them to do; give them the information they need to do it. Including questions in your copy is a good way to get people thinking about their current situation and how your law firm may be able to help them, whether that is in their current state or in the future.

For example, if Webster, Webster & Cohen wants to target truck victims with a conversion-focused Facebook photo ad, it might say:

**Post:** Injured in a truck wreck? Our Victims' Guide outlines all of your legal options.

**Headline:** Webster, Webster & Cohen

**Description:** Take back control with advice from our trusted injury lawyers.

**Call to Action:** Learn More

When creating your ad for each particular objective, just know that you will not create a perfect, "unicorn" ad on the first try. As much as you try, you will not know exactly what ad copy and what imagery is going to resonate with that audience, so you should always be testing.

Create multiple sets of ad copy and multiple creatives and test them against each other to let the user tell you what they are interested in.

- Does your audience convert more when you provide statistics or numbers?

- Are they more likely to watch a video when you ask a question?
- Will someone be more likely to download an e-book on tips after a car accident when they see an image of a car wreck or they see a mock-up of the e-book?

All of these questions can be answered with testing and analytics. If you don't have the capacity to run a detailed data analysis and testing program, work with an advertising agency that can help.

## Measuring Success and Adjusting Your Campaigns

Creating exciting social media ads is not the end of the story. To make sure your advertising is successful and reaches your law firm's goals, you need to measure the success of the campaign. Its success should not just be based on an arbitrary number of clicks or video views, but should focus on your original goals that you set out to accomplish when creating the campaign.

You'll have a variety of social media metrics to assess. If you want to generate more brand awareness, then use metrics such as reach, impressions, video views. If you want to increase engagement with your brand, then measure comments, retweets, shares. If you want to increase traffic to your website, then measure the clicks, **cost per click** (CPC), and **click-through rate** (CTR).

Once you know what you're measuring, create reports based on those metrics and identify benchmarks based on industry standards or previous campaigns. Make sure you are looking at the entire story and not just one metric that may support your goals.

Finally, take all the information from your testing and analytics and use it to improve your campaign. This may involve adjusting an individual ad's copy or imagery. Other times, you'll need to adjust your demographic targeting or budget at the campaign level. Regardless, you should use data to make these adjustments.

# Checklist for Social Media Marketing

- Optimize social media profiles.
- Install tracking pixels.
- Create conversion-focused assets.
- Articulate your campaign's goals.
- Know your target audience.
- Determine your budget for paid social advertising.
- Create compelling social media ads.
- Always be testing.
- Measure success based on business goals.

# 13

# Paid Advertising: Pay per Click

## Setting Yourself Up for Sustained Success

Paid advertising is everywhere on the internet: your search results pages, news sources, and social media platforms. These ads are the primary income source for companies like Google and Facebook, and they can be a powerful tool for your law firm.

In the right hands, pay-per-click advertising is a powerful tool that can boost your law firm's brand awareness and convert leads into clients. However, paid advertising, especially PPC, is notoriously complex and can be expensive. If you dabble in PPC, you'll likely waste your time, money, and resources.

Before you enter the world of PPC advertising, you need to educate yourself and build a comprehensive paid advertising strategy. Over the next two chapters, we're going to explain how to plan and execute smart PPC campaigns that expand your client base and grow your firm.

# What Is Pay-per-Click Advertising?

Pay-per-click advertising is the practice of purchasing text- and image-based advertisements on search engine result pages, websites, blogs, pop-ups, and mobile applications to promote some aspect of your law firm. Every time a user clicks on that advertisement, the platform host (Google and Bing being the most common) charges the advertiser a fluctuating rate determined by auction-style, real-time bidding. Ad placement varies based on your bid amount, the overall quality of your ad, and other important factors.

Ultimately, the goal of PPC, like most digital marketing efforts, is to direct your audience to perform a desired action (conversion)—such as completing a form to download a legal e-book or request a consultation with your firm. It also can help boost awareness of your website while you build up its organic page rank and domain authority.

All effective PPC campaigns share one common attribute: value. Your job is to entice your potential leads by presenting your firm's unique value proposition in a way that aligns with their specific needs. You need to get the right messaging with the right offer in front of the right audience at the right time. Sometimes this can be a difficult objective, but when you build your strategy on the proper foundation, cost-effective, long-term PPC success is within your grasp.

# Is PPC Right for Your Firm?

The short answer to this question is yes, but implementing a successful legal PPC campaign poses many challenges. Paid digital advertising can be expensive, especially in the legal industry. Legal PPC terms are consistently among the most expensive to bid on in popular search engines, such as Google and Bing. According to a 2019 WordStream blog article detailing some of the most expensive keywords, the average

CPC of lawyer-related keywords is $54.86, which ranks fourth on their list.[1] Further, PPC Protect's analysis of the most expensive keywords found that legal search queries accounted for three of the five most expensive searches. The word *claim* came in fifth at $238 while *attorney* was second at $499 and *lawyer* was first at a whopping $564 per click.

Before you start spending your advertising budget on PPC, ask yourself the following questions:

- Does our law firm have the time and skills necessary to research cost-effective long-tail keywords that appeal to our ideal clients? (We discussed long-tail keywords in chapter 5, "Upgrade and Optimize Your Website.")

- Do we have compelling content, like an e-book or white paper, that we can leverage in our ads?

- Can we articulate specific goals for our campaigns, focusing on metrics like our conversion rates, click-through rate, and ROI?

- Do we have the time and patience necessary to test and update our ads based on their performance?

If you're not ready to create highly targeted campaigns and reinforce those campaigns with compelling and relevant content, then PPC probably isn't for you (at least not yet). Spending money on haphazard campaigns without a clear objective and developed strategy isn't a wise investment. If you want to reap the benefits of PPC and get a meaningful return on your investment, you should have either an external marketing partner who can handle your campaigns or a dedicated in-house staff member who can devote significant time (twenty-plus hours for campaign setup plus a few hours a week for maintenance and tweaking—assuming the person is already well trained and experienced in PPC) to manage everything.

1. Elisa Gabbert, "The 25 Most Expensive Keywords in Google Ads," *The WordStream Blog* ,https://www.wordstream.com/blog/ws/2017/06/27/most-expensive-keywords.

PPC is not a silver-bullet solution or cure-all—you need to put the time and effort into your campaigns to see results. However, a thoughtful PPC strategy and diligent optimization can bring you success at almost any budget.

## Set Your Foundation by Mastering the Basics

Before anyone sees your ads, you must clearly define your goals and objectives. They will inform your entire strategy and help ensure a quality ROI. More than 96 percent of Google's revenue is generated through their ad platforms, and an alarming amount of that money is spent by advertisers who are in over their heads and never see a discernible return on investment. They're effectively donating their budget to the software giant.

Anyone promising amazing conversion rates at a low cost-per-click within the first few months of a campaign is likely being disingenuous or outright lying to you. When embarking on your PPC efforts, you should always start simple and then build your way up based on the knowledge you gain and the story the data tells.

## Pay-per-Click Campaign Types

There are three main PPC campaign types:

- **Search ads**

- **Display ads**
- **Remarketing** ads

Each of these campaigns can work well on their own, but we usually achieve the most success when we implement and coordinate multiple campaign types in conjunction with a content marketing strategy. Below, we'll examine what each of these campaigns consists of and how they work. In the next chapter, we'll walk you through exactly how to create and optimize each campaign type.

## Search Campaigns

Search ads are what you see when you are using search engines. For example, if I search "lawn service" in Google, the results at the top of the page will almost certainly be ads:

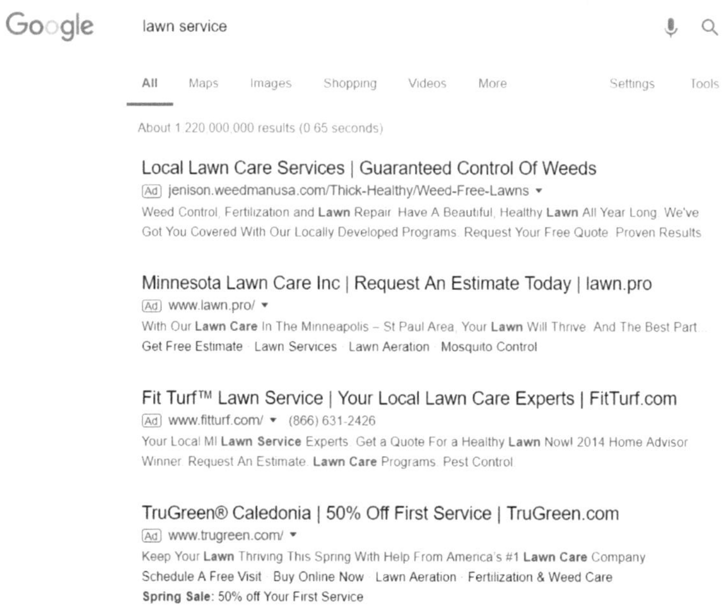

These are text-based ads that look strikingly similar to organic results, and that's deliberate. You can see from this example that some of these companies may be spending a lot of money, but they haven't dedicated much time to strategy. For example, Minnesota is over five hundred miles away from my current location. I may ignore that ad completely because it's irrelevant. Or I might click on it only to discover that they don't serve my area; Google would then send a bill to that company for my click on that ad, even though it was ineffective.

Long before I searched for a lawn service, landscaping companies created their ads, selected specific keywords, and set their maximum budgets. If they outbid their competitors *and* had a high quality score on their ads, they got placed higher in my advertising results.

In order to keep costs down and optimize your return on investment, you should pay close attention to **keyword match types** when structuring your search campaigns. Failing to properly identify your keywords' match types could result in a wasted marketing budget and even more wasted opportunities. Currently, these are the keyword match types:

- broad match
- broad match modified
- exact match
- phrase match

## Broad Match

*Broad match* ads appear whenever a user searches any keyword you're bidding on, in any order. This match type can generate a lot of irrelevant traffic (especially since ad platforms frequently match queries with synonyms), so use it sparingly and keep a watchful eye on all of your broad match keywords. Also note that broad match keywords are the *default* setting in **Google Ads**, so unless you specify otherwise, your keywords will be considered broad match.

**Example:** car accident

**Potential matches:** auto accident chiropractor, Geico accident, had an accident, auto pedestrian, car wreck in Chicago today, car accident repair, pay car accident ticket, fatal car accident near me, car accident traffic

## Broad Match Modified

The *broad match modified* keyword match type allows more control over your user audience by including terms within the larger key phrase that *must* be included in a **search query** in order for your firm's ads to appear on the search engine results page. (Queries and keywords are essentially the same—they are the words the user types into a search engine's search box to begin a web search. Some marketers would argue there is a difference between a query and a keyword, but the distinction is semantic and you don't need to worry about it.) You can add a plus symbol before your chosen keyword to communicate to the ad platform that this term should be included as a *broad match modified* keyword.

**Example:** +car accident

**Potential matches***:* car accident lawyer, t bone car crash, average settlement for a car accident back injury, derek underwood car crash, fix airbags after car crash

## Exact Match

*Exact match* is the optimal match type for firms looking to reduce costs. You can denote exact match keywords by placing brackets around your terms when entering them into ad groups. This match type ensures your ads will only appear on the search engine results page when a potential client searches a query including those terms (along with close variants, such as synonyms or plurals).

We recommend using exact match for *all* key phrases when you first launch your campaign. You can then expand match types as you determine which terms are having the most (and least) success.

**Example:** [car accident]

**Potential matches:** car accident, auto collision, in a car accident, vehicle wrecks

## Phrase Match

*Phrase match* is similar to broad match modified in that it allows for more specific targeting than broad match and less than exact match. Phrase match key phrases will only appear when the search query is entered in the exact sequence of your choosing (by placing quotation marks at both ends of your key phrase), although other terms can be included before or after the phrase. It's a flexible match type that should highlight the essence of your firm to capture a wide, yet targeted, audience.

**Example:** "car accident"

**Potential matches:** best car accident lawyer, car accident repair shop, what to do after a car accident, car accident traffic delays

# Display and Remarketing Ads

Compared to search campaigns, display ads are typically less expensive. Whereas the cost per click for many legal search terms can extend well into the hundreds of dollars, clicks on display placements (the ad slots on pages where your display ads are placed) rarely exceed more than a few dollars, and they often cost much less. And while search campaigns are more likely to reap trackable conversions, display ads can significantly increase brand awareness by getting your ads placed on popular websites, such as online retailers, prominent news outlets, and streaming video sites.

A vital extension of display advertising is **remarketing**. Remarketing ads appear on various websites (and even email servers) after a user has already visited your website or other web properties. Best practices dictate that you should create a separate set of display ads for your remarketing campaign that maintain brand guidelines but are distinct from the messaging of your other display ads. Whereas display ads for users who have never visited your site should be more general in nature (redirecting to your home page) or divided by practice area (redirecting to corresponding practice area pages), remarketing ads should focus on providing something that a visitor may have missed on their first trip to your website.

For example, in its remarketing campaign, Webster, Webster & Cohen advertises a free downloadable e-book, *Steps to Take Following a Car Accident*. After Cathy Client visits the law firm's car accident page, she begins to see ads on other sites, like her favorite news source, offering her this free e-book. After seeing the ad several times, she decides to click. She's sent to a landing page, where she provides some contact information (email address, first name, and possibly an optional phone number) in exchange for the resource. She's also automatically signed up for the law firm's lead-nurturing newsletter.

In the next chapter, we will provide a roadmap to set up, launch, test, and optimize your PPC campaigns. Before you dig into advertising platforms and start spending money, though, you'll want to determine your approach and carefully plan your user's journey from start to finish.

# Start with an Initial Strategy Session

Even if you're familiar with the lingo and basic PPC concepts, online advertising can be a tough nut to crack. If you don't set clear objectives and goals from the outset, there's no way to achieve (much less measure) success.

The first step in any paid campaign is to meet with key stakeholders and develop a plan that clearly identifies your team's goals, a timeframe in which to achieve those goals or alter your approach, and how this initiative fits into your larger marketing strategy.

## Basic Strategy Questions

Ask yourself these basic strategy questions to get started:

- **Which marketing campaigns are we currently running?**

  Are you active on social media or do you have a PR strategy in place? Maybe you have billboards or bus-backs around town that you'll need to coordinate with your online efforts.

- **Who are our main competitors, and what are they doing to promote their firms?**

  The legal field is saturated and competitive, so you need to understand what you're up against before diving in.

- **What e-books, infographics, videos, and other collateral do we already have?**

  Even if these pieces are a bit outdated or are in a draft state, updating and polishing content that's already in existence will make the most of your time, energy, and budget. And if you need to create entirely new content, think about how these pieces will support what your firm wants to achieve. That is, don't tailor the campaign to the content; tailor the content to the campaign.

- **Why are we implementing a pay-per-click campaign?**

  Law firms implement PPC campaigns for numerous reasons, but in most cases, launching a paid initiative is critical to achieve these goals:

  » Driving traffic to a landing page.

  » Generating conversions in the form of contact information or revenue.

  » Securing RSVPs to webinars or other digital or in-person events.

  » Increasing brand awareness online with a limited budget.

  » Maintaining brand positioning on search engine results pages.

  If you're looking to do any or all of the above, paid digital advertising can be a great strategy to reach a select group of people who are especially likely to become clients and introduce them to your brand. However, keep in mind that once your payments stop, so do your ads—and their results.

- **What are our fundamental expectations for this campaign?**

  When discussing this question, you don't need to develop clearly defined goals or objectives (at least not yet). Just work together to identify what you're hoping to achieve. Do you want to build up your email newsletter list? Do you want to drive more traffic to a specific practice area page of your website (in hopes of attracting more potential clients)? The important thing is to make sure the general purpose of the campaign is universally understood and agreed upon.

- **Do we have the right personnel and resources to succeed?**

  This is a critical question. At the risk of sounding melodramatic, if you don't have the right people, the proper tools, and a comfortable budget, you're doomed from the start. Creating, managing, testing, and optimizing pay-per-click campaigns is very difficult and requires painstaking attention to detail and constant vigilance. This is not a task for an intern, and it's not an entry-level position. You should have experienced, capable people overseeing your paid campaigns. And you should provide them with the tools and budget they need to succeed and be strategically aggressive.

- **Should we use custom dedicated landing pages, or can we use existing conversion-optimized organic pages?**

  The answer to this question will depend on the types of campaigns you're planning to run and the resources at your disposal. For most PPC campaigns, we recommend directing your clicks to a **dedicated landing page**, but things can get tricky when running multiple campaign types at once.

- **What additional resources do we need to create to complement the campaign?**

  Every type of PPC campaign can benefit from relevant, targeted content that helps encourage users to convert, whether that's just providing an email to get your newsletter or scheduling a consultation to meet with one of your attorneys. Here are just a few of the potential assets you will need to create:

» display ads

» search ad copy

» dedicated landing pages

» informative and useful white papers or infographics

» testimonials

» professional videos and photos

» website forms (and notifications)

» email drip campaigns

The list could go on much further, which is just one reason you truly need to understand your fundamental goals and what resources will be necessary to achieve them. Namely, you need dedicated content marketing staff who can develop valuable assets that speak to your potential clients' primary pain points. We'll talk more about how to decide which marketing strategies and tasks you can reasonably handle in-house and which are best outsourced to an agency in chapter 17, "Working with an Agency."

- **Are we willing to see this campaign through potential challenges and obstacles?**

Regardless of how much planning and research you conduct, the first two to four weeks of a PPC campaign can be brutal, especially if you're not exercising the degree of caution we've been stressing so far. Money can disappear into thin air with almost no return on investment, and while your ads might be receiving a lot of traffic, those clicks are worthless without a healthy conversion rate. Maybe you haven't identified the right personas? Maybe you're not targeting the proper regions? Some of this is basic human error, but it can also be the initial kinks getting worked out of a campaign.

All marketing initiatives suffer growing pains—perhaps none more than pay per click. The question is whether you are truly committed to seeing your efforts through the tough times. In our experience, almost every law firm that sticks to the plan, making smart, data-driven updates along the way, starts achieving success within six to twelve weeks.

- **What types of campaigns do we want to run?**

If you're looking to be aggressive in the marketplace, you might want to create broad-match keyword search campaigns, highly targeted display campaigns, or even email remarketing campaigns. Typically, search campaigns are focused on end-stage buyer conversions, display campaigns are meant to drive traffic and raise brand awareness, and remarketing campaigns are meant to generate softer conversions, such as an e-book download. When combined into a single strategy, these campaign types can work together to produce amazing results. Knowing *what* you want to achieve will inform *how* you pursue that success.

- **What negative keywords or other potential conflicts have we not yet considered?**

It's possible (even likely) that your firm name, practice areas, and branding elements could appear in searches that will not bring you any business, which will result in wasted money spent.

# Moving from Brainstorming to Planning

Once you have answers to each of these questions, it's time to begin planning your campaign. At this point, the conversation moves from basic expectations to desired outcomes. You might be expecting to drive traffic or generate conversions, but to what extent and to what end?

Answers to questions about your goals for the campaign are going to rely on your purpose, tactics, and budget. Every campaign should be designed to create as much interest in your firm as possible, and you want to make sure the leads you are generating are *qualified* leads. Conversions are great, but what's the point of adding someone to your list if they're not actually interested in retaining your firm's services or referring cases to you?

The best way to attract qualified leads is to use targeted keywords and placements and tailor your copy for your ideal audience segments.

When establishing your PPC goals, it's best to work in reverse. Determine the amount of revenue, traffic, conversions, and so on that you want to achieve. Next, consider the variables necessary to reach those goals. For instance, let's assume your law firm wants to add twelve new personal injury clients next year specifically using PPC advertising.

First, you need to estimate how many of your paid advertising leads become bona fide clients. If you don't have that data, you can use estimates from your other web-based leads. Depending on your law firm's focus, you might expect approximately 30 percent of your web leads to become clients. So, you need to get at least forty people to fill out the form on your PPC landing page over the course of the year.

Next, you need to estimate how many visitors convert. Usually, your conversion rate is a much smaller percentage. Again, depending on your law firm's focus, you might expect 3.75 percent of your visitors to complete a form on your page. So, you need to get at least 107 people to your landing page throughout the year. That means 107 clicks. The cost per click varies widely by practice area, geography, campaign type, and more, but if you are paying an average of $60 per click, you'll need to budget at least $6,420 for the year (not including the costs of your staff to build and manage your campaigns); that's about $535 per month.

Zooming out one more layer, consider how much visibility you need to achieve in order to get those clicks. In other words, how many **impressions** (instances in which a person sees your ad) do you need in order to get 107 clicks? Like conversion rate, the click-through rate is usually quite low for law firms. It's around 2 percent on average. So, that means 5,350 people need to see your ads over the course of a year. That's 446 impressions per month.

We'll get further into the weeds discussing how to calculate and plan to achieve those numbers—and reduce your client acquisition costs. But having a baseline understanding of the numbers early on in the planning stage will help you determine an adequate budget and also let your team know the expectations from the outset.

As you go about developing a plan for your paid search initiatives, be sure to include the right people in all relevant conversations. This way, you can get quality input from multiple perspectives and rely on the people you trust most to provide the information you need for great campaigns that meet and eventually exceed your goals.

# Tools and Resources for PPC Research

Pay-per-click advertising is constantly changing and evolving to meet the needs of both consumers and advertisers. Here are some powerful (and free) tools that can help you create, launch, and optimize your PPC campaigns.

## Google Keyword Planner

The Keyword Planner is a free resource located under the "Tools" option in the **navigation** of every Google Ads page. It helps users research the best keywords for their campaigns based on objective data. It even provides suggested bids so you can make informed decisions based on your budget. Keyword Planner also allows you to conduct competitive research and focus on niche industries by selecting product categories.

To use the Keyword Planner, simply enter keywords related to your service area (for example, "car accident" for personal injury attorneys) or enter your final destination URL (likely your website's home page or a dedicated landing page). You can refine your search to target a certain region, language, or even a Google network search engine, such as AOL. In addition, filter your search to specify a desired cost per click or hide keywords you know are technically relevant but will result in wasted spend (and, thus, should be considered as candidates for your negative keyword list, which we'll talk more about in a minute).

## Google Ads Editor

Like the Keyword Planner tool, Google Ads Editor is a free tool you can use to help maximize your PPC potential. Just download the application to your computer and use it to manage your Google Ads campaigns offline. This tool is most useful for law firms running a lot of different campaigns because it allows the user to make bulk changes quickly. So, if you are part of a diversified firm, you should definitely be using Google Ads Editor.

Additional benefits include the ability to do the following:

- Export and import files.
- View stats and metrics for all campaigns and subsets.
- Manage multiple accounts simultaneously.
- Move items at the ad group and campaign level.

- Develop drafts before uploading new elements live to the account.

- Undo/redo multiple changes while editing.

When you make changes to existing campaigns in Google Ads, those changes take effect in real time. Using Google Ads Editor allows users to create draft versions of their campaigns and then review them before setting them live. Save money. Reduce stress. Download and use Google Ads Editor.

## Google Trends

Another free tool from our friends at Google, Trends is a simple way to identify the most effective keyword or key phrase in sets of up to twenty-five terms. Just visit the site and enter a search term and any variable of that term. Trends will generate a graph that shows which key term is the most popular over a defined time period. You can also adjust by region, category, and which *type* of search you want to focus on.

For example, if we're still using our personal injury attorney from above as our example, we might be unsure which is the most commonly used keyword of this bunch:

- car accident lawyer

- car crash lawyer

- car wreck lawyer

Many personal injury attorneys prefer *not* to use the term *accident* because it suggests an unavoidable mistake when, in fact, at least one person is almost always responsible for a car wreck. But people who have been in a crash clearly prefer to use the term *accident*:

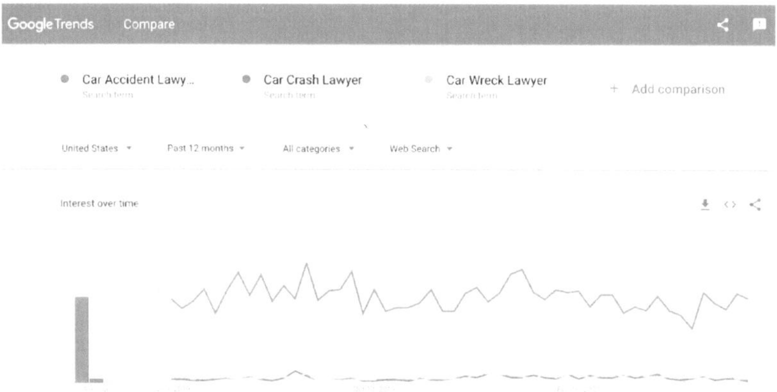


Even though most attorneys we interact with are loath to use the term *accident*, it is far and away the most commonly used descriptor according to Google Trends. And this is where Google Trends is so helpful. Like all great data sources, it eliminates opinion and delivers objective facts.

# Planning Is Only Half the Battle

Once you've decided that pay-per-click advertising fits well into your firm's holistic marketing strategy, it's time to begin piecing your campaigns together. In the next chapter, we're going to walk you through how to structure, launch, test, and optimize your campaigns—and also provide some innovative tips and best practices to achieve optimal results.

# Checklist for PPC Advertising

- Set your PPC goals and expectations.
- Identify resources that you can use in PPC campaigns, such as videos and downloadable e-books.
- Use online tools to study your competitors' ads.
- Determine which PPC ad types meet your needs.
- Set your campaign budget.

14

# Paid Advertising: Monitoring

## Building, Executing, and Monitoring Paid Campaigns

Pay-per-click (PPC) advertising has an intimidating reputation. You may have heard of law firms that spend thousands of dollars in a blink of an eye—with minimal results. However, you've probably also heard of lawyers who have leveraged PPC advertising and boast about their remarkable ROI. Whom do you believe?

While well-trained professionals can create PPC campaigns that have an exceptional return on investment, doing so requires attention to detail, patience, and a sophisticated strategy. That doesn't mean you need to hire a PPC expert (although it helps), but you will need to commit a significant amount of time and effort into getting your campaigns right.

Unfortunately, too many law firms (and other businesses) fall prey to shady PPC firms that make astounding promises but deliver subpar results. If you're going to hire a marketing agency, make sure that you carefully vet it and look for an agency that's a certified marketing partner for your preferred advertising platform.

While there are many paid advertising platforms, Google holds more than 90 percent of the market. For this reason, we'll focus on building Google Ads campaigns. Now, let's explore the campaign process in more detail.

# Step 1: Open a Google Ads Account

Before you can create a single PPC ad, you need to create an account on your chosen platform. This is a relatively simple, but essential, process. If you already have a Google account (that is, you have a Gmail account), you can use it to log in to Google Ads.

However, we think it's best not to mix your personal and private email accounts. Rather than use your personal Google account, open a new one for your legal practice. For example, Webster, Webster & Cohen could open a Google account using "webstercohen@gmail.com" as its address. Then they use this account only for their marketing efforts on Google Ads, Google My Business, and Google Analytics.

Once the law firm has a Google log-in and password, it should review its earlier **keyword research** and then head to ads.google.com and start building ad campaigns. (For more about your underlying PPC strategy, refer to chapter 13, "Paid Advertising: Pay per Click.")

# Step 2: Create a Campaign and Define Your Budget

Now that you have a Google Ads account, you should log in to the platform and create your first campaign. Once you're on the platform, Google will start asking you questions about your campaign and its goals.

For example, suppose Webster, Webster & Cohen wants to generate more drunk driving accident leads. Their marketing assistant logs in to Google Ads and sees the following screen.

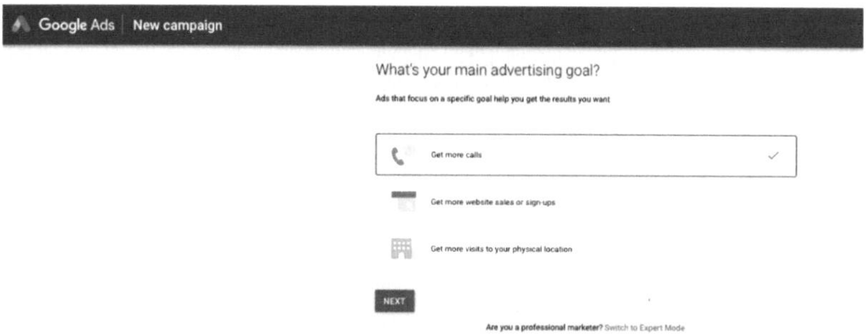


He clicks on "Get More Calls." Next, he's asked to describe his business and provide the firm's website URL.

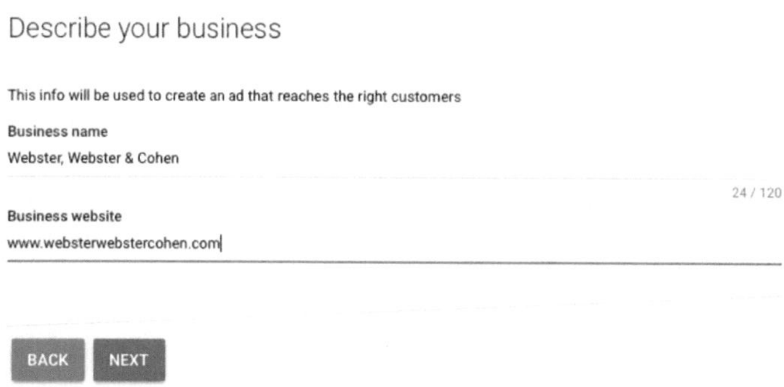

Then Google asks him to define his ideal customers' location. The law firm can either specify precise areas or a radius around their business. The law firm decides to focus on specific communities.

The firm's marketing assistant can list specific zip codes, and cities, or Nielsen® DMA® (Designated Market Area) regions. *Designated market areas* cover a specific media market and typically include a broad metropolitan area, including suburbs and sometimes neighboring counties. For example, the DMA for New York City includes the city itself as well as nearby Pike County, Pennsylvania.

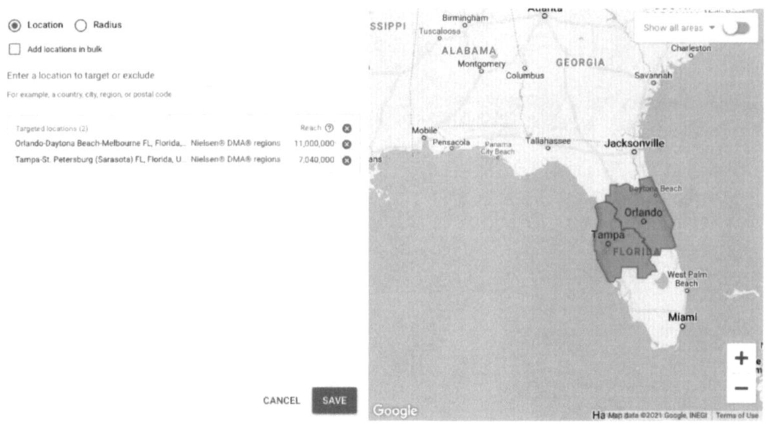


Now that the marketing assistant has identified his geographic targets, he'll need to provide Google Ads with information about their keywords and budget. While we'll delve into keywords in more detail in just a moment, it's important to understand how Google Ads budgets work.

## Managing Your Campaign Budget

Google auctions off its **ad spaces** through a complicated process that considers your bidding strategy, the campaign's quality, and other factors. In Google Ads, you can set an average daily and a maximum monthly budget for your ads. In the past, you also needed to identify your maximum bids.

While you can manually set your Google Ads bidding strategy, most people decide to use the platform's automated bidding systems. When you use these systems, which let you identify specific goals, like maximizing clicks or conversions, Google's algorithms will optimize your bids for you. Even if you're comfortable with the basics of a PPC campaign, we'd recommend you use automated bidding.

# Step 3: Research Your Keywords and Build a Long-Tail Strategy

Although you've done preliminary keyword research, you now need to build your **ad groups**, or the lists of keywords that may trigger your ad to appear on a search engine results page.

Creating an ad group is both a science and an art. As mentioned in chapter 13, "Paid Advertising: Pay per Click," they can include a variety of keyword match types:

- **Broad match:** The default setting in Google Ads, a wide variety of related keywords can trigger your ad, including synonyms, misspellings, and possible variations. However, your ad may appear for many unwanted searches, like "drunk driving crash statistics" or "celebrity DUI."

- **Broad match modifier:** Listed keywords and close variants trigger your ads, but you can designate words that must be included in the search, such as "accident" or "injury."

- **Phrase match:** The search must include your keyword or a very close variant; additional words can proceed or close the search terms.

- **Exact match:** Only your keyword or very close variants will trigger your ads; they cannot contain additional words.

- **Negative keywords:** These are words that you want to exclude from your campaigns.

While it's tempting to use very broad keywords, like "injury lawyer," it's not always the best option. First of all, many broad keywords, like "truck accident" and "lawyer" are incredibly expensive and competitive. Even more targeted keywords, like "Oklahoma truck accident lawyer" can cost hundreds of dollars per click.

Instead, we recommend using long-tail keywords, longer keyword phrases that specifically target a demographic, in your PPC campaigns. As we discussed before, these longer keywords offer significant benefits.

First, you can select keywords that specifically address your ideal personas. If your ad appears for the search "drunk driving," many of your readers may not be in the market for a personal injury lawyer. They may be shopping for a DUI defense attorney, researching blood-alcohol concentration laws, or learning about crash statistics.

For example, Webster, Webster & Cohen may decide to include the following keywords in a drunk driving injury campaign:

- drunk driving accident lawyer
- drunk driving accident claim
- drunk driving victim
- drunk driving death
- hurt by a drunk driver
- drunk driving insurance claim
- need lawyer for drunk driving accident
- drunk driving injuries
- typical settlement amount for drunk driving accident
- injured because of drunk driving
- drunk driving lawyer near me
- settlement for drunk driving
- dram shop claim drunk driving
- -DUI defense (negative keyword)

Second, many of these long-tail keywords are more accessible for small and mid-sized law firms. If fewer people are bidding on "typical settlement amount for drunk driving accident," you will have a better chance of appearing in one of Google's top spots—and you may end up paying less per click.

# Step 4: Build and Optimize Your PPC Ads

Now that you have chosen your keywords, you can start building ads that are relevant and appealing to your ideal clients. While this process may seem simple, since you're only writing a few lines of text, you need to make sure that you meet Google Ads' strict requirements and deliver high-quality content.

## The Essential Parts of a PPC Search Ad

There are five primary components to your Google search ad:

- **Headline 1:** Ideally includes one of your keywords and cannot be more than thirty characters.
- **Headline 2:** Content that includes another targeted keyword, again, it cannot exceed thirty characters.
- **Headline 3:** May not show up in all searches, but a great place to include one of your value propositions, like "Free Consultation" or "24/7 Hotline."
- **Display URL:** Directs readers to the website address that you want them to visit.
- **Descriptions:** Summarizes your value proposition and offerings, often including a call to action and a total of 180 characters in these fields.

While Google occasionally changes its character limits for each field, we've listed its current specifications. You should include more than one ad in each of your ad groups. This can also help you improve the campaign's relevance and quality.

For example, Webster, Webster & Cohen's drunk driving injury campaign could include the following ads:

Hurt By A Drunk Driver | Drunk Driving Accident Lawyer | Free Consultation
Ad www.websterwebstercohen.com

Our Injury Lawyers Fight For Drunk Driving Victims And Have Recovered Millions In Damages. Get The Compensation And Answers You Deserve. Our Lawyers Make Hospital Visits.

Drunk Driving Victim | Settlement For Drunk Driving | 24/7 Injury Law Hotline
Ad www.websterwebstercohen.com

Local, Respexted Injury Lawyers. Millinons Recovered For Survivors And Families. Take Back Control With Our Help. No Fees Unless We Win. Free, No-Risk Consultation

The headlines appear above Webster, Webster & Cohen's URL, and the descriptions are below. Most PPC professionals will suggest capitalizing the first letter of each word, since it looks cleaner.

## How Relevance and Performance Impact Visibility

If you're new to PPC, you probably don't realize that Google considers more than your budget when placing search ads. Instead, it assigns your ads a **quality score**, which is based on the following factors:

- The average click-through rate for your selected keywords and your ad's performance.

- Your ad's relevance and consistency with your selected keywords.

- Whether your landing page is relevant, original, and easy to navigate.

That means that even if you're willing to spend a little more than your competitors, but your ads are poorly built, you may not get the top ad spot.

How do you bolster your ad's quality score? Sometimes, you'll need help from a PPC expert. However, there are some simple ways you can try:

- Include only related and highly relevant keywords in your ad group.

- Use your keywords in the ad text, especially in the headlines.

- Make sure your landing page's content is well aligned with your ads and keywords.

- Avoid using distracting design elements, like pop-ups, that can make navigating your landing page difficult.

Google's algorithms scan your ad and landing page content, making sure that they're directly relevant to your selected keywords and easy to use. For example, Webster, Webster & Cohen should choose only keywords that align with their ad group, like "injury lawyers near me" and "drunk driving accident lawyer." They shouldn't add keywords like "auto body shops near me" or "high school football rankings," since they don't directly align with the ad's content and will result in a poor quality score. They should also make sure that they include those keywords in the actual ads. Consider this ad:

**We Make Drunk Drivers Pay | Get The Money You Deserve**
[Ad] www.websterwebstercohen.com
Millions Recovered For Victims. A DUI Is Not Enough! Get Paid For Your Injuries. Our Lawyers Aren't Afraid To Fight. Learn How Much Your Case Is Worth.

While the "We Make Drunk Drivers Pay" ad may grab your attention, it likely won't get a high-quality score because its headlines don't include a single keyword listed in Webster, Webster & Cohen's ad group.

Now, suppose when someone clicks on the ad, they're sent to a page that is filled with pop-ups that ask them to subscribe to the WWC newsletter, request a consultation, and download an e-book. The page's content also is overly broad, talking about car accidents in general (instead of drunk driving wrecks), and the advertised "Request a Consultation" form is buried at the bottom of pages of text. Google's algorithms won't understand the connection between the ads and the landing page, lowering the quality score even more. And because the user experience is so horrible, thanks to the overwhelming pop-ups and a hard-to-find form, the ad's quality score will drop again.

## Ad Extensions: Provide a Richer User Experience

Depending on your ad's **Ad Rank**, which Google calculates based on your bid, quality score, and other factors, you can sometimes add more information to your PPC ads through extensions. You may be able to include the following information in an **ad extension**:

- phone number
- office location
- callouts, like "free consultation"
- website links, like practice area pages
- reviews

If you have the option to include extensions in your ad, you should do so. It won't cost you additional money to insert them into your ad, although if someone clicks on an extension, like a practice page link, you will be charged for that click.

Notably, Google Ads favors ads that use these extensions, so using them may increase the likelihood that your ads appear in the search engine's top placements. In the ad below, the law firm includes a review extension and a website links extension.

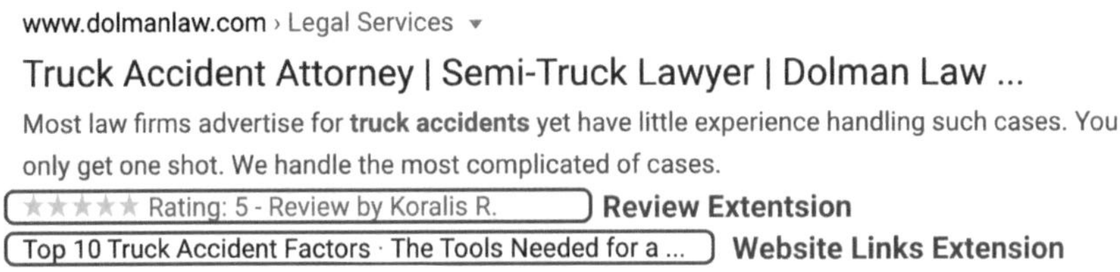


## Using Machine Learning to Build Your Ads

If you're struggling with your PPC ad copy, you might want to consider using responsive or dynamic search ads. Rather than creating each ad yourself, you can use Google's algorithms and **machine learning** capabilities to build your PPC ads.

- **Responsive search ads:** You write multiple headlines and descriptions, and Google combines them for you, based on the search query.

- **Dynamic search ads:** Google scans your landing page and creates headlines based upon the search query and your page's content.

While both options can save you time and effort, we've seen broader success with responsive search ads (especially for law firms).

However, crafting a responsive search ad involves more than writing down a series of headlines. You need to ensure that all of your possible headlines work together and can display in any order. The biggest potential problem is that your various headline options involve too much repetition of words and phrases, and when Google tries to assemble a variation, the result is highly repetitive. Google will reject these repetitive ads and refuse to display them.

## What **Not** to Do: Too Much Repetition

Here's an example of what not to do when building headline options.

- Webster, Webster & Cohen
- Experienced Personal Injury Lawyers
- Injury Lawyers in Hazardville, Florida
- Client-Focused Injury Law Firm
- Client-First Representation

These headline options would form these possible ad combinations (likely to be rejected by Google for excessive repetition):

- Webster, Webster & Cohen | Experienced Personal Injury Lawyers | Injury Lawyers in Hazardville Florida
- Client-First Representation | Client-Focused Injury Law Firm | Webster, Webster & Cohen

## What **to** Do: Avoid Excessive Repetition

To avoid this problem, you need to vary the words and phrases you use in your headlines. A little bit of repetition is okay, as long as Google can assemble viable ads that aren't overly repetitive. The following are some headline options:

- Webster, Webster & Cohen
- Experienced Personal Injury Attorneys
- Handling Injury Cases in Hazardville
- Get a Free Case Evaluation
- 24/7 Free Case Evaluations
- Client-Focused Representation
- A Track Record of Success
- We Win Tough Cases
- No Fees Unless We Win

These headlines would form the following possible ad combinations:

- Webster, Webster & Cohen | Experienced Personal Injury Lawyers | 24/7 Free Case Evaluations
- A Track Record of Success | No Fees Unless We Win | Webster, Webster & Cohen

# Step 5: Create PPC Landing Pages

When readers click on an ad, they should head to a **landing page**, which is specifically designed and written for the campaign. Unlike a typical website page, a landing page often does not include additional navigation, like links to your blog, attorney bios, or other practice areas.

Instead, it provides the reader with essential information about the ad's subject matter, expresses your law firm's unique value, and offers a call to action and a contact form. Here's what a typical landing page includes:

- Headline
- Tagline (a subheading below your primary headline)
- General information discussing your ad group, focusing on your law firm's unique value proposition
- A testimonial that builds trust
- Call to action
- Contact form
- Compelling images that reflect your landing page's subject matter

On the next page, you'll see an example that includes these elements.

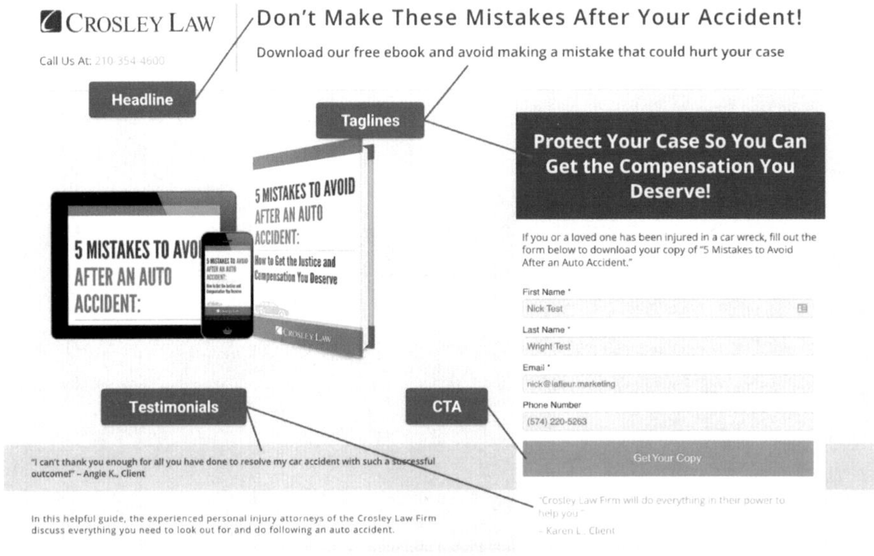


Depending on your ad strategy, you may offer an asset like an e-book, infographic, or checklist on your landing page.

While you can use your home page or a practice page as a PPC landing page, that typically isn't your best option.

First, these generic pages may not speak directly to your ideal clients. For example, suppose a reader clicks on Webster, Webster & Cohen's drunk driving injury ad. They're routed to the firm's home page, where there's plenty of information about its diverse practice areas, location, and value proposition—but very little about drunk driving accidents. Unfortunately, there's a good chance that this reader will "bounce" quickly and head back to the search results page.

Second, most of your website's pages are filled with distractions: your blog, links to other internal pages, and pop-ups about your email newsletter. When someone clicks on a PPC ad, you want to limit their options and keep them focused on the task at hand: completing your contact form and hitting the "Submit" button.

Finally, your landing page should improve your ad's quality score. If the page doesn't clearly address your ad group's subject matter, Google will lower your quality score, making it less likely that people will see your PPC campaigns.

## Step 6: Launch Your PPC Campaign

Once you've built your PPC ads, the process of finalizing them is again relatively simple. You'll need to provide Google with your billing information. Typically, Google will automatically charge your credit card every thirty days or when you reach a designated billing threshold.

You'll also need to set an ad rotation. While you can rotate through all your ads, we suggest that you optimize your ads, letting Google give your preference to your best-performing ads.

Finally, we suggest that you enable Google Ads tracking features. Like a social media ad tracking pixel, you will need to insert snippets of code into your website. However, once you've done this, you can track conversions, phone calls, and user activity when someone clicks on one of your PPC ads. You can ask your webmaster or website partner to insert the Google Ads **tracking code** for you, or if you'd like to do it yourself, just do a Google search for "set up google ads conversion tracking for my website." You should get a top result from Google Ads Help, which will walk you through two different options for how to install the Google Ads tracking code.

## Step 7: Track Your Ads' Performance and Adjust Your Tactics

Like any marketing tactic, you can't leave your PPC campaigns unattended. Instead, you'll need to carefully assess their performance, looking at metrics like your cost per click, quality score, and conversion rate. If your ads aren't performing well, you should incrementally change them, continually assessing what is (and isn't) working.

For example, you may want to rework your headlines and landing pages to improve your quality score. Or you may discover that certain keywords or responsive ads seem to attract more high-quality leads than others. Based on your review, you can revise your strategies and focus on only high-performing ads and content. For more information about data analytics, refer to chapter 16, "Going Beyond the Basics: Analytics."

## When in Doubt, Consult a Trusted Marketing Agency

While some lawyers love the complexity and technicality of PPC advertising, many discover that they don't have the time or expertise that their paid campaigns require. If you're feeling overwhelmed or simply don't want to slog through lists of potential keywords, it's best to collaborate with a respected PPC agency.

You should always insist on using a marketing agency that is certified by your preferred platform as a PPC partner. These credentials indicate that the marketing firm meets specific performance, training, and budget requirements.

In 2020, Google changed its requirements for Partner status, making it even more difficult to obtain this designation. In the past, an agency could become a Google Partner as long as one of their PPC team members was certified in Google Ads. Now, at least 50 percent of the agency's "eligible users," people who are either admins or users on its Ads Manager account, must have an updated Google Ads certification. Other Partner criteria have also become more rigorous. So, if the agency you're working with is certified as a Google Partner, you can feel confident they've devoted significant time and resources to building up and maintaining their expertise in Google Ads.

# Checklist for Launching PPC Campaigns

- Review your PPC goals and expectations.
- Open a Google Ads account.
- Create a campaign.
- Define your budget.
- Craft a long-tail keyword strategy and define your ad group.
- Build your ads and consider their quality score.
- Create landing pages for your PPC ads.
- Launch your campaign.
- Assess the campaign's performance and make adjustments.

# 15

# Practical Client Acquisition Strategies

Congratulations! You've followed all of our recommendations and you're seeing a boom in calls, emails, and high-quality leads. Your administrative team is continually scheduling consultations and responding to your leads' questions. In fact, they're absolutely swamped.

Identifying and connecting with your leads is just one step in the client journey—you still need to convert them into clients. The stark reality is that only a small fraction of your law firm's leads will become clients.

Thankfully, you can improve your chances with a strong, customizable client acquisition strategy. Your client acquisition process should build trust and demonstrate your law firm's value at every step.

To do this, you'll rely on many of the fundamental concepts we've already addressed, including email automation, brand ambassadorship, and content strategy. However, a single tactic cannot successfully move your leads further down the funnel. Instead, you need a holistic, multipronged acquisition process.

# Don't Shy Away from Business Development

As a legal professional, you may consider *sales* a four-letter word. You're not selling something; you're providing nuanced legal advice and services! However, that doesn't mean you can't learn from sales-driven organizations and improve your business development processes.

Business development involves activities that identify growth opportunities and foster high-value relationships. For a law firm, client acquisition is an essential part of business development; it also can involve identifying and nurturing referral sources. While you shouldn't violate your bar association's solicitation rules, you certainly can nurture leads and do your best to convert them into clients.

Building a robust client acquisition strategy is essential to your firm's survival. In 2000, there were 1,022,462 practicing lawyers in the United States, according to the ABA's *National Lawyer Population Survey*. By 2019, this number had grown to 1,352,027. In fact, the number of attorneys in the United States has consistently increased every year since 1915![1] You're also facing an increasing number of DIY services, like LegalZoom and Rocket Lawyer, that want to chip away at your market share.

Furthermore, your consumer base is increasingly sophisticated. They're evaluating your online reviews, reading your blog, and looking for proof that you're the lawyer for them. To thrive, you need to consistently demonstrate your expertise and dedication to your clients—and that requires a comprehensive business development plan.

1. American Bar Association, *ABA National Lawyer Population Survey*, 2019, https://www.americanbar.org/content/dam/aba/administrative/market_research/total-national-lawyer-population-1878-2019.pdf.

# Your Leads Expect Almost Instantaneous Service

Remember what we talked about in chapter 9, "Nurture Leads with Email Automation"? Online leads have incredibly short shelf lives, but too many law firms refuse to adapt to this fact. In case you don't remember the details, let's brush up. In 2011, the *Harvard Business Review* published a study assessing 2,241 businesses' online response times.[2] The study findings were shocking. While 37 percent of companies responded to an online query or form fill within an hour, their average response time was forty-two hours.

Let that sink in. Suppose Cathy Client contacts your law firm. Her husband was involved in a crash with a commercial vehicle and recently got an initial settlement offer from the insurance company. She fills out a contact form and waits. In the meantime, the insurance adjuster leaves a message, pressuring the family for a response.

Since she hasn't heard from your office, she decides to do some more research. Cathy requests a free consultation from Webster, Webster & Cohen. Within fifteen minutes, a legal assistant at the firm calls her back, collects her information, and schedules the Clients for a face-to-face meeting with a lawyer. Within an hour, Cathy receives an email confirmation of their appointment, directions to their office, and the attorney's bio.

Your administrative assistant calls Cathy hours after her initial form fill, but she declines an appointment. "I didn't hear from you, so I hired someone else," she explains.

In the past, many attorneys thought that as long as they called potential clients back within twenty-four hours, they could still convert.

2. James Oldroyd, Kristina McElheran, and David Elkington, "The Short Life of Online Sales Leads," *Harvard Business Review*, March, 2011, https://hbr.org/2011/03/the-short-life-of-online-sales-leads.

Those days are long over. According to the same 2011 *Harvard Business Review* study, firms that waited more than an hour to respond to an online query are almost seven times less likely to have meaningful contact with the lead (such as an initial consultation). If you wait for twenty-four hours or more, you are sixty times less likely to book a consultation or speak with the potential client.

# Essential Tools for Client Acquisition

How do you ensure lightning-quick response times and a consistent client experience? Part of the equation is a commitment to customer service. If you have an intake coordinator, they should be checking their inbox for form fills every hour (or more). If you don't have a designated person in charge of client acquisition, consider rotating the responsibility through your administrative team.

However, technology can also help alleviate this burden. Below, we've listed several tools that can streamline client acquisition.

## Customer Relationship Management (CRM) Platforms

You likely have a case management system or client database, but these systems typically don't have the ability to track your leads' and clients' experience. That is why an increasing number of law firms are turning to customer relationship management (CRM) platforms.

A CRM, when used consistently, helps you track your lead's engagement and all of your interactions with them. Typically, you will input your leads into a database, which includes tools that help you track their activity. For example, suppose Cathy Client calls Webster, Webster & Cohen and speaks with an intake coordinator, but she decides not to schedule a consultation. After their first interaction, an intake coordinator or legal assistant inputs Cathy's email and contact information in its CRM; they also sign her up for their newsletter.

In the weeks after their initial phone call, the Webster, Webster & Cohen team can see that Cathy has visited their website repeatedly, downloaded an e-book, and clicked on every article in their newsletter. She even registered for a TBI survivor webinar that the law firm is hosting. Based on Cathy's intense level of interest, the intake coordinator asks one of their partners to follow up with her in a phone call.

While Cathy appreciates the lawyer's call, she's still not ready to hire a lawyer. Webster, Webster & Cohen's intake coordinator notes these interactions in their CRM and sends Cathy a drip campaign that includes insurance claim FAQs, client success stories, and other helpful information. Finally, after months of reading every email and watching multiple videos, Cathy calls for her free consultation. The intake coordinator sees her entire history in the firm's CRM and schedules her with the partner from her early phone call.

While some of this interaction could be possible without a CRM, these platforms streamline the process and provide powerful insight into your leads' engagement and activity.

Unfortunately, many small and mid-sized law firms have been slow to adopt customer relationship management platforms. In its 2019 *The State of CRM at Law Firms* survey, Ackert (a legal consulting firm) noted that 40 percent of small to mid-sized law firms do not have a CRM, while 88 to 95 percent of large law firms use one.[3]

Even if you've already invested in a CRM, you should assess your law firm's implementation. According to the 2019 Ackert survey, in most law firms, 0 to 5 percent of the lawyers regularly used their CRM platforms to track leads! Instead, they used a patchwork of email

3. David Ackert, LindseyMartin, and OliviaWatson, *The State of CRM at Law Firms (2019)*, Ackert, https://info.ackertinc.com/crm-for-law-firms-2019-white-paper.

reminders, spreadsheets, and paper notes. Unfortunately, it's easy to lose that sticky note or ignore an email reminder.

When asked why they resist using their CRM, the majority of the lawyers' responses were cultural. For example, 63 percent of those surveyed didn't understand or care to learn about the CRM. Another 59 percent didn't bother to adopt their firm's CRM because there was no accountability or mandate. It's likely that many of these law firms failed to create clear CRM standards and processes.

Your law firm needs to take advantage of this opportunity. You can assume that most of your competitors either do not have a CRM or are haphazardly implementing their platform. If you can commit yourself to fully implementing your CRM, maintaining your contact lists, and tracking leads, you may be able to convert more high-value clients.

Importantly, you can find CRM systems at numerous price points. While a free CRM may not be as easy to use or powerful as Salesforce, there's probably a solution that meets your needs on the market. At LaFleur, we're big fans of SharpSpring, a moderately priced CRM platform.

## Lead Scoring: Track Engagement and Lead Relationships

Not all leads are created equal. You may already rank cases based on their potential value, aiming to get as many "four-star" or "A" cases as possible. However, digital marketing tools can give you even deeper insight into your leads.

With most CRM and email automation platforms, you can gain insight into your leads' engagement. Using **tracking pixels** and other tools, you can see how frequently they open your drip campaigns, which blogs they read, and how often they download your e-books and infographics. This can help you even further refine your client acquisition strategies, putting the most time and effort into those clients with desirable cases who demonstrate real interest in your law firm.

## Email Automation

As discussed in chapter 9, "Nurture Leads with Email Automation," when a form fill or another action triggers an automated email campaign, your team can gain a little extra time and build trust. Rather than having to manually send a message, an automation system personalizes your templated emails and sends them automatically.

There are several benefits to using email automation as part of your client acquisition process:

- Automatically triggered emails may satisfy your leads' desire for an immediate response.
- You can anticipate your leads' questions and answer them in drip campaigns, saving you time while building trust.
- Consistent, on-brand messaging can keep your firm at the top of your leads' minds.

## Online Chat Systems

Online chat is becoming increasingly common on law firm websites. In most cases, an automated **chatbot** responds to the initial query and asks a series of qualifying questions. If the lead meets specific criteria, the chatbot will connect them with one of your staff members. However, if you are a personal injury lawyer and they have a family law question, the chatbot may refer them to your state bar association's referral service.

When done well, leads may not even realize that they're interacting with a chatbot. Instead, they experience a seamless and fast intake process—and your team has more time to spend with qualified leads.

For example, suppose Cathy Client visits Webster, Webster & Cohen's website and clicks the "Chat" button.

**Chatbot:** "Welcome to Webster, Webster & Cohen! How can I help you today?"

**Cathy:** "I just got t-boned, and I'm not sure what to do."

**Chatbot:** "I'm so sorry to hear that. Were you injured?"

**Cathy:** "I broke my leg, and my shoulder is really sore."

**Chatbot:** "Again, I'm sorry you're hurting. I can schedule you for a free consultation with one of our lawyers. I know they'd love to help."

**Cathy:** "I do have some questions."

**Chatbot:** "One moment, and I'll connect you with a lawyer."

However, a poorly written chatbot script and process can detract from your potential clients' experience. Let's replay Cathy's chat, but with a weaker script:

**Chatbot:** "How can I help you today?"

**Cathy:** "I just got t-boned, and I'm not sure what to do."

**Chatbot:** "It sounds like you were in an accident."

**Cathy:** "I broke my leg, and my shoulder is really sore."

**Chatbot:** "I'm sorry. I didn't understand. Were you in an accident?"

**Cathy:** "I told you. I was in a truck wreck, and I need a lawyer."

**Chatbot:** "It sounds like you need a lawyer. Would you like to talk to one?"

In this case, Cathy closes the chat, frustrated and annoyed that the firm was clearly using a bot.

When you're writing or editing your chatbot scripts, put time and care into them. The more empathetic and human they sound, the better. At the end of this chapter, we've provided some additional resources that will help with choosing a chatbot platform and guide you through the (often time-consuming) process of creating chatbot scripts. The top names in chatbot software tend to change every few years, so it's also a good idea to ask your marketing partners about their preferred chat systems; they may be able to guide you to the best possible option.

Also, if you don't feel comfortable with an automated system, there are more hands-on chat solutions that let you and your staff converse with potential clients online.

## Texting and SMS Platforms

Today, many people prefer texting to phone calls or email. While we would discourage a lawyer from sharing privileged information via text, since many systems are not encrypted, you certainly can communicate minor information via text. Luckily, that doesn't mean you need to share your personal cell phone number with every lead. Instead, there are software programs that can help you connect with your leads safely over text, sending them short messages and reminders. Some software platforms, like Apex, even allow your potential clients to initiate contact, provide basic information, and schedule their initial consultation, all via text message.

## Establish Clear Intake Procedures and Protocols

From your first interaction with a potential client, every communication or touchpoint should reflect your values. This involves more than crafting on-brand content; it also requires clear intake standards and training.

For example, suppose Webster, Webster & Cohen's brand focuses on how their clients benefit from a team that goes "above and beyond" to help them. Unfortunately, the law firm hasn't fully trained their newest intake coordinator.

A prospective client, Otto Angst, calls the firm. He's scheduled for an independent medical examination (IME) and isn't sure what he should do. He's so worried that he's nearly in tears. During the call, the coordinator puts him on hold repeatedly to take other calls. Then they simply say that they'll send his message to a lawyer. The coordinator neglects to collect his email, and there isn't any follow-up for twenty-four hours. By the time a Webster, Webster & Cohen's lawyer calls Otto back, he's consulted with a different law firm that was "way more compassionate."

Nothing about this interaction expressed Webster, Webster & Cohen's commitment to their clients' experience. Here's what the coordinator should have done instead:

- Empathetically listened to Otto's story without interruption.
- Collected all of his contact information, including his email.
- Scheduled him for the earliest possible appointment.
- Put the lawyer or the lawyer's assistant on the line to discuss the IME process.
- Inputted his contact information into the firm's CRM.
- Followed up with a welcome email drip campaign and other resources.

Don't leave your intake process to chance. Set a clear process and fully train your team. That way, you're more likely to deliver a consistent and high-quality experience.

# Consistently Express Your Law Firm's Value

As we discussed in chapter 1, "Foundations: Your Brand," your law firm brand is more than a logo, color palette, and catchphrases. While these elements may attract your leads' eye, they aren't the reason that they hire you. Rather, they've decided that your law firm's culture and approach meet their unique needs.

Your value proposition is even more important now that legal consumers can choose from an array of legal services and DIY options. You need to convince today's skeptical consumers that you have the credibility, competence, and unique perspective that sets you apart from your competition.

Even little things, like offering to meet leads at the hospital or a more convenient location, like a private meeting space in a library, or a handwritten thank-you note can speak volumes about your law firm's brand and commitment to service.

However, these subtle gestures should supplement your comprehensive content strategy, which demonstrates your firm's unique value through informative e-books, client guides, email campaigns, blogs, client stories, and videos. (To learn more about building a content strategy, refer to chapter 8, "Email Newsletters That Engage Your Followers.")

Reviews are also an important part of your narrative. As discussed in chapter 11, "Networking and Creating Brand Ambassadors," modern legal consumers typically won't take you at your word. Instead, the majority of people rely heavily on reviews and client testimonials when they're shopping for a lawyer. If permitted by your state bar association, you should always encourage your satisfied clients to share their experience on Google My Business and social media platforms.

# Be Patient

While some legal claims, especially those nearing the statute of limitations, require immediate attention, many people aren't ready to hire a lawyer right away. In fact, according to a 2015 Avvo/Martindale survey, about 37 percent of people tried to solve their legal issue on their own first.[4] When they felt overwhelmed or outnumbered, they turned to a lawyer. Notably, of those who tried to represent themselves, the survey reported that 32 percent of them at least consulted with a lawyer—and 25 percent decided to retain counsel.

So, don't give up on your leads who don't immediately convert, especially if they maintain a high lead score on your CRM. Instead, nurture them with drip campaigns, monthly newsletters, and the occasional phone call, consistently expressing your law firm's value. When they decide they need a lawyer, they'll hopefully turn to you.

# Checklist for Client Acquisition

- Identify and train your client intake team.
- Use email automation and chat to quickly connect with leads.
- Consider implementing a customer relationship management (CRM) platform.
- Connect with your leads via chat and SMS/Text.

4. Nika Kabiri, *Sink or Swim: How to Adapt to the New Legal Consumer*, (Avvo: 2015) https://www.martindale-avvo.com/wp-content/uploads/how_to_adapt_to_the_new_legal_consumer_avvo_whitepaper_2016.pdf.

- Create emails and other assets that encourage conversion.
- Score your leads and target your biggest fans.
- Express your value during every interaction with a lead.
- Collect reviews that highlight your law firm's value proposition.

## Additional Recommended Resources

- https://www.consumersadvocate.org/chatbots.
- Ben Beck, "How to Write a Script for a Chatbot: Key Elements for Good Dialogue Flow," ClearVoice, Inc. (January, 2019), https://www.clearvoice.com/blog/how-to-write-a-chatbot.
- Hillary Black, *Conversation Design: How to Design a Chatbot Script from Scratch,* (2019), https://gumroad.com/l/conversationdesign.

# 16

# Going Beyond the Basics: Analytics

Have you seen the film *Moneyball* (2011)? In it, Brad Pitt plays baseball manager Billy Beane, who manages the Oakland A's. Beane has a limited budget, yet he has to assemble a team that can compete with rich major-market ball clubs.

Instead of using traditional eye-test methods to recruit ball players—Beane famously doesn't even watch baseball games throughout the film—he uses data analysis to find diamonds in the rough that other managers have overlooked. His team wins their division and makes the playoffs against the odds, although they lose in the first round. Still, the unexpected success of the A's turns heads around the league, and Beane gets an offer to manage a team with a much larger budget, which he declines.

It's a fun film because it makes data analysis sexy, which is rare. And if you haven't seen it, you should watch it, because Billy Beane's situation and solution are much like yours. In fact, the practice of data analysis that Beane uses in the film is based on the same principles as digital marketing **analytics**.

Most likely, you've got to compete online against law firms that have much bigger budgets, and if you go toe-to-toe with them using their methods, you'll lose every time. But analytics are your out card; they let you do much more with far less.

# What Is Marketing Analytics?

Yes, analytics is a singular noun, like *gymnastics*. Analytics is the practice of managing and studying data so you can determine the return on investment (ROI) for marketing strategies and identify ways to improve.

Let's also clarify what analytics is not. Applying analytics doesn't mean letting a computer make all your decisions. Instead, analytics is about using data to see trends and patterns you wouldn't see otherwise, so you can make better, more informed choices. The insights from analytics should work in service to your judgment, your legal experience, and your core values, not replace them.

The one thing you can always predict about people is they're unpredictable. When you're creating a website page or other marketing asset, even something as simple and seemingly irrelevant as the color of a button can affect conversions and ROI. Using your own judgment to try and optimize all these tiny factors that affect performance is a recipe for failure, at least unless your ideal clients are other attorneys your same age and gender who look and think just like you. So, the best legal marketers use data to make informed decisions about their strategies rather than just trusting their intuition.

Creating a digital marketing strategy and executing the various tactics is enough work on its own (we already devoted fifteen chapters to it, after all), so no one could blame you if you get a campaign out the door and feel like never thinking about it again. But the process of succeeding at digital marketing is less like planting a tree in your backyard—get it in the ground and clean up the branches every couple years—and more like the Japanese art of bonsai, where you're constantly monitoring and making adjustments to keep things on course.

Monitoring the analytics data from your marketing campaigns can help you do the following:

- Identify and monitor trends in your marketing campaigns.
- Determine which strategies are working and find out why.
- Apply insights from successful strategies to improve ones that aren't getting results.
- Understand exactly what returns you're getting for your investment in each marketing strategy and campaign.
- Predict future costs and returns.

## Digital Marketing Metrics and Key Performance Indicators

The other important terms besides *analytics* you need to understand are **metrics** and **key performance indicators** (**KPIs**). You'll see these terms a lot in any resource that discusses digital marketing analytics.

Metrics are values you can measure. We've mentioned many different digital marketing metrics throughout this book so far. Here are some examples of common metrics:

- Website and content marketing:
  - » **Traffic:** The number of people who visit a given page on your website or the site as a whole.
  - » **Conversion rate:** The number of people who perform a desired action (like filling out a form and becoming a lead) after visiting a web page or viewing an asset.
  - » **Bounce rate:** The number of people who visit a page and then leave without taking any other actions or navigating to any other pages.
  - » **Time on page:** The average amount of time people spend viewing a given website page.
- Email marketing:
  - » **Open rate:** The percent of email recipients who open an email.
  - » **Click-through rate** (**CTR**): The percent of email recipients who open an email and click on at least one link within the email.
  - » **Bounce rate:** The number of contacts who didn't receive an email.
  - » **List growth rate:** The number of new subscribers to your email list minus the number of unsubscribes over a given time period.
- Social:
  - » **Impressions:** The total number of times your content was displayed in people's feeds, whether they saw it or not.

- » **Reach:** The total number of times people actually saw your content (different platforms calculate reach in different ways).

- » **Engagement:** Likes, comments, shares, mentions, and clicks.

- Pay-per-click advertising:

  - » **Clicks:** The number of times people click on your paid ads.

  - » **Click-through rate (CTR):** The percent of people who click on your ad after seeing it.

  - » **Cost per click (CPC):** The average amount you spend to receive one click.

  - » **Conversion rate:** The percent of people who take a desired action (like filling out a form and becoming a lead) after clicking on one of your ads.

  - » **Quality Score:** Google's measurement of the quality and relevance of your ads, keywords, and landing pages.

Finally, key performance indicators (KPIs) are metrics that you identify as vital to the success of your marketing campaigns and your business goals. Most metrics can tell you something, but not all of them make good KPIs in every situation. For example, website traffic has value, but it's not a good choice for a KPI that you can use to evaluate the overall success of your marketing strategy.

Why? Well, let's say you write a lengthy, fascinating blog about the history of the law as a passion project. When you finally publish your blog, it ends up performing well in Google search or even getting a link from a major publication. Now, many people who Google "history of the law" wind up on your blog, and you're seeing a huge surge in traffic on your website.

However, all of these visitors are law school students or other unfortunate souls who have term papers to write. None of them are actually potential clients who have cases, so none of that traffic translates to web leads, phone calls, or signed clients. (This isn't a fantasy exercise, by the way—we had almost this exact situation occur on our LaFleur blog, so we know from experience.)

So, website traffic in itself is not a terribly useful KPI for your overall strategy. It often correlates with success, but you can get a huge increase in website traffic without moving any closer to achieving any kind of meaningful business goal. Now, if you launched a campaign to boost traffic to a particular page or set of pages that you know tend to produce valuable leads, then traffic makes sense as a KPI for that individual campaign.

Even your total number of leads makes a sketchy KPI for your overall strategy, since large numbers of leads don't necessarily translate to good results. Generating lots of low-quality leads can make more work for your staff while moving the needle very little in terms of revenue.

## Good Key Performance Indicators

What kinds of metrics *do* make good KPIs for your digital marketing strategy as a whole? Here are some examples:

- **Total marketing spend:** The first marketing metric you should always track is how much you spend on marketing each month. You need to know how much you're spending on different campaigns and channels. If you spend $2,000 per month on digital marketing, don't just write down "$2k" and call it a day. You need a detailed budget sheet with recorded figures for every strategy, campaign, and channel: $300 per month on blog marketing, $200 developing e-books, $80 creating regular Facebook posts, $150 on paid Facebook advertising, $200 on this PPC campaign and $180 on that one, and so forth.

- **Number of qualified leads and clients generated:** We said overall leads weren't a great metric for success, but *qualified* leads are a different story. Qualified leads are much more likely to become valuable cases, so they're a much better predictor of success. And once you know how many qualified leads you're getting, you can figure out what percent of your total leads from digital marketing become qualified leads and which tactics are most likely to generate qualified leads. You can also calculate what percentage of qualified leads become clients, which can give you insights into how successful your team is at qualifying leads and then following up with those leads.

- **Average cost and revenue per client and per lead:** Knowing how much revenue you get per client helps you assign a monetary value to leads. As an example, let's say the average revenue you see per client obtained via digital marketing is $2,000. Your conversion rate for qualified leads is 50 percent, so for every two qualified leads you get one client; that means each qualified lead has a value of $1,000. One out of every five leads you receive from digital marketing channels becomes a qualified lead, so the average value of each lead is $200. Now you know the value of each lead, qualified lead, and client; meanwhile, you can divide your total marketing budget by the total number of leads, qualified leads, and clients to determine the average cost for each.

- **Conversion rate:** A conversion rate is the percentage of people who go on to become leads after interacting with a marketing asset or campaign. So, if one thousand people visit a pay-per-click (PPC) landing page, and one hundred of them fill out the page's form and become leads, that page's conversion rate is 10 percent. Calculating conversion rates can help you identify which campaigns and assets do the best job at generating leads. However, it's important to remember that conversion rates tend to be relative—blog content will have different conversion rates than practice area pages, which will have different conversion rates than PPC landing pages, and so on.

Also, conversion rates only become a useful KPI once you've fleshed out the other KPIs we've described and assigned a value to digital marketing leads. If you don't know whether the leads you're getting translate to revenue, then you can't say whether getting larger numbers of those leads really matters.

- **Marketing return on investment** (**ROI**)**:** This is the ultimate digital marketing metric. Once you know how much total revenue you're generating from clients that come via digital marketing channels, you can see how much money your digital marketing strategy generates and how that compares to the money you're putting in.

One thing you'll notice about these KPIs is that many of them require data you can't get from digital marketing tools alone. You'll find it impossible to calculate your average cost per client and revenue per client, for example, if you aren't tracking which leads come in from digital marketing campaigns and then following them until their case resolves and you can assign a dollar value. However, the analytics data you'll get from digital marketing tools stops once a potential client starts interacting with your firm directly through phone calls or direct email messages. So, getting useful data for your most important KPIs usually requires additional tools, like case management software, to fill in the picture from that point on.

One of the biggest challenges we face at LaFleur involves working with small firms that don't have systematic methods for tracking leads and monitoring client relationships. Without these systems in place, digital marketing campaigns generate lots of data, but leads go into an abyss and never come out. You can't assign value to digital marketing leads, so you can't tell whether the leads you're generating are good ones, and marketing ROI becomes impossible to calculate. The best you can do at this point is to rely on lesser metrics like web traffic, conversion rates, and total number of leads. To make a baseball analogy in tribute to Billy Beane, that's like getting box scores that include only one team's scoring and stats.

Also, the KPIs listed above represent your most important metrics, but that doesn't mean the many other metrics like email click-through rates and traffic to web pages can't tell you anything useful. You'll use these types of metrics as KPIs to evaluate the success of individual assets and campaigns; meanwhile, the marquee KPIs like total spending, cost and revenue per lead, and overall return on investment make sure that success with individual assets and campaigns actually translates to more clients, cases, and revenue.

# How Do I Get Analytics Data?

Even though the data from digital marketing tools alone won't give you enough information to calculate the most important KPIs, you certainly need that data—it's a big part of the picture. So, how do you go about getting analytics reports you can understand?

First, analytics reports are built into many of the software tools and platforms we've already mentioned in previous chapters, like SharpSpring (chapter 8, "Email Newsletters That Engage Your Followers"), Facebook Ads (chapter 12, "Paid Advertising: Start with Social"), and Google Ads (chapter 13, "Paid Advertising: Pay per Click"). However, we haven't yet talked about one of the most important analytics tools, which is **Google Analytics** (GA). This tool offers so many insights and such data-crunching power that it's almost hard to believe it's free—like mailing in a postcard and getting a space shuttle in return. Here's what Google Analytics can do:

- Show you the total traffic for your website and for any individual page or collection of pages.

- Show you how users navigate through your site (which pages they tend to visit and in which order).

- Tell you how users arrive at your site (organic search, paid search, links from other websites, or typing in your URL in their browser).

- Categorize users into groups based on demographic information and prior behavior so you can see how the groups behave differently.

- Tell you which websites organic users visit before and after arriving at your site.

- Provide custom analytics reports and dashboards based on your unique goals and the metrics you care about most.

- Diagnose technical issues on your site, such as slow loading times.

Of course, nothing truly comes for free. Google gives you GA at no charge in part because they want your data. The company won't serve you ads or anything of that nature while you use GA, but presumably they use the enormous amounts of website data they gather via GA to optimize their own tools and platforms, such as making improvements to Google search. GA also integrates with Google Ads in a lot of ways; Google hopes that using Analytics will convince you to try paid advertising with Google Ads, which definitely does cost money.

We won't try to walk you through how to set up and use Google Analytics in this chapter, mainly because Google already offers free online resources that will show you how to do all this. To get started, go to the Google search home page and do a search for "get started with google analytics." The top result should be a Google support page titled "Get started with Analytics." This page will walk you through the four steps required to set up a GA account and start collecting data. The page also includes links that elaborate on each step as well as a tutorial video.

Keep in mind that Google Analytics requires you to install a tracking code on your website before the platform can begin gathering data (the tutorial explains how to install the tracking code, and if you're still struggling, try searching YouTube for "how to install google analytics tracking code"). You can't set up GA and then ask Google to go back and get data from before you completed the setup process. Google will begin collecting data only from that point forward, so you'll have to wait at least a couple weeks for data to build up before you can get any useful insights about site performance and user behavior.

Once you've set up GA, you should get familiar with the platform by completing Google's free video-based course "Google Analytics for Beginners"; you'll find it as the top result if you perform a Google search for the phrase. The course assumes very little prior technical knowledge, and it includes four units, which take about an hour each to complete.

# How Do I Use Analytics Data?

Google Analytics can provide truckloads of data, and learning to sift through it all takes time, practice, and education. However, there are a few easy-to-view metrics that will pop up whenever you view a page within Analytics, and these beginner-level metrics often provide everything you need to make significant improvements to web pages:

- **Page views:** The total number of times that users viewed a page over the specified time period. Repeat views of the same page by the same user count.

- **Unique page views:** Like pageviews except repeat views of the same page by the same user don't count.

- **Average time on page:** The average amount of time users spend viewing the page. More time on page is usually good. Ideal time on page varies widely, but a couple of minutes is usually considered a good time on page for many types of content.

- **Bounce rate:** The percent of users who arrive at the page as the first page in their **session** and then leave the site without taking any other actions (like clicking on a link and visiting another page). High bounce rate is usually bad. However, bounce rate is relative; some pages, like blog articles, have a naturally high bounce rate. It's normal for your blog articles to have a bounce rate of, say, 85 to 90 percent while your home page has a bounce rate in the area of 30 to 40 percent.

- **Percent exit:** The percentage of users who leave the site after viewing a particular page. Percent exit and bounce rate are similar, but percent exit refers to the percentage of users for whom the page in question was the last page they saw on your site. In contrast, bounce rate refers to the percentage of users for whom the page in question was the first and last page they visited. Just like bounce rate, some pages have a naturally higher percent exit. For example, a basic Contact Us page that includes your address and phone number will normally have a high percent exit. Usually, pages that need attention will have a high bounce rate and a high percent exit; on its own, a high percent exit is rarely anything to worry about.

So, how do you use these metrics to optimize pages? As an example, let's say Webster, Webster & Cohen (WWC) has a blog article that's performing exceptionally well and getting lots of traffic. However, the blog article has a high bounce rate even compared to other blogs on the site, which means visitors tend to read the blog article and then leave instead of checking out other pages on the site.

First, WWC needs to ask the question: Are the people visiting the blog potential clients at all? If the high-traffic blog fails to target potential clients, like the "history of the law" blog we mentioned earlier, then the high bounce rate probably results from the fact that visitors don't need legal services and have no further reason to hang around on a law firm website. The best solution is to focus future blog articles on issues that affect potential clients and not write more pieces that generate meaningless traffic.

However, if the high-traffic blog seems like a topic that's likely to attract potential clients—something like "How Can a Lawyer Help Me After a Car Wreck?"—and still has a high bounce rate, then WWC may need to make other adjustments to the page. For example, WWC might include a "related article" link after the end of the first section to try and funnel people to another useful piece of content rather than leaving (since very few people will end up reading any blog article to completion). Or they might add a link to the firm's car wreck practice area page early in the copy. WWC could also check whether the article's headline matches its title tag (to make sure users don't see an on-page headline that's drastically different from the title they clicked on in the web search), try adding a sidebar form so visitors can contact the firm without scrolling down, or embed a video on the page to encourage users to stick around longer and check out more content.

In addition, let's say WWC notices a pay-per-click (PPC) landing page (like the ones we discussed in chapter 13, "Paid Advertising: Pay per Click") that's receiving lots of traffic but almost no conversions. WWC needs to review this page and ask what's preventing people from fulfilling the conversion goal for the page, which is to fill out a form and provide contact information so the user can get a free e-book. Is the form demanding more information than users are willing to give? (Remember, more form fields means fewer form fills.) Is the call-to-action for the form clear and user focused? ("Email me a link to my free e-book" should perform better than "Get e-book"; calls-to-action written in first person tend to perform well, and so do those that let the user know exactly what happens next when they perform the desired action.) Does the page have a prominent, concise headline and an attention-grabbing image to hook the user as soon as they arrive?

When you're making improvements to a page, whether it's a blog article, a practice area page, or a paid search landing page, it's usually best to make one adjustment at a time, wait, and watch for changes in results rather than make a lot of changes to the page all at once. If you make many changes at the same time and see an improvement, you won't know which of those changes made the difference, so you won't be able to apply that insight to any other pages.

As we mentioned earlier, sometimes a change as small as the color of a call-to-action button (like "Download Now") can affect the performance of a page in significant ways. But if you take this fact to heart completely, it can lead you down the path to madness. How do you know what color your button should be in the first place? Red, blue, green, yellow? If you're already getting good results from a page with a blue button, could they be better if you changed the button to red? Or would they get worse? And if you change to red and the results get better, how do you know the improvement happened because of the change and not because of some other factor, like a seasonal fluctuation in web traffic?

First, remember there is no such thing as a perfect web page. Marketing does not happen in a laboratory, and it's impossible to test every variable of a page in every possible permutation. So, you do not need to lie awake at night tossing, turning, and mopping tiny beads of sweat from your brow because you haven't tried turquoise buttons and links on your web pages yet.

Second, a practice called **A/B testing** can make the process of optimizing web pages much more coherent. A/B testing involves creating two different versions of a page and then showing them to users at random. So, if you decide to A/B test the blue versus red button issue, you would set your web page up so that half of the visitors who arrive at the page see a version with the blue button and half see a version with red. Through this type of A/B testing, you can know whether any given change you implemented made the difference in a page's performance, because you can still see data from the original version of the page for the same time period.

Unfortunately, we can't walk you through the process of setting up A/B testing because it varies so much depending on how your website is set up and what platform your site uses. With WordPress, for example, there are a variety of plug-ins you can download and add to your site that will open up options for A/B testing. You'll need to search the web for a guide on how to implement A/B testing for whichever platform you use to maintain your website.

These are the common elements of digital marketing campaigns that you'll want to A/B test:

- headlines
- page title tags
- calls to action
- prominent images
- email subject lines

Again, remember that a web page is more like a painting than a chemistry experiment. The universe will not give you a sign that your work is complete, so it's done when you put down your tools and walk away. If you do a couple A/B tests with red versus blue CTA buttons and red wins, and then you do a few more with yellow and red still wins, it's okay to assume that red is probably the best choice for all your buttons and apply that logic sitewide. Maybe next year, you can revisit and test a few more colors or make sure red still wins against the colors you've tested already. Just test as many elements as often as you reasonably can, and remember to change only one element at a time.

# Summary

The ability to get analytics data and use it to improve digital marketing assets and campaigns is what differentiates online marketing from more traditional advertising methods like radio spots, television commercials, and billboards. The insights you get from platforms like Google Analytics help you squeeze more value out of every web page, blog article, and other asset you create, which makes analytics a key pillar of online law firm marketing that you can't afford to ignore.

# Analytics Checklist

- Identify key performance indicators (KPIs) for overall strategy and for individual campaigns (blog marketing, social media, and so on).
- Set up Google Analytics.
- Complete the "Google Analytics for Beginners" course.
- Implement A/B testing for key site pages (home page, practice area pages, PPC landing pages).

# Additional Recommended Resources

- https://www.marketo.com/marketing-analytics
- Iain Blaire, "The Definitive Guide to Marketing Analytics," buildfire.com, https://buildfire.com/marketing-analytics.
- Google Analytics Academy (https://analytics.google.com/analytics/academy)
- Mike Grigsby, *Marketing Analytics: A Practical Guide to Improving Consumer Insights Using Data Techniques,* 2nd ed. (2018).
- Kevin Hartman, *Digital Marketing Analytics: In Theory And in Practice,* 2nd ed. (Ostmen Bennettsbridge Publishing Services: 2020).

17

# Working with an Agency

Hopefully, we've made the case by now that digital marketing is an essential element of your law firm's long-term strategy for growth and success. If you've accepted that premise, then there are three ways to make sure the actual work gets done:

1. Handle it yourself.

2. Hire an in-house marketing staff.

3. Partner with a digital marketing agency.

Throughout this book, we've tried to help you accomplish your marketing goals via option number one. You can save plenty of money by managing your own digital marketing campaigns, and it's certainly doable without formal training. Digital marketing is not like chemistry—I and many of my colleagues don't even have a college degree in marketing. And no matter how badly your online experiments go, they will not literally blow up in your face.

However, marketing your business always involves costs. If you aren't paying money, then you're paying time—and as the scope of this book has probably made clear, the time investment is significant. For most small business owners with young businesses, burning the midnight oil is a normal and expected part of the process. Living like a superhero—mild-mannered attorney by day, dynamic digital marketing guru by night—may seem tolerable for a long time.

Eventually, you'll probably reach a point where you tire of this double life and begin to want your time back. As your law firm grows and survives the early lean years, hours spent with family, friends, and favorite pastimes may come to seem more valuable than cutting every cost to the bone and squeezing every last drop of profit. At this point, it makes sense to pass the marketing torch to either an in-house staff member or an outside agency.

Both options have potential benefits and downsides. First, let's examine the option of expanding your team to include a dedicated in-house marketer.

## The True Cost of Hiring In-House

Many law firms, once they hit a certain size, dive into the hiring process for dedicated marketing staff. It's a natural outgrowth of many previous decisions about scaling up that involved in-house hires for other positions.

Unfortunately, many law firms don't consider whether their investment in a new staff member to handle their marketing needs could deliver better returns somewhere else. Often, it could.

According to the most up-to-date data from the website Glassdoor (pulled on March 13, 2020), the average base pay of a marketing manager in the United States is $65,539.[1] That figure doesn't include benefits or the costs associated with the hiring process. So, hiring someone new is a significant investment.

But hiring an in-house marketing manager requires more than just the investment in the person's salary, payroll taxes, and benefits. There's also the time investment of everyone involved in the hiring, interview, and training processes. To perform their duties, your new marketing manager will need office space and equipment, including a computer and smartphone. They'll also need access to some of the specialized software we've described in previous chapters.

When you add up these costs, hiring an in-house marketing manager is a serious investment. And cost is only one of many factors to consider as you seek to delegate the work of digital marketing.

## The Inherent Limitations of Marketing Staff Members

Whether you're considering an in-house or freelance marketing professional, you need to consider not only the cost but what you're getting for that cost. The big question you need to ask here is, "How much can one person truly do?"

As in any other field that requires lots of different skillsets, marketing professionals specialize in one aspect of the field or another. Take me, for example—I'm an experienced writer, editor, and content marketer, and I've also dabbled in design and web builds, but I've never so much as touched Google Ads or managed any aspect of a pay-per-click campaign. (Don't worry, I didn't write that chapter.)

1. "Marketing manager," Glassdoor Incorporated, updated March 13, 2020, https://www.glassdoor.com/Salaries/marketing-manager-salary-SRCH_KO0,17.htm.

So, if you're hoping to hire a single marketing professional who executes in every area at a professional level, you'll probably end up disappointed. That's simply not how the field works. Instead, you'll have to incur additional costs to cover the gaps in their skillset or to make up for shortages in their workload capacity.

# Maximize Your ROI by Partnering with a Digital Marketing Agency

As you're considering all the resources required to bring on and support an in-house marketing professional, it's also worth investigating what you'll get if you invest the same amount of resources in a partnership with a digital marketing agency. Usually, the answer is "more." There are a few important reasons why an agency is a better bet to give you the best return on your marketing budget:

- **Comprehensive marketing services:** Successful agencies don't look for jack-of-all-trades marketing professionals. Instead, they hire specialized and certified marketing professionals who focus in each service area. For essentially the same cost as the expertise of one accomplished professional, you get the experience and versatility of a well-rounded team.

- **Faster results:** A successful agency employs a team that's designed to hit the ground running. They have established onboarding practices, where they get to know their clients' goals and priorities, and they'll have a full team working on the reporting, investigation, and analysis required to craft and launch a digital marketing strategy. With one person doing all this work, this process will naturally take much longer—even without considering the length of time involved in the hiring and training processes.

- **Experience with similar law firms:** The agency you partner with should have extensive experience working specifically with law firms. If so, they'll have volumes of data about what works and what doesn't for law firms similar to yours and in similar geographic regions.

  Meanwhile, unless your in-house marketing manager comes over from a direct competitor firm with similar business goals, they'll have to figure out what works via experimentation, incremental adjustment, and occasional failure—an extended process that will play out on your dime.

- **Access to tools and platforms:** Any digital marketing agency worth its salt should already have access to the essential software tools and platforms we mentioned throughout earlier chapters of this book. The costs for these tools are rolled into your agency's fees, but they're also paid by the agency's other clients, so you pay a small fraction of the cost of each tool rather than the full freight.

- **Workplace chemistry:** Conflicts naturally arise in workplaces as teams grow in size. Adding a new person to your team always raises the possibility that they won't play nice with someone already on your staff.

## In-House Staff Can Complement an Agency

For some law firms, it may still prove worthwhile to hire a marketing manager. If you've got a larger firm with a lot of institutional knowledge and complex communication networks, an in-house marketing professional can make a lot of sense. However, it remains unlikely that this person will arrive with all the skills and tools needed to handle every aspect of a well-rounded digital marketing strategy.

The good news is that in-house staff and agency partnerships often pair very well. An in-house marketing manager can actually help you get more out of your agency partnership by serving as a single consistent point of contact and translating their institutional knowledge into actionable marketing insights.

So, rather than trying to find that unicorn digital marketing professional who's mastered (and stays up-to-date on) every area of the field, you can focus on finding a candidate who fits your culture and who brings formidable skills in a particular area. (Content marketing often makes a lot of sense to bring in-house since it requires the most institutional knowledge.) Then you can supplement their core skills with a customized plan from an agency.

# Agency Partnerships Aren't Always Made in Heaven

Despite all the compelling benefits, the process of hiring a marketing agency comes with potential pitfalls too. We've met many clients who have been burned in the past by failed agency partnerships. If this happened to your firm, you might still feel a little sour toward agencies in general, and that's understandable.

A big part of finding the right partner is knowing what to avoid. To help, we've put together a list of potential red flags that can steer your ship away from the rocks and narrow your search to the digital marketing agencies who can get you the best results for your budget.

## Red Flag #1: No Clear Reporting

A lack of transparent reporting is how bad agencies paper over bad work. With the amount of data produced by tools like Google Analytics, email automation platforms, social media networks, and customer relationship management tools, there's no excuse for your agency partner not to deliver clear reports that explain exactly what results you're getting for your marketing spend.

Also, remember the metrics we talked about in chapter 16, "Going Beyond the Basics: Analytics," and don't let the agency hide behind vanity metrics like web traffic, clicks, and impressions. Instead, make sure they can prove success in the areas that matter: number of qualified leads, average cost and revenue per lead, conversion rates, and marketing ROI. (But don't forget that getting this kind of valuable data requires information and organization on your part too. Review chapter 16, "Going Beyond the Basics: Analytics" if you need a refresher.)

## Red Flag #2: Byzantine Billing

If there's one complaint we've heard over and over from law firms who had bad agency partnerships, it's that they received bills they couldn't understand for projects and initiatives that never seemed to materialize.

The marketing agency you work with should be able to break down your bill in a clear manner that's easy to understand, and they should attach concrete, realistic timelines to projects and then adhere to them. They should also, at any time, be ready and willing to prepare a report that shows you what they've achieved for you (both recently and since the beginning of your relationship) and how they're allocating your money.

## Red Flag #3: No Experience in Your Industry

Every agency has to branch out into an industry with an initial client—but that doesn't mean that client has to be you. Your limited marketing budget is too valuable to burn up on someone's first foray into a new field. And law firms market their services under some unique conditions (confidentiality, highly specialized practice areas, bar association advertising rules), so it's important that your prospective agency has specific experience with the nuances of legal marketing.

Ask the agency to provide proof of results and references from other law firms they've worked with—preferably firms that practice in areas similar to yours. If the agency waffles or can't deliver, you should try to find a different partner who has experience that's directly applicable to the legal industry and your business goals.

## Red Flag #4: Ugly Assets

Would you hire a carpenter who lives in a house that's falling apart at the seams? An auto mechanic who drives a muffler-dragging rust bucket? A marketing agency's website is their showcase for their vision, philosophy, and reason for being, and if it doesn't make an instant impression and entice you to learn more about them, then you shouldn't expect better results when they create a website for you.

During the vetting process, check out every aspect of an agency's online presence—not just their home page, but their service area pages, their blog, their social pages, their press releases, and anything else you can dig up. The devil's in the details, and if things get sloppy around the edges of an agency's web presence, you shouldn't trust them to handle your digital marketing strategy.

## Red Flag #5: Questionable Reputation

Hopefully, any time you consider a marketing agency for a partnership, you're looking at their online reviews from platforms like Google and Twitter. However, ask anyone who's bought a crappy appliance on Amazon because it had ten thousand five-star reviews, and they can tell you: sketchy companies know bad reviews are their Achilles' heel, and they'll do whatever they can to cover them up, which may include posting scores of fake reviews to drown out the real ones.

Since it's easy for companies to post fake positive reviews, you'll have to go deeper during your vetting process. For starters, ask for the agency's case studies, view examples of work they've done for clients in the past, and look them up on the Better Business Bureau website.

Also, request from your prospective partner a list of both past and current clients you can call for a reference. If they have any problem with this reasonable request, that's a bad sign. When you talk with the agency's references, don't just pose yes-no queries about whether the reference liked the agency. Instead, ask open-ended questions about what business challenges the reference experienced before the partnership and how the agency addressed those issues with practical solutions.

## Red Flag #6: Hoarding Assets

If you get burned by an agency because they didn't make the best use of your budget, the story will end like a bad fling—you lose time and money, and there will be pain, but you get a fresh start. However, if you let an unscrupulous agency get a hold of your website, social accounts, and other marketing assets, you could find yourself in a breakup that's more like the divorce from hell.

Some unsavory agencies try to maintain exclusive access to your most important assets just so your firm is effectively held hostage. And these aren't just fly-by-night companies, either—some of them have been around for a while and look perfectly legitimate. These parasite agencies know they don't deliver a good ROI at competitive pricing, so instead, they make their living by grabbing hold of their clients' websites and other key assets and never letting go.

To avoid this trap, make sure your marketing agency can promise that you'll have free and unfettered access to all your important digital marketing assets—especially your website and your site's domain name—if you decide to change agencies or move your marketing in-house. A stand-up marketing partner not only won't balk at this request but will help you make the transition if you decide to make a change.

## What Should the Agency Hiring Process Look Like?

The process of hiring an agency will look a bit different from agency to agency and firm to firm. For example, many larger agencies may be used to working with larger clients with a long history of agency relationships, so these larger agencies may ask for a **request for proposal (RFP)**. An RFP identifies and documents a company's needs and gives the prospective agency insight into the company's business goals.

However, at our smaller agency, most of our legal clients don't submit RFPs because they haven't done the necessary background work and organized the information. Instead, we hold discovery calls to get the information we need to create a detailed proposal.

The advantage of creating an RFP is that it can save you from having to go over the same information repeatedly in discovery calls. If you're looking at only a couple potential agencies, it might not be worth the work to create an RFP; if you're going to evaluate a lot of prospective marketing partners, an RFP will probably save time in the long run.

If you want to create an RFP, it should include the following essential information:

1. **Background/introduction:** Provide a few paragraphs of useful background about your firm: your story, who founded the firm, where you're located, what types of clients you serve and cases you handle, and what sets you apart from competitors. (No need to write this from scratch—you can draw from the branding information we established in chapter 1, "Foundations: Your Brand.")

2. **Scope of services and project goals:** Make sure the agency knows what you're trying to accomplish. For example, do you just want to hire the agency for a one-off website build project, or are you looking to establish an ongoing partnership? Make sure to outline the specific tasks you expect the agency to handle.

3. **Deadline:** Make sure to include your timeline for selecting a partner so the agency knows whether they can get a comprehensive proposal together in time.

4. **Timeframe:** For any projects with a specific end date (like a website build), you should specify the time frame you have in mind. This will eliminate any agencies who can't work within your time constraints.

5. **Evaluation criteria:** Explain how your firm will choose from among the agencies who submit a proposal. You can mention the criteria we discussed earlier in this chapter for evaluating an agency: examples of past work, case studies, references, and reports that detail results achieved for similar law firms.

6. **Challenges:** Every business has marketing challenges and obstacles they need to overcome. The more up front you are about yours, the better an agency can address them with practical solutions.

7. **Budget:** The agency needs to know how much you can pay for their services before they'll create a proposal.

## Example RFP

1. **Background/introduction:** Webster, Webster & Cohen is a personal injury law firm in Hazardville, Florida. Our practice is based around handling complex cases other injury attorneys can't by using cutting-edge investigative techniques and the best expert witnesses. We also have some of the most efficient and streamlined client communications practices in the industry thanks to technology that we use to schedule consultations, bring clients on board, and stay in touch throughout cases. We want to focus on the people who need our help the most, so we want to reach severely injured victims of negligence in and around Hazardville, especially people with brain injuries and those who have suffered serious injuries in car accidents and truck wrecks.

2. **Scope of services and project goals:** Our primary goal is to execute a redesign of our website to update the overall design and create a more inviting and intuitive user experience. Our new site will need to be mobile-responsive and accessible for persons with disabilities. These are the services we'll require:

    » project management
    » graphic design
    » web development
    » content migration
    » content strategy
    » on-site SEO
    » quality assurance and testing
    » copywriting/content creation

3. **Deadline for proposal:** May 15, 2021.

4. **Timeframe:** We would like to launch our new website by September 2021.

5. **Evaluation criteria:** We will make our selection based on agency experience, portfolio, examples of relevant projects, and references.

6. **Challenges:** We have two competing firms in our area who are able to outspend us in paid advertising and consistently outrank our current website in organic search results. We are looking for a partner who can help optimize our website for search, including content strategy and creation of additional content.

7. **Budget:** $50,000 for the initial website build; $15,000 annually for website hosting, support, and maintenance; $35,000 annually for content creation (blogs, videos, e-books).

Regardless of whether the agency gathers information via discovery call or RFP, the next steps should be the same: the agency should schedule a call to go over some initial recommendations. If the recommendations seem reasonable and practical and both sides feel like it makes sense to move forward, the agency will create a detailed proposal.

When it comes time to evaluate a proposal, the knowledge we've provided in this chapter and throughout this book should give you a strong foundation for understanding the elements that go into a successful digital marketing strategy. In general, it's difficult to give prescriptive recommendations for evaluating a proposal—finding the right one is often more of a "you know it when you see it" experience.

The most important element to look for in a marketing proposal is specificity: make sure the proposal describes all the services and deliverables provided in detail, with specific budgets and timelines attached to each. If the proposal includes a major project, like a website build, make sure each phase of the project is outlined and broken further into steps, with as much detail around timelines as possible.

If you and the agency agree on the terms of the proposal and decide to work together, you'll sign an agreement. Fortunately, since you're reading a guide to law firm marketing, you most likely have experience reviewing contracts or know someone who does. As we mentioned earlier, the single most critical step to protect yourself throughout this process is to ensure you maintain sole control of your website and any other assets produced if and when the partnership with the agency ends.

# Secrets to a Successful Marketing Marriage

Partnering with an agency shouldn't feel like hard work on your part—the whole point of hiring them is to make your life easier! However, the agency will require occasional information, input, and communication from you, and you can certainly take some proactive steps to maintain a productive, efficient, and even enjoyable relationship with your new partner. Here are a few tips to help.

## Give Them a Clean Slate

If you had a bad experience with an agency before, it's okay to communicate that to your new partner. They've probably heard similar stories before, so you're unlikely to shock them with the details. And finding out what led to a breakdown in a previous partnership can give them valuable insight into your preferences and values.

However, you shouldn't saddle your new agency with baggage from a previous partnership. It's okay to ask probing questions, call for detailed reporting, and even treat statements of results with healthy skepticism—this is a business relationship, after all, and the agency's ability to deliver profits for your law firm is what matters. But it's not appropriate or helpful to treat employees at your new agency with hostility or assume bad intentions on their part without a valid reason.

## Transparency and Communication Are Key

The more your agency partner knows about your business and your goals, the better they can serve you. So, if your firm is facing serious challenges or needs immediate results, it's vital to say so. If you chose an agency that has experience working with other firms, they should have insights into how those firms operated, and they may be able to provide advice and diagnose issues that extend beyond your marketing strategy.

You also have an obligation to clearly outline your expectations for the agency and define what marketing success looks like for your firm, if you haven't already done so during the proposal and onboarding process. If you don't clearly communicate what your firm needs, then you can't complain when your agency partner fails to deliver it.

Of course, transparency and communication are two-way streets, and your agency has obligations too. They should be able to provide the following:

- Detailed reporting that identifies results for agreed-upon key performance indicators (KPIs).
- A clear breakdown of your budget and how they allocate resources to individual strategies and campaigns.

- Clear delineation between their spending on paid ads and costs associated with managing them.
- Easy access to artwork, content, and other created assets.
- Access to project management, campaign, and website tools.
- Ability to verify and approve deliverables before they go live.
- Access to tracking tools so you can pull reports as needed.

## Get with the Times

Nothing can suck the efficiency out of your communications with your marketing partner like outdated communications practices. Many lawyers are confirmed paper-and-pen addicts, but trust me: it pays to go digital, even if you have to grit your teeth while you get used to it. I can tell you from excruciating experience that there's no more pointless or frustrating waste of agency employees' time and your valuable resources than trying to clarify illegible handwritten feedback and comments on scanned documents sent by an attorney who refuses to modernize their communication habits.

## Verify and Approve Work Before It Goes Live

No matter how busy you are, you need to make sure you or someone from your firm reviews every asset, deliverable, and piece of content, at least early in the relationship. Your partner can't hone their approach and internalize your preferences if you don't provide detailed feedback. As you begin to trust the agency more and they show the ability to consistently represent your brand, you can take a slightly more hands-off approach at your discretion.

# Summary

Hiring an agency to handle your digital marketing strategy and campaigns has potential drawbacks, but the benefits of a relationship with the right agency partner are extraordinarily powerful and can deliver enormous value for your budget. An in-house marketing manager can make sense too, especially for large firms, and bringing a marketing manager on to your team doesn't prevent you from partnering with an agency to complement the in-house manager's core expertise.

Even if an agency partnership doesn't unfold as you hoped, you should be able to move on and find a better fit without too much trouble—as long as you maintain control over your digital marketing assets, especially your website. Never let someone from outside your firm gain exclusive access to or control over your website or your site's domain name.

# Marketing Agency Checklist

- Identify key performance indicators (KPIs) for overall strategy and for individual campaigns (blog, marketing, social media, and so on).

- Set up Google Analytics.

- Complete the "Google Analytics for Beginners" course.

- Implement A/B testing for key site pages (home page, practice area pages, PPC landing pages).

# Conclusion

## Building on Your Digital Marketing Success

This book has laid the groundwork for establishing your law firm's online presence, generating new leads from the web, and honing your digital marketing strategies to maximize the return on your budget. We've covered the foundations of digital marketing success and the factors involved in developing and launching a website. We've also delved into content strategy, social media, outbound communications, lead nurturing, different content types, and paid efforts, and we've explained how to evaluate whether or not your efforts are gaining traction.

The adage "good things come to those who wait" requires an addendum in the digital marketing world: "but only the good things left behind by those who hustle and get there first." The first person or firm to implement a successful new strategy has a distinct advantage over their competitors. The first firms that scooped up keyword-match domains (example: "floridainjurylawyer.com" instead of "websterwebsterandcohen.com") found incredible success. The first firms that took an education-based approach toward content marketing suddenly and drastically outpaced those that relied on old-school content development farms, which produced low-quality content stuffed with keyword spam.

When new issues emerge, like new mass tort cases, the first firm to the table with high-quality, readable content tends to have at least a temporary advantage. You and your team should be in the group that hustles—chooses to act and apply the tactics in this book. Move early and look for opportunities to stay on the leading edge of new platforms, new technology, and new tactical approaches.

Machine learning and predictive analytics, in which systems learn from data, identify patterns, and improve without human intervention, are the next horizons in digital marketing as of this writing. As these applications of artificial intelligence start to take off, keep an eye on developments that can provide you with that early advantage. Be cautious and skeptical, but also stay open-minded and maintain an appreciation for new technologies that can help you make the best use of your marketing budget.

Digital marketing success is a moving target, and the emergence of technologies like those mentioned above will ensure that it stays so. However, by watching for new software features, processes, tactics, and technologies, and by choosing to learn and discuss with your peers and with others involved in the digital marketing world, you can stay at the front of the pack and identify those tools that will help you continue to succeed.

Often, preparing for what's next will involve monitoring the new developments in tools and software at the enterprise level—in other words, at the level available to only large organizations with massive budgets. We consistently see technologies emerge as a part of marketing initiatives at the enterprise level, only to trickle down within a few years to platforms accessible to businesses and firms like yours.

In writing this book, I wanted to provide you first and foremost with the framework and philosophy that informs all successful digital marketing strategies and campaigns. In general, the principles behind those successful efforts don't change, even if the tactics and execution do. So, even though digital marketing success is a moving target in terms of metrics and tactics, we consistently find that taking an audience-based approach and employing empathy in all that we do stands the test of time.

As an example, Google constantly changes and tweaks its search algorithms, but we generally find that these changes rarely hurt websites that focus primarily on providing a good user experience. If people spend a lot of time on your site, they're doing it because your site addresses their needs; whether consciously or not, users appreciate that you had them in mind when you created the site and its content. And for all the sophistication of Google's algorithms, all they're really trying to do is serve users with helpful and accessible content.

Of course, the legal field has distinct requirements and quirks when it comes to online advertising. Besides new technologies, platform updates, and shifting audience preferences, legislation and changes to bar association rules can significantly affect the way you market your firm. But none of these changes should affect your fundamental approach. The best way to build on your digital marketing success is to keep testing, keep learning, and stay curious.

I bet that while you've been reading this book, you've probably received a robocall telling you that your website cannot be seen by Google, about five spam emails pitching SEO services, and at least one call or personalized email from a marketing firm promising to change your world with their one special trick. Above all, I hope this book gives you the vocabulary and understanding to sift through these communications and differentiate the ones that could lead to a productive partnership from the ones that will only waste your time.

You deserve to achieve success through digital marketing, especially because you've chosen to invest your two most valuable resources, your time and energy, into reading this book toward that pursuit. I hope that, in return, we've delivered the value you anticipated, and I hope that you use the tools, tactics, and ways of thinking described throughout to outperform your own expectations.

# GLOSSARY OF DIGITAL MARKETING TERMINOLOGY

The digital marketing world has its own unique language, just like the law. Our comprehensive glossary of digital marketing terms is explained in plain English. Flip to these pages whenever you run into digital marketing lingo you're not familiar with. And if you can't find a definition for the term you're looking for, check our continually updated online version: lafleur.marketing/dictionary.

## Marketing Terms

#: The symbol for a hashtag (see hashtag).

**301 redirect:** A tool that automatically redirects a visitor from one web page to another. (Example: you own cats.com and dogs.com, but you decide that you want to merge both sites into a new site, pets.com. You would set up a pair of 301 redirects that send all the traffic from both the old sites to the new one.)

**302 redirect:** A temporary version of a 301 redirect.

**404 error:** The error message you receive when you try to visit a web page that doesn't exist. Sometimes the page actually says "404," while other times it will display customized text.

# A

**A/B testing:** A method of marketing research that involves showing users two different versions on a web page or other asset with minimal variables and then comparing the results.

**Above the fold:** The section of a web page you can see without scrolling. Many people never scroll down on any given web page they visit, so the content that's above the fold is most important. The term comes from newspapers.

**Ad blocking:** The blocking of web advertisements, often via software or browser features.

**Ad campaign:** The set of related ad groups that compose a specific pay-per-click initiative. Each ad group will have the same budget, campaign type, and ad settings. If you want separate initiatives with distinct settings, you'll need to create additional campaigns.

**Ad extensions:** When you see a Google Ad, it may contain extra bits of information—like an address, pricing info, a click-to-call phone number, and more. These are all types of ad extensions. Adding extensions generally increases click-through rates (CTR) on ads.

**Ad groups:** Ad groups include distinct keyword sets that all relate to the same topic, theme, and objective. They should include only keywords that relate directly to the ad's destination page—organic or dedicated.

**Ad rank:** Ad rank determines your ad's position on a search engine results page (SERP). Google and Bing (as well as other, smaller search engines) do not disclose how they calculate ad rank, but it involves some proprietary combination of bid amount and quality score.

**Ad space:** The space on a web page available for advertisements.

**AdSense:** See Google AdSense.

**AdWords:** The previous name for Google Ads.

**Algorithm:** A sequence of instructions that tell a computer or program what to do. Search engines use complex and carefully guarded algorithms to determine which results to show their users.

**Analytics:** An umbrella term for digital marketing processes and practices that focus on using data to optimize strategies and campaigns. (See also, Google Analytics.)

**Application:** A software program that's primarily designed to be used by a person, meaning it has a user interface (as opposed to behind-the-scenes software that the user never interacts with directly).

**Asset:** Any type of marketing material, including email messages, flyers, websites, videos, e-books, and other content.

**Audience:** Short for target audience.

**Audience segmentation:** Breaking a broad audience down into smaller groups, based on their demographics and specific needs.

**Authority:** Different services use different proprietary metrics to measure authority. For example, Moz uses page authority (PA) and domain authority (DA) while Ahrefs uses URL rating (UR) and domain rating (DR).

**Automation:** See email automation.

**Average time on page:** A Google Analytics metric that measures how long the average visitor spends on a given page.

# B

**B2B:** Short for business-to-business; refers to transactions between two commercial entities.

**Badge:** A logo or symbol from a known and respected organization (like Avvo, Martindale-Hubbell, or Super Lawyers) that you display on your site to assure a visitor that your firm is legitimate and capable.

**Bandwidth:** The amount of data a communications channel can handle, often expressed in kilobits per second (kbps).

**Banner ad:** A web ad that displays in rectangular fashion, like a banner; 468 pixels by 60 pixels is a common standard size.

**Banner blindness:** The tendency of a web user to become fatigued by banner ads and ignore them, even when they contain relevant info the user is actively looking for.

**Banner exchange:** An internet advertising network where the websites work together and place banner ads at the top of one another's pages.

**Below the fold:** The section of a web page that is not immediately visible upon loading and can only be viewed by scrolling down. Many people never scroll down on any given web page they visit, so the content that's above the fold is the most important. The term comes from newspapers.

**Bid:** The maximum amount advertisers are willing to spend on each ad they serve to potential prospects.

**Bing:** Operated by Microsoft, Bing is the second most popular search engine in the world, behind Google.

**Bing Ads:** A service that provides pay-per-click (PPC) ads on both Bing and Yahoo! Search.

**Blog:** Short for "weblog." An online journal of information made up of discrete articles that appear from most recent to oldest. Also can be used to refer to the individual articles or as a verb to refer to the act of writing them (so you could say, "I found some time to blog and posted a blog on my blog"—hey, we don't make these rules).

**Blog article:** One of the individual articles that make up a blog. Also sometimes referred to as just a "blog" for short.

**Blurbs:** Short statements that are included in a newsletter or another marketing asset. They often summarize a longer-form article and are followed by a link to full content.

**Bounce:** A visitor who leaves a web page without completing an action or visiting another page.

**Bounce rate:** 1.) In website analytics, the percentage of visitors who leave after viewing a single page on the site. 2.) In email marketing, the percentage of emails in a campaign that get returned as undeliverable.

**Brand:** Your brand is more than a logo and a color palette, although these elements can help define your brand. Instead, it is how your clients, leads, and the community perceive your law firm.

**Brand awareness:** The extent that people are familiar with your law firm, its unique characteristics, and your services.

**Branding guidelines:** Sometimes called brand standards or a style guide, this document outlines rules about how you present your law firm to the community. They often specify how your firm and marketing partners should use colors, fonts, logos, your brand's tone, voice, and taglines.

**Brand positioning statement:** A single succinct statement that defines your overall target audience and the benefits you offer them over the competition.

**Browser:** See web browser.

**Button ad:** Like a banner ad but usually smaller and more square or circular than rectangular.

**Buyer's journey:** The process by which a client learns about you, gathers information, and chooses you from among their potential options. See also, funnel.

## C

**Call to action:** The part of a marketing communication that tries to entice someone to perform a desired action (for example, "Call us today" or "Download now").

**Campaign:** A series of advertising messages or assets that share a common theme, such as their target audience or placement.

**Chatbot:** A computer program that uses AI to simulate interactive conversation with a human (often a customer service representative).

**Clicks:** When someone visits your content by clicking on a link, marketers typically track the number of clicks that a call to action or paid ad get.

**Click-through rate (CTR):** A metric that shows how often people click on an ad after they see it. CTR is measured by dividing the total number of impressions by the total number of clicks.

**Contact form:** A section on a website that contains fields like name, phone number, and email address. Visitors can complete the fields and click a button to send their contact information to the website's owner.

**Content:** Information or experiences that are directed toward an audience. An umbrella term that includes all manner of digital marketing assets—such as blogs, infographics, e-books, videos, and so on.

**Content marketing:** Creating and publishing targeted content that appeals to your audience, educates them about your law firm, and aims to convert them into clients.

**Conversion:** A conversion occurs when a user takes a desirable action, like filling out an online form or subscribing to receive an email newsletter.

**Conversion rate:** The percent of website visitors who complete a desired goal, like downloading an e-book.

**Cookie:** A piece of information that a website stores on a user's computer so the website can remember their preferences.

**Cost per Click (CPC):** The amount of money spent to get each click on an ad in a pay-per-click (PPC) campaign.

**Crawler:** See web crawler.

**CTA:** An abbreviation for a call to action.

**CTR:** An abbreviation for click-through rate.

**Custom audience:** In Facebook advertising, a defined group of people who already have a relationship with your business, such as past clients, people who have visited your website, or people who have watched a video.

**Customer relationship management (CRM) software:** Sophisticated software that helps you keep careful track of your leads and potential clients.

## D

**Dashboard:** A web page that gathers and displays data about the performance of a website or digital marketing campaign.

**Dedicated landing page:** A standalone web page that a user arrives at after clicking on an ad or promotion. They are dedicated to a single goal: conversions. They rarely have any navigation leading readers away from the page.

**Dedicated tracking phone number:** A unique phone number that is assigned to a specific marketing tool, like your website. When someone calls this tracking number, it forwards to your normal business phone number, but you'll collect data about where the person found your contact information.

**Density:** Short for keyword density.

**Directory:** A website that provides an organized, categorized listing of information.

**Display advertising (display ad):** Advertising on websites, apps, or social media platforms. Display advertising may include banner ads, videos, audio, text, images, and other formats.

**Domain:** Shorter term for domain name.

**Domain name:** The URL where users can access your website (usually the homepage URL). Example: Google's domain is google.com.

**Drip campaigns:** A series of automated emails that are sent over a period to a lead or client. They aim to build brand awareness and lead them further down their buyer's journey (with the ultimate aim of converting them into a client or a referral source).

**Duplicate content:** An instance where the exact same content exists in two places on the web. Google has designed its algorithms to identify duplicate content, figure out which site published the content originally, and punish the duplicator in search rankings.

## E

**Email automation:** A marketing practice that uses software to send emails to target audience members based on predefined triggers.

**Email list:** A collection of email addresses that you can use to send out email marketing communications.

**Email marketing:** Using email for marketing purposes.

## F

**Facebook:** The world's most popular social media platform.

**Facebook Ads Manager:** Facebook's tool for creating and managing ad campaigns.

**Facebook advertising:** Facebook's ad network, which allows advertisers to reach Facebook users with various types of ads.

**Facebook profile:** An individual Facebook user's account.

**Facebook page:** The page that represents a business or other entity on Facebook.

**Footer:** The bottom section of a web page; often features the name of the company that manages the web page, contact information, and basic navigation links.

**Form fill:** When a visitor fills out a contact form on a website.

**Funnel:** Marketers often liken a person's journey from lead to client as a funnel. At the beginning, they are considering a variety of options, and slowly they eliminate them based on their research and interactions. This process typically has four stages: awareness, discovery, consideration, and conversion.

## G

**GCLID (Google Click ID):** A tag that Google Ads uses to communicate information to Google Analytics.

**Geotargeting:** The practice of delivering content to a user based on their geographic location.

**GIF:** A compressed image file format that supports animated images. All the goofy animated images you see on social media and the web are GIFs.

**Google Ads:** Google's online advertising platform. Formerly called Google AdWords.

**Google Analytics:** Google's platform for tracking and reporting on website traffic and trends.

**Google My Business:** A free tool from Google that helps businesses appear in both Google searches and Google Maps.

**Google Search Console:** A free web service from Google that helps webmasters check their websites' indexing status and improve visibility.

**Google Trends:** A free web tool from Google that analyzes the popularity of Google search keywords across various regions and languages

**Guest blog:** A blog post published by a featured author who doesn't normally write for the blog.

## H

**H# (H1, H2, H3, etc.) tags:** HTML tags that categorize text headings on a web page. The H1 heading displays as a large title at the top of the page. The larger the H number, the smaller the heading text. Ideally, you use H2s to divide your page into subsections, H3s to divide your H2s into smaller subsections, and so on.

**Hard bounce:** The number of emails in your list that are invalid, resulting in a returned newsletter.

**Hashtag:** A word or phrase beginning with the "#" symbol. Hashtags provide a way for users on social platforms (especially Twitter, where hashtags originated) to tag content and conversations for other users to find.

**Header (web page):** The top part of a web page that usually contains the logo and menu.

**Header tags:** See H# tags.

**HTML:** The coding language for creating web pages and web apps. Short for Hypertext Markup Language.

**HTTP:** The set of rules for transferring files and information on the web. Short for Hypertext Transfer Protocol.

**HTTPS:** A more secure version of HTTP (the "S" stands for secure).

## I

**Image alt tag:** Text that helps search engines and people with vision impairments understand and identify what is in a picture on your website.

**Impressions:** A pay-per-click (PPC) advertising term that refers to how many times an ad is shown on search results pages.

**Index:** 1.) As a noun, all the web pages that a search engine can access. 2.) As a verb, the act of a search engine "noticing" a website and beginning to include it in search results.

**Influencer:** A person who has the power and credibility to impact other's buying decisions. While many people associate influencers with social media, you could also consider a law firm's referral sources (such as other attorneys and past clients) as influencers.

**Instagram:** A popular social media platform that focuses on sharing images and videos.

## J

**Java:** A programming language used to create applications that run on digital devices.

**Javascript:** A scripting language that web designers use to create interactive elements on web pages. Often confused with Java.

## K

**Key performance indicator (KPI):** A quantifiable measurement (metric) that you have identified as important to the success of a marketing campaign or business goal.

**Keyword:** A word or phrase that indicates the topic or theme of a piece of online content. For PPC purposes, keywords relate to specific queries advertisers include in ad groups and bid on in online PPC auctions.

**Keyword match types:** A feature in Google Ads that helps control which searches on Google can trigger your ad. Keyword match types examples include broad match, broad match modified, exact match, and phrase match.

**Keyword phrase:** A string of multiple words that operate together as a single keyword.

**Keyword research:** The process of researching popular search terms. Keyword research helps marketing professionals learn which search terms people use and care about so the marketers can create content that matches those interests.

## L

**Landing page:** Any web page that a user lands on when they click a link.

**Lead:** A potential customer who has made some type of contact with your business.

**Likes:** A metric on Facebook that describes how many separate users have clicked the "like" button on a page.

**Link:** Shorter term for a hyperlink.

**Link text:** See anchor text.

**LinkedIn:** A social networking site geared toward connecting professionals and businesses with peers in their fields or industries.

**List growth rate:** A performance metric that tracks the size and growth of your email subscriber lists.

**Listing:** An entry in a directory site. See directory.

**Long-tail keyword:** A longer keyword phrase that represents the interests of a niche demographic. The philosophy of targeting long-tail keywords is an adaptation of the long-tail theory of marketing for SEO.

**Lookalike audience (Facebook):** A targeting option from Facebook advertising that identifies common characteristics of existing or desired customers and then targets users with similar characteristics.

## M

**Machine learning (ML):** Branch of computer science that aims to create software programs that can use data to teach themselves new tricks that haven't been explicitly programmed.

**Marketing automation:** See email automation.

**Meta description:** An HTML tag that tells Google what copy to display for a web page when it appears on a search engine results page.

**Meta keywords:** A specific meta tag that displays the keywords a page of content supposedly addresses. Google and other search engines used to take these tags into account, but people quickly began abusing them, so almost all search engines now ignore meta keywords tags.

**Metric:** A quantifiable measurement used to track the results of a marketing campaign. For example, bounce rate is a website metric, and cost per click (CPC) is a metric for PPC advertising.

## N

**Native advertising:** Ads, sponsored articles, or links that appear to be part of a web page rather than an obvious ad.

**Nav:** Short for navigation.

**Navigate:** Common verb for the act of getting around a website.

**Navigation:** The menu section(s) at the top (and often bottom) of a website where users can click on various options to explore the site. Navigation should be kept to a minimum on dedicated landing pages because the purpose of the page is to receive prospect contact information via a form fill.

**Negative keywords:** When you create your keyword lists, you can use negative keywords to prevent your ad from triggering for unwanted terms.

## O

**Open rate:** The percentage of email recipients who open an email.

**Organic:** Adjective that refers to digital marketing results that occur "naturally"—that is, without taking measures like paying for clicks or spending money to boost posts. Also see organic traffic.

**Organic search results:** The pages that appear on a Google search results page, excluding the paid entries marked "ad" at the top and bottom.
**Organic traffic:** Visitors who arrive at a website by clicking on the organic search results in a search engine.

**Over-the-top advertising:** Targeted video ads on streaming devices, gaming platforms, and internet-connected smart TVs.

## P

**Page authority:** The weight search engines give to a page to determine how well it ranks.

**Page views:** An instance of an internet user visiting a particular web page.

**Pay per click:** See pay-per-click advertising.

**Pay-per-click (PPC) advertising:** A model of online advertising in which the advertiser pays a fee each time someone clicks on one of their ads.

**PDF:** A file format for documents that looks like a digital version of a printed document. Popular because it provides consistent formatting and viewing across different viewing software and devices and because it's difficult to alter.

**Penalty (Google):** An infraction issued by Google for violating its guidelines. Can hurt performance in Google search results or get a site kicked off Google entirely.

**Percent exit:** The percentage of users who leave the site after viewing a particular page. **Persona:** A fictionalized representation of a desired customer, ideally based on research and data.

**Podcast:** A program that's like a radio show but is released and downloaded over the internet.

**PPC:** An abbreviation for pay-per-click advertising.

**Pop-up ad:** An online ad that displays in a new browser window.

**Preheader:** Used in email, preheaders are short summaries or statements that follow a subject line.

# Q

**Qualified lead:** A lead who is especially likely to become a client, often because they have expressed some interest in your law firm (for example, by downloading an e-book, reading a few of your blog articles, or providing some info about their situation via a contact form).

**Quality score:** A Google Ads metric that measures how relevant your landing page and ads are to the keywords you've chosen. Working on a scale of 1 to 10, Google's Quality Score rates how closely your keywords and landing pages align with your ads.

**Query:** The word or string of words that a user types into a search engine's search box.

## R

**Ranking:** A term for where a site appears in a search engine's results for a given keyword. Rankings constantly change and are specific to each keyword, so a site can rank highly for some keywords while ranking lower or not at all for others.

**Redirect:** A web technique that tells web browsers to take users who try to visit one web address to another web address instead.

**Referral:** A Google Analytics metric that represents users who arrive at your website via another site.

**Remarketing:** A digital marketing tactic that lets you position ads in front of potential customers who have already visited your website.

**Request for proposal (RFP):** A document that announces and provides details about a project in order to solicit proposals from potential partners.

**Retargeting:** Another word for remarketing.

**Robots.txt:** A text file that a webmaster creates to tell search engines and web crawlers which pages to crawl for information.

**ROI:** Short for return on investment. A positive ROI means earning more money than you're spending on a given campaign or initiative.

## S

**Search ad:** A text-focused ad that appears on a search engine results page (SERP). These ads appear above organic results, and some research suggests that more than half of search engine users do not realize they are advertisements.

**Search engine:** A program that searches an index of information and returns results to the user based on keywords the user enters.

**Search engine optimization:** The process of trying to increase a website's rankings in search engines to attract more organic traffic.

**Search engine results page:** The page you arrive at when you type words into a search engine and click "search."

**Search query:** See query.

**SEO:** See search engine optimization.

**SSL (Secure Sockets Layer) certificate:** An SSL certificate is a digital certificate that authenticates the identity of a website and encrypts information sent to the server. Having an SSL certificate makes your website more secure, and it also gives your site's URL an "https" designation, so visitors will know you've taken extra steps to secure their data.

**Session:** A Google Analytics metric that measures one user interacting with your site for a given time period. The default session is thirty minutes. If a user visits your site and clicks on fourteen different pages in twenty minutes, it still counts as only one session.

**SERP:** Abbreviation for search engine results page.

**Sharing rate:** How frequently your subscribers hit a "share" or "forward" button on your newsletter.

**Sitemap:** A visual or textually organized representation of a website's content and structure.

**Snapchat:** A multimedia social networking platform. Popular with Millennials and younger generations.

**Social engagement:** How frequently your followers engage with your social media content, either by liking, sharing, commenting, or engaging in another activity.

**Social impressions:** A social media advertising term that refers to how many times an ad is shown on a platform.

**Social proof:** A psychological phenomenon where people mimic others' behaviors, assuming that is sometimes called "herd behavior." In the world of digital marketing, online reviews and testimonials can encourage social proof.

**Social reach:** How many people your content and ads reach across a social media network.

**Source:** A piece of information in Google Analytics that helps you see where web traffic is coming from.

**Spam:** Unsolicited communications, especially low-quality and low-value advertising messages.

**Spider:** Another term for a crawler.

**Stock photography:** Images that you purchase or license from an artist or company. While most law firms use stock photography in their marketing, you should always make sure the images align with your brand guidelines.

**Style sheet:** Another term for a CSS.

# T

**Tag:** A keyword or term assigned to a piece of information.

**Target audience:** The intended audience for a piece of content, advertising campaign, or other marketing initiative.

**Target market:** The group of consumers most likely to buy a company's products or services.

**Time on page:** See average time on page.

**Title tag:** An HTML element that describes the topic of a web page. If a search user conducts a search and one of your pages shows up in their results, the page's title tag is what they'll see (along with the meta description underneath).

**Touchpoints:** The places where your potential clients interact with your law firm's brand.

**Tracking code:** A website script that passes information along to software programs to gather data about users.

**Tracking pixel:** A tiny snippet of code that allows you to gather information and track behavior for users who visit your website or interact with your social media ads.

**Traffic:** See website traffic.

**Tweet:** A post on Twitter.

**Twitter:** A social networking site based around users posting short public messages.

**Twitter Ads:** Twitter's advertising platform.

## U

**Unique pageviews:** The total number of times that unique users view a page over a specified period.

**Unique visitors:** A metric that shows how many individual users visit a website over a given period by tracking users' IP addresses. If the same user visits a website on two separate occasions, it will count as only one unique visitor.

**Unsubscribe rate:** How frequently people opt out of your newsletter.

**URL:** The address of a web page, it stands for Uniform Resource Locator.

## V

**Visits:** An old analytics term. Generally replaced by "sessions."

**Visitors:** See unique visitors.

**Vlog:** Short for video blog. A blog that publishes video content.

## W

**Web hosting:** The business of providing the storage, connectivity, and other services necessary to maintain a website.

**Website traffic:** The number of visitors and/or visits that a website receives. There is no one metric for website traffic; instead, website traffic is an umbrella term that encompasses more specific metrics like visits, unique visitors, and sessions.

**Webinar:** An online seminar.

**Website:** A document or collection of documents accessible via the World Wide Web.

**Widget:** A standalone, web-based application that can be embedded on a website to perform a specific task. Often used to create dynamic page elements like clocks, counters, calendars, weather reports, etc.

**Working title:** A preliminary, tentative title for a blog, web page, or another asset. It gives the writer direction and helps them understand the purpose of the piece. Writers and editors often change working titles to make them more appealing to readers.

## X

**XML:** A language for formatting and sharing information via the internet or a private network. Stands for Extensible Markup Language.

**XML sitemap:** A document in XML format that lists all your website's important pages for a search engine and helps the engine understand your website's structure.

## Y

**YouTube:** A video sharing website and one of the most popular sites in the world.

**Yahoo!:** The world's third most popular search engine. Powered by Bing (which means it will display ads created through Bing Ads).

# Z

**Zzz:** The sound you make after poring through a glossary of a couple hundred digital marketing terms.

# ABOUT THE AUTHOR

Chip LaFleur became involved in website development early on when he used a dialup connection to explore the bulletin board system (a precursor to the World Wide Web). Soon, he was learning HTML and building websites. While working for an advertising agency, Chip became convinced that digital marketing's trackability made it more effective and powerful than traditional marketing platforms. He began to focus more on data-driven digital solutions.

In 2015, Chip founded LaFleur. The Grand Rapids-based marketing agency has focused on legal marketing from the beginning, helping law firms nationwide build effective marketing plans, empower their communities, and reach their ideal clients. LaFleur quickly became a recognized name in the legal and digital marketing industries. Today, the agency focuses on digital marketing for professional services, with deep specializations in heavily regulated industries like legal, healthcare, and financial services.

In his spare time, Chip loves spending time with his wife and sons, building things out of wood and metal, and being outdoors.